24™ UNDERGROUND

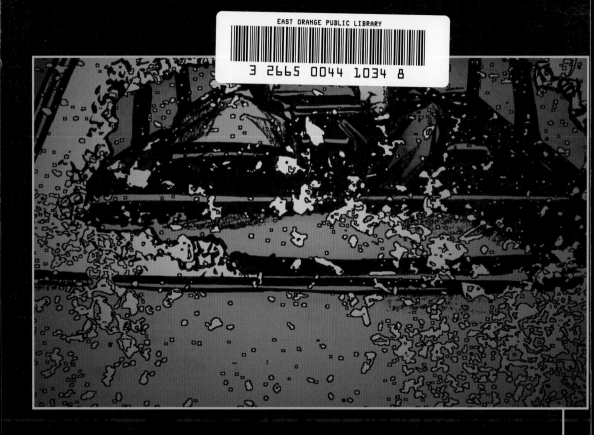

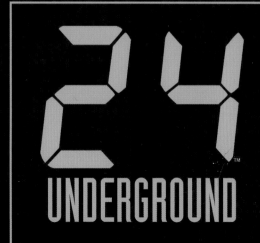

Art by Michael Gaydos

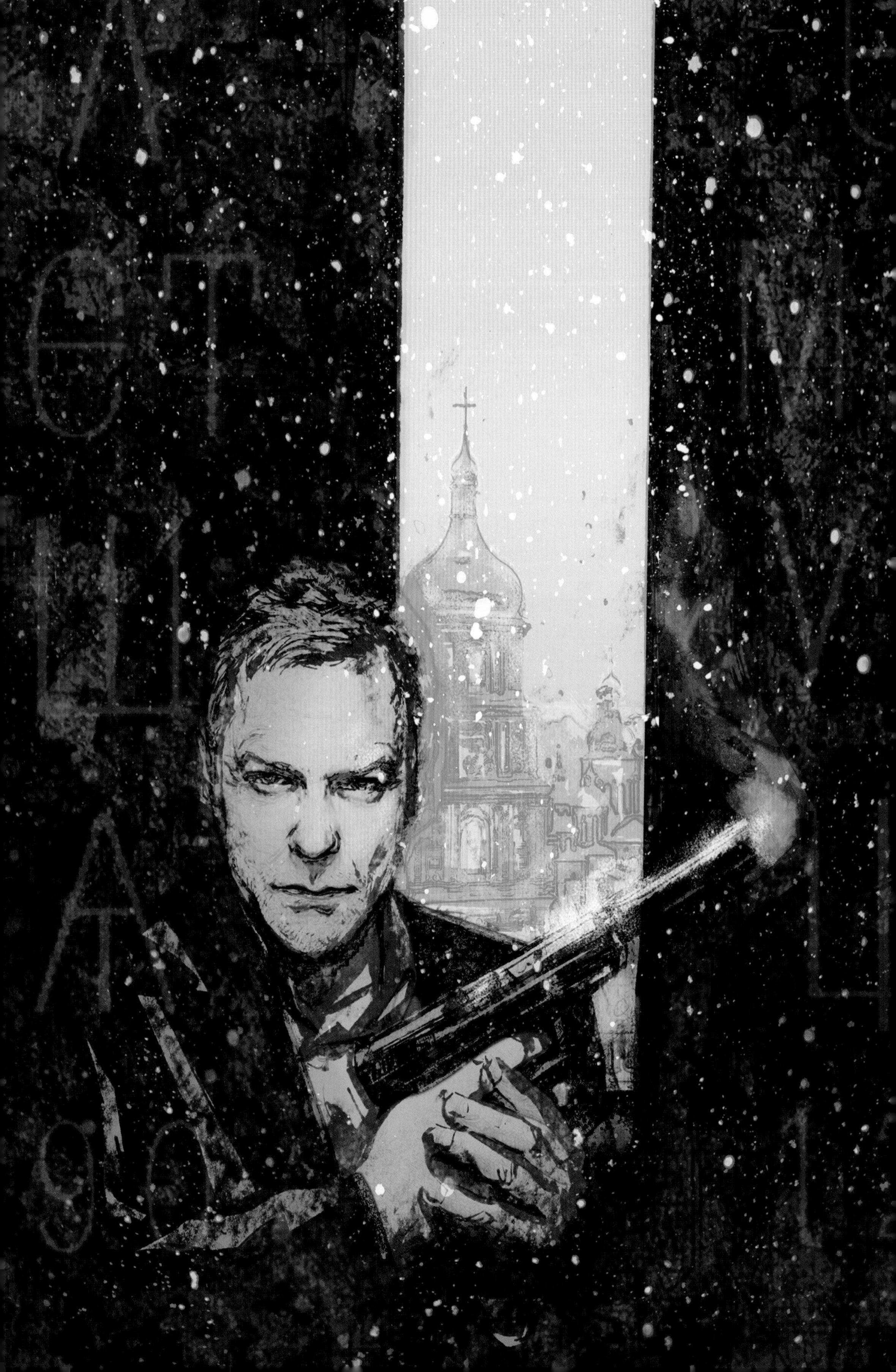

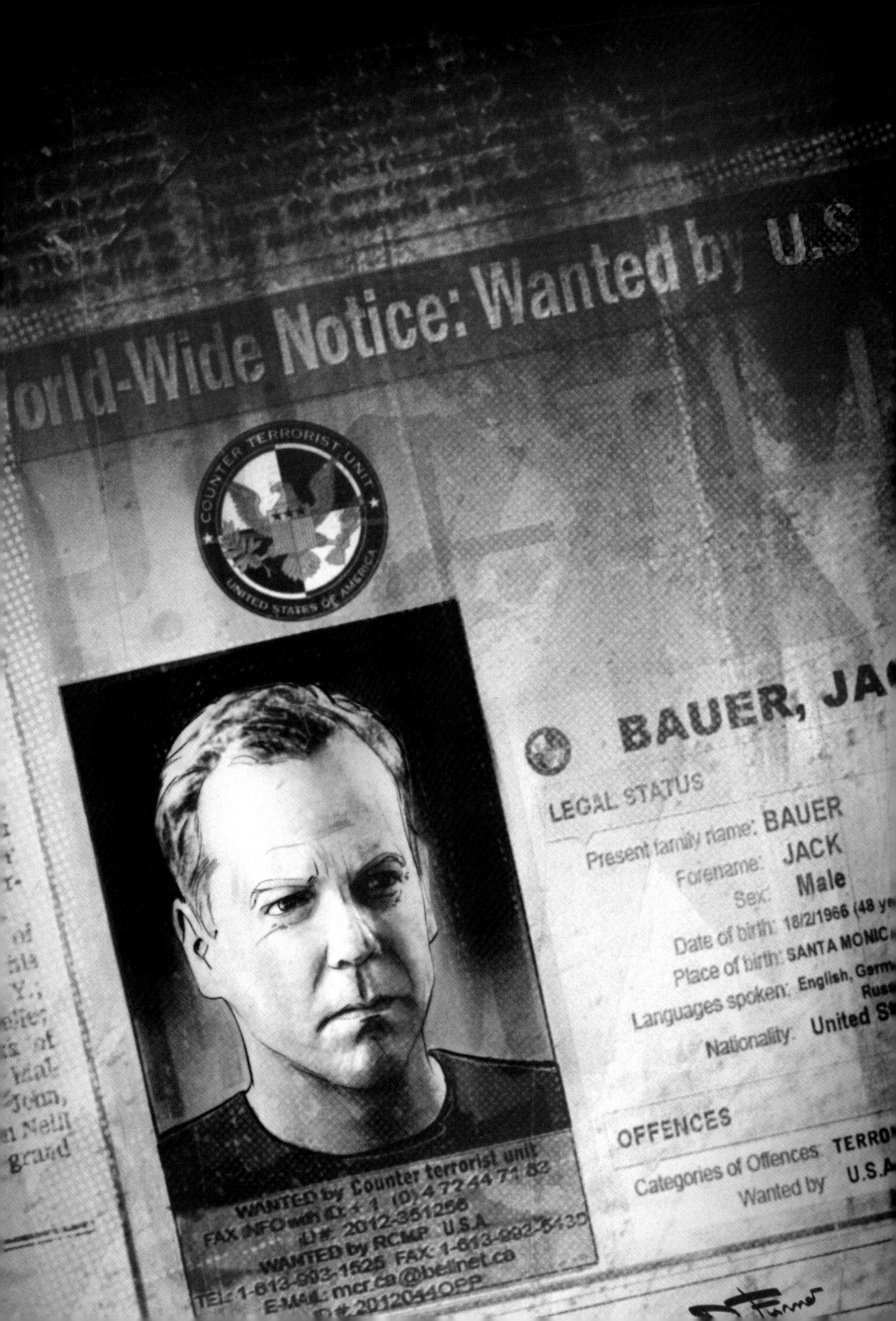
orld-Wide Notice: Wanted by U.S
COUNTER TERRORIST UNIT
UNITED STATES OF AMERICA
BAUER, JA
LEGAL STATUS
Present family name: BAUER
Forename: JACK
Sex: Male
Date of birth: 18/2/1966 (48 ye
Place of birth: SANTA MONIC
Languages spoken: English, Germ
Russ
Nationality: United St
OFFENCES
Categories of Offences: TERRO
Wanted by: U.S.A
WANTED by Counter terrorist unit
WANTED by RCMP U.S.A.

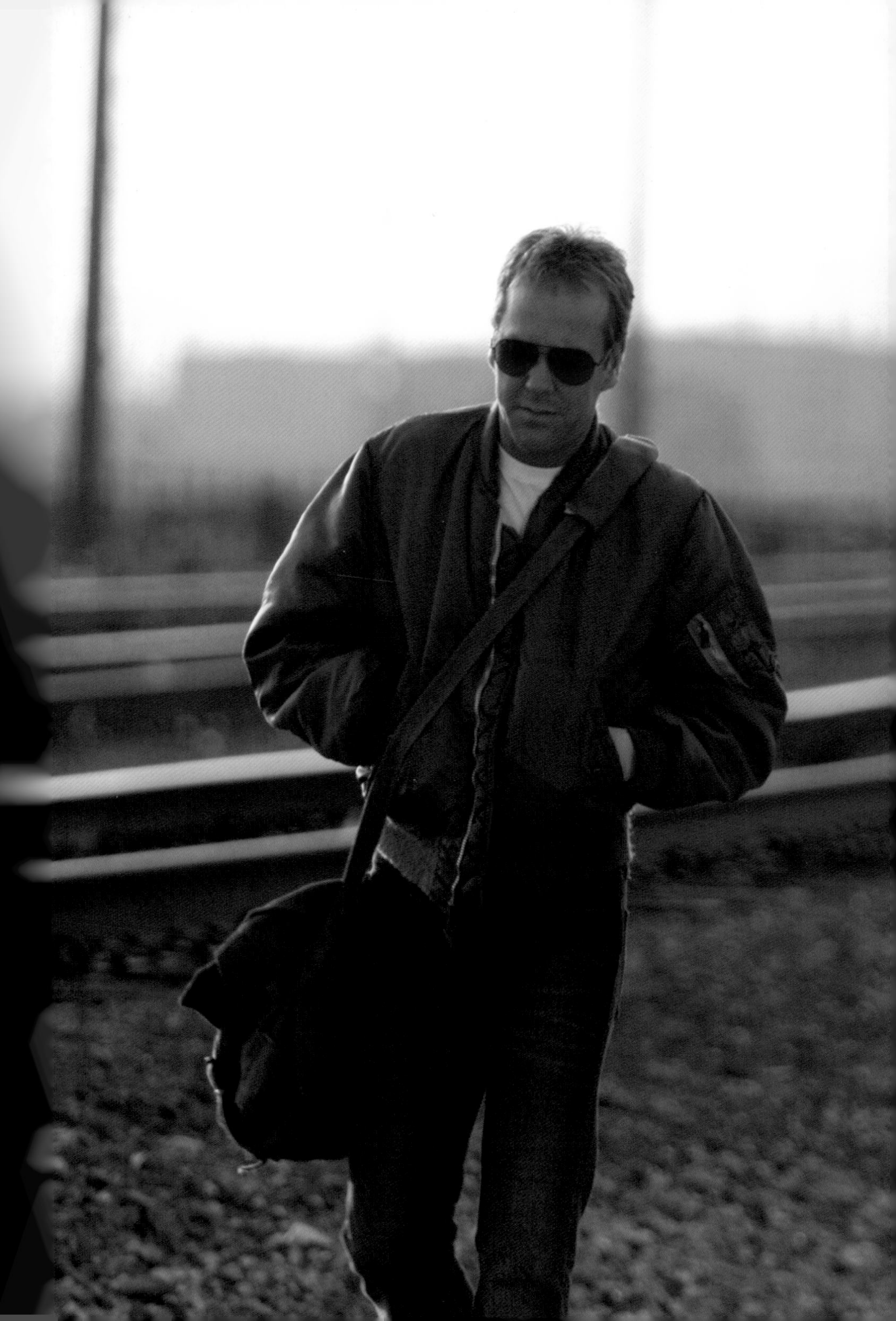

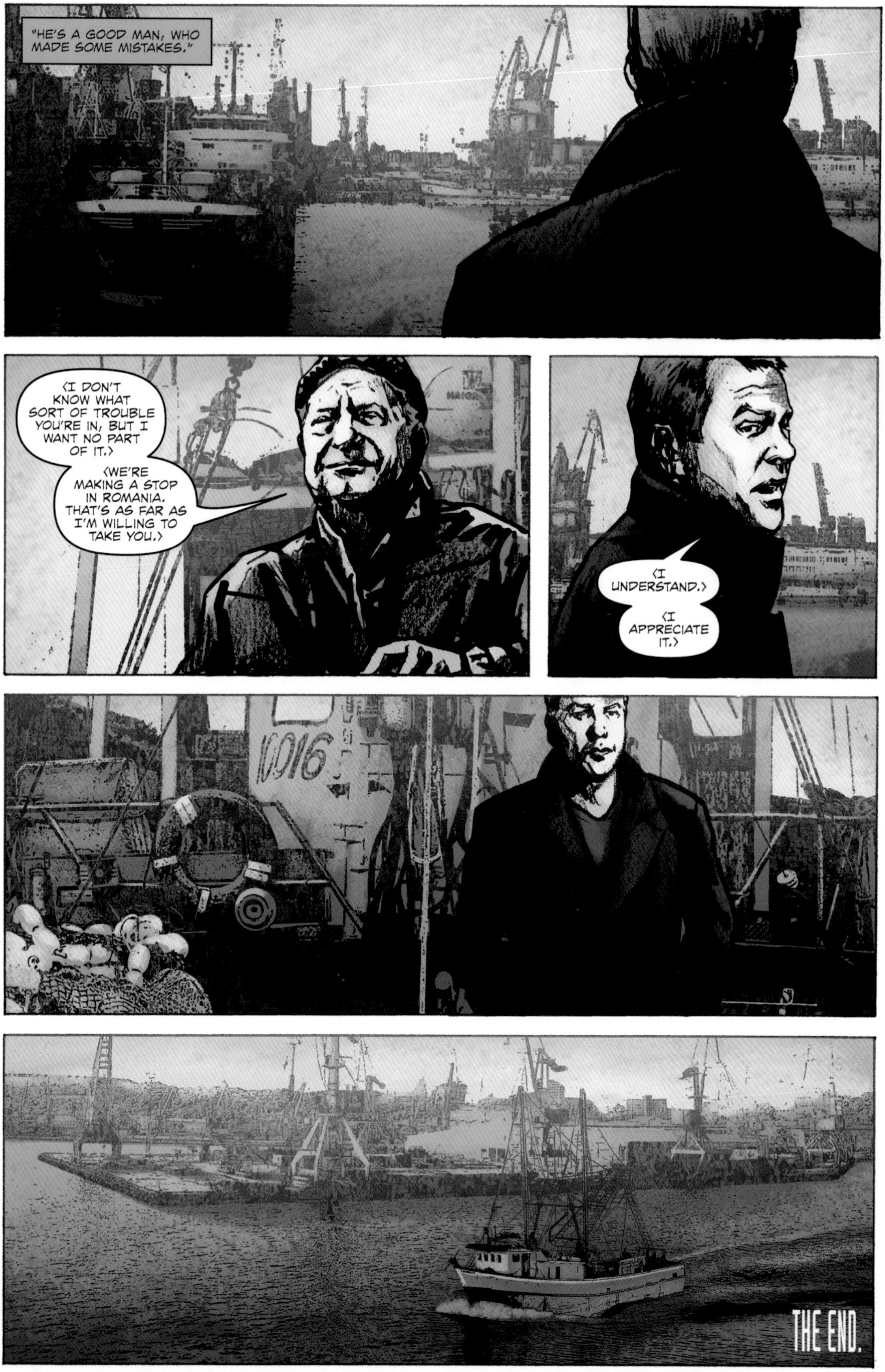
"HE'S A GOOD MAN, WHO MADE SOME MISTAKES."
‹I DON'T KNOW WHAT SORT OF TROUBLE YOU'RE IN, BUT I WANT NO PART OF IT.›
‹WE'RE MAKING A STOP IN ROMANIA. THAT'S AS FAR AS I'M WILLING TO TAKE YOU.›
‹I UNDERSTAND.›
‹I APPRECIATE IT.›
THE END.

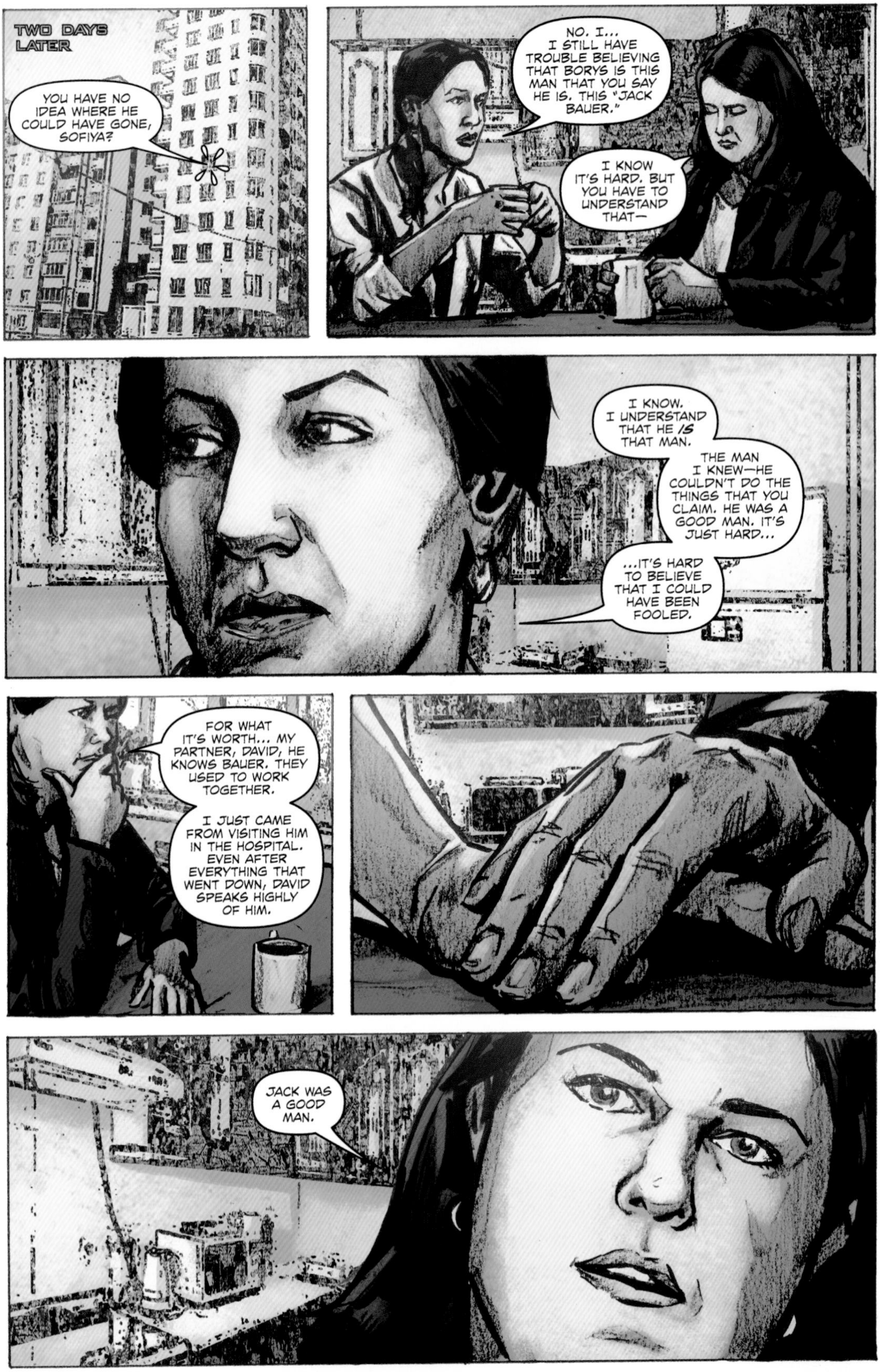
TWO DAYS LATER
YOU HAVE NO IDEA WHERE HE COULD HAVE GONE, SOFIYA?
NO. I... I STILL HAVE TROUBLE BELIEVING THAT BORYS IS THIS MAN THAT YOU SAY HE IS. THIS "JACK BAUER."
I KNOW IT'S HARD. BUT YOU HAVE TO UNDERSTAND THAT—
I KNOW. I UNDERSTAND THAT HE *IS* THAT MAN.
THE MAN I KNEW—HE COULDN'T DO THE THINGS THAT YOU CLAIM. HE WAS A GOOD MAN. IT'S JUST HARD...
...IT'S HARD TO BELIEVE THAT I COULD HAVE BEEN FOOLED.
FOR WHAT IT'S WORTH... MY PARTNER, DAVID, HE KNOWS BAUER. THEY USED TO WORK TOGETHER.
I JUST CAME FROM VISITING HIM IN THE HOSPITAL. EVEN AFTER EVERYTHING THAT WENT DOWN, DAVID SPEAKS HIGHLY OF HIM.
JACK WAS A GOOD MAN.

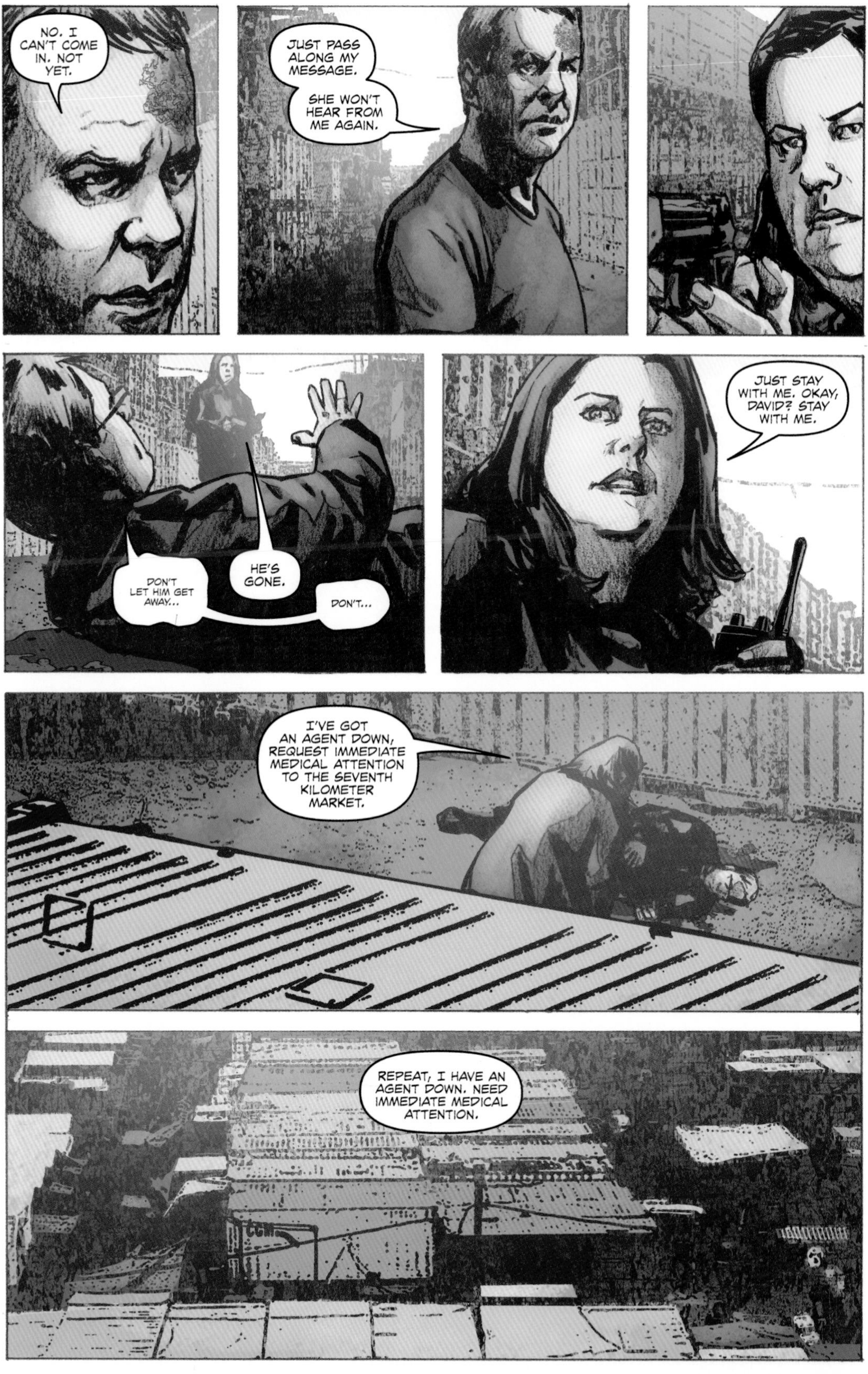
NO. I CAN'T COME IN. NOT YET.
JUST PASS ALONG MY MESSAGE.
SHE WON'T HEAR FROM ME AGAIN.
DON'T LET HIM GET AWAY...
HE'S GONE.
DON'T...
JUST STAY WITH ME. OKAY, DAVID? STAY WITH ME.
I'VE GOT AN AGENT DOWN, REQUEST IMMEDIATE MEDICAL ATTENTION TO THE SEVENTH KILOMETER MARKET.
REPEAT, I HAVE AN AGENT DOWN. NEED IMMEDIATE MEDICAL ATTENTION.

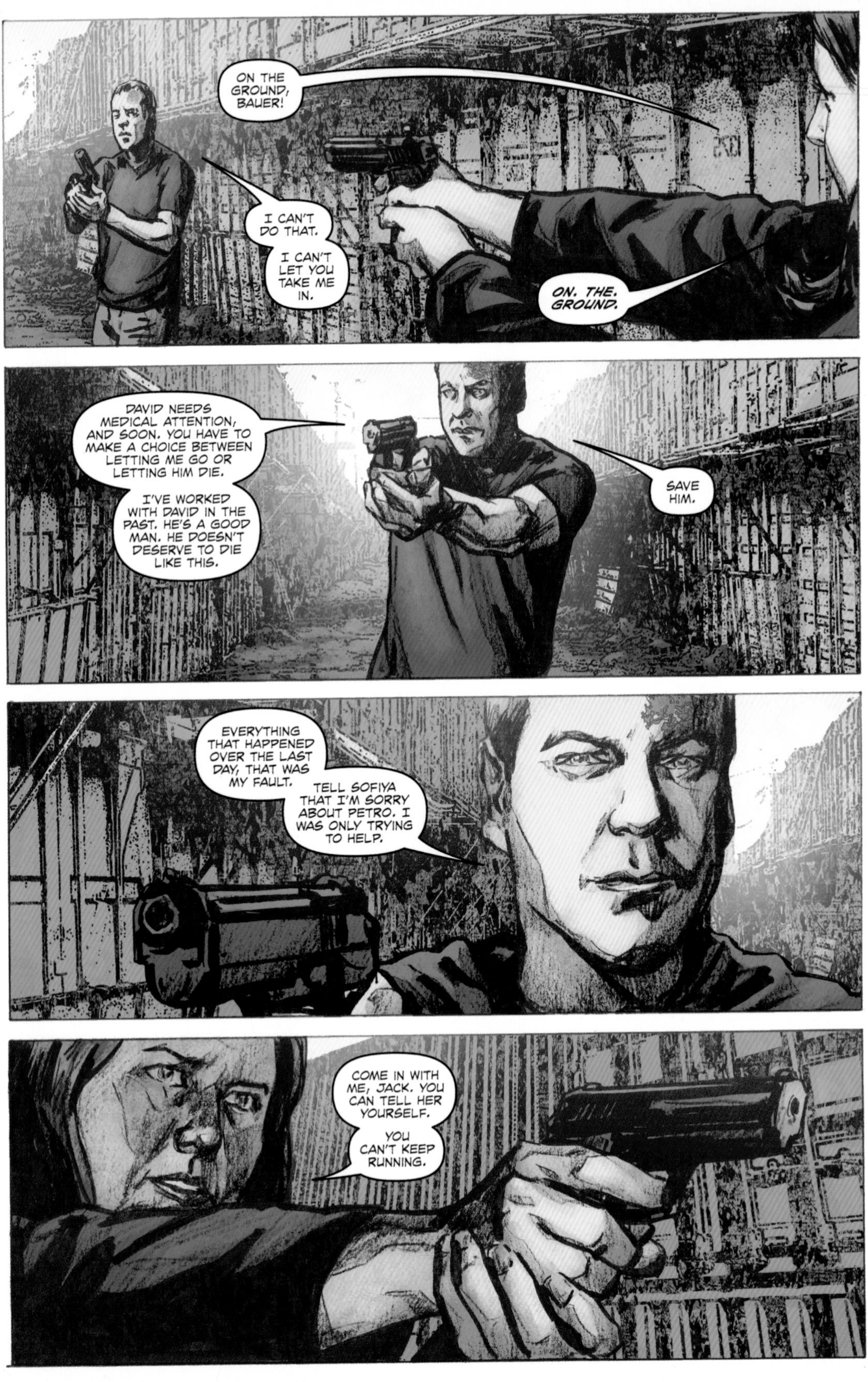
ON THE GROUND, BAUER!
I CAN'T DO THAT.
I CAN'T LET YOU TAKE ME IN.
ON. THE. GROUND.
DAVID NEEDS MEDICAL ATTENTION, AND SOON. YOU HAVE TO MAKE A CHOICE BETWEEN LETTING ME GO OR LETTING HIM DIE.
I'VE WORKED WITH DAVID IN THE PAST. HE'S A GOOD MAN. HE DOESN'T DESERVE TO DIE LIKE THIS.
SAVE HIM.
EVERYTHING THAT HAPPENED OVER THE LAST DAY, THAT WAS MY FAULT.
TELL SOFIYA THAT I'M SORRY ABOUT PETRO. I WAS ONLY TRYING TO HELP.
COME IN WITH ME, JACK. YOU CAN TELL HER YOURSELF.
YOU CAN'T KEEP RUNNING.

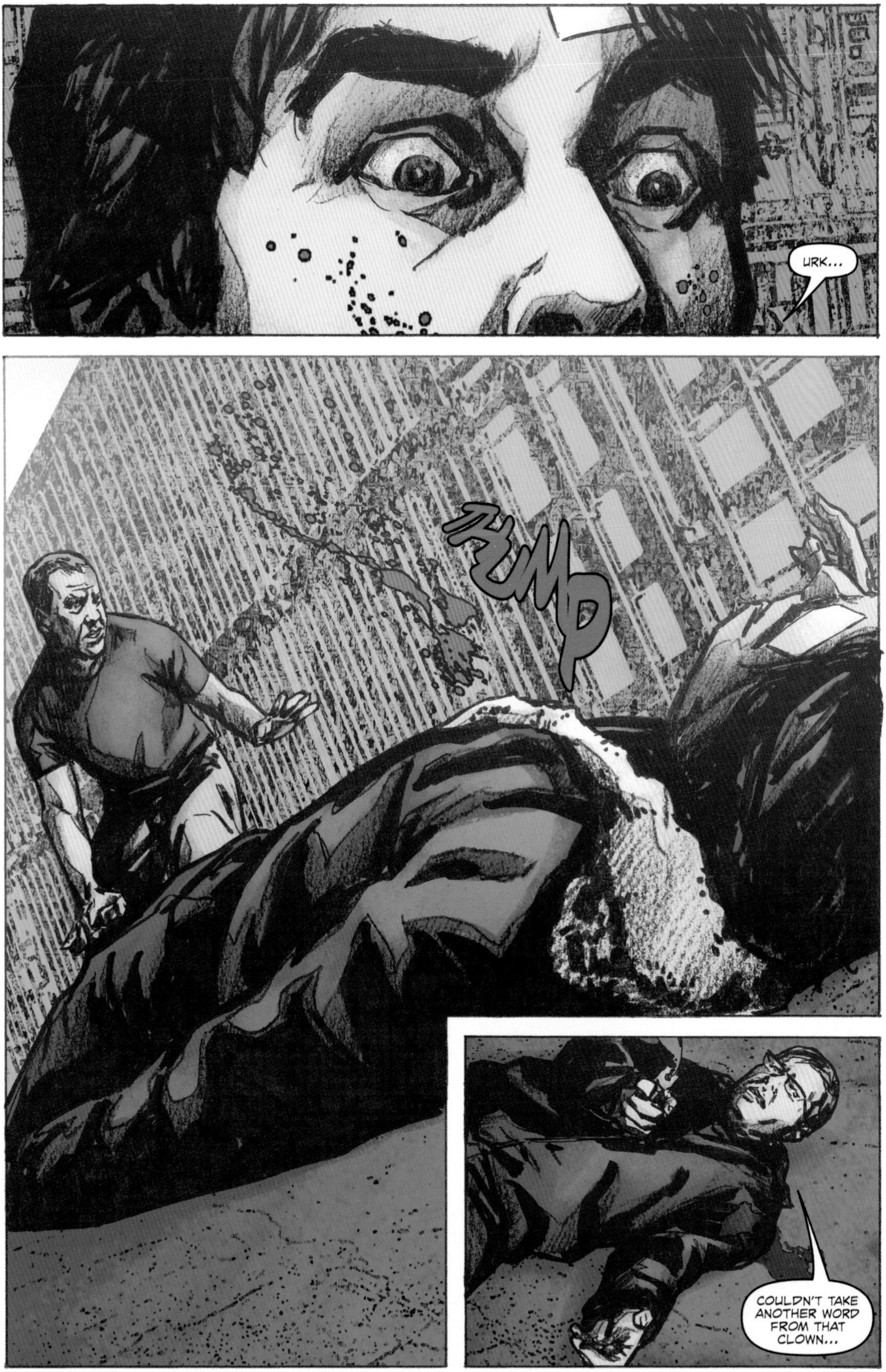
URK...
THUMP
COULDN'T TAKE ANOTHER WORD FROM THAT CLOWN...

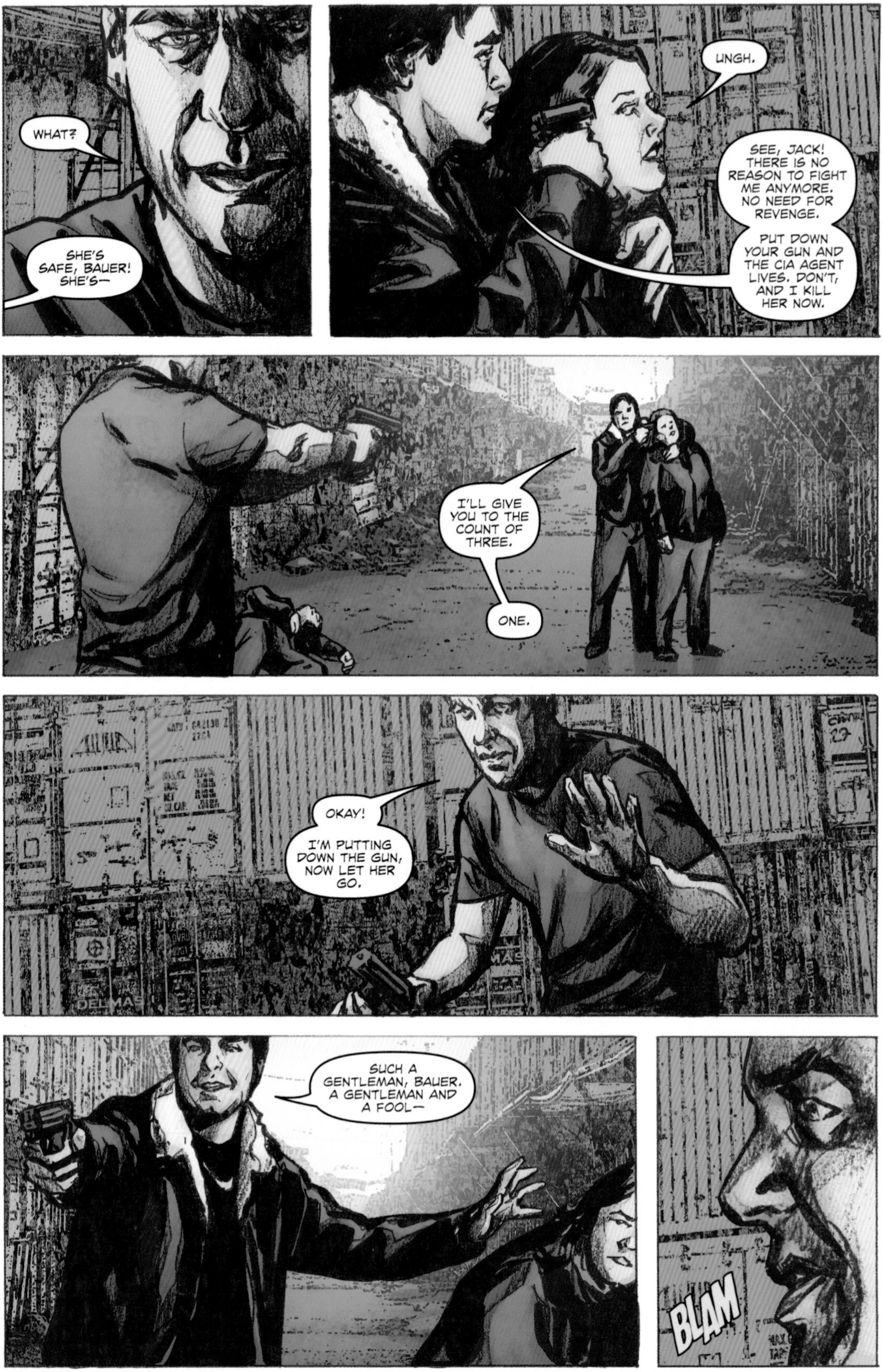
WHAT?
SHE'S SAFE, BAUER! SHE'S—
UNGH.
SEE, JACK! THERE IS NO REASON TO FIGHT ME ANYMORE. NO NEED FOR REVENGE.
PUT DOWN YOUR GUN AND THE CIA AGENT LIVES. DON'T, AND I KILL HER NOW.
I'LL GIVE YOU TO THE COUNT OF THREE.
ONE.
OKAY!
I'M PUTTING DOWN THE GUN, NOW LET HER GO.
SUCH A GENTLEMAN, BAUER. A GENTLEMAN AND A FOOL—
BLAM

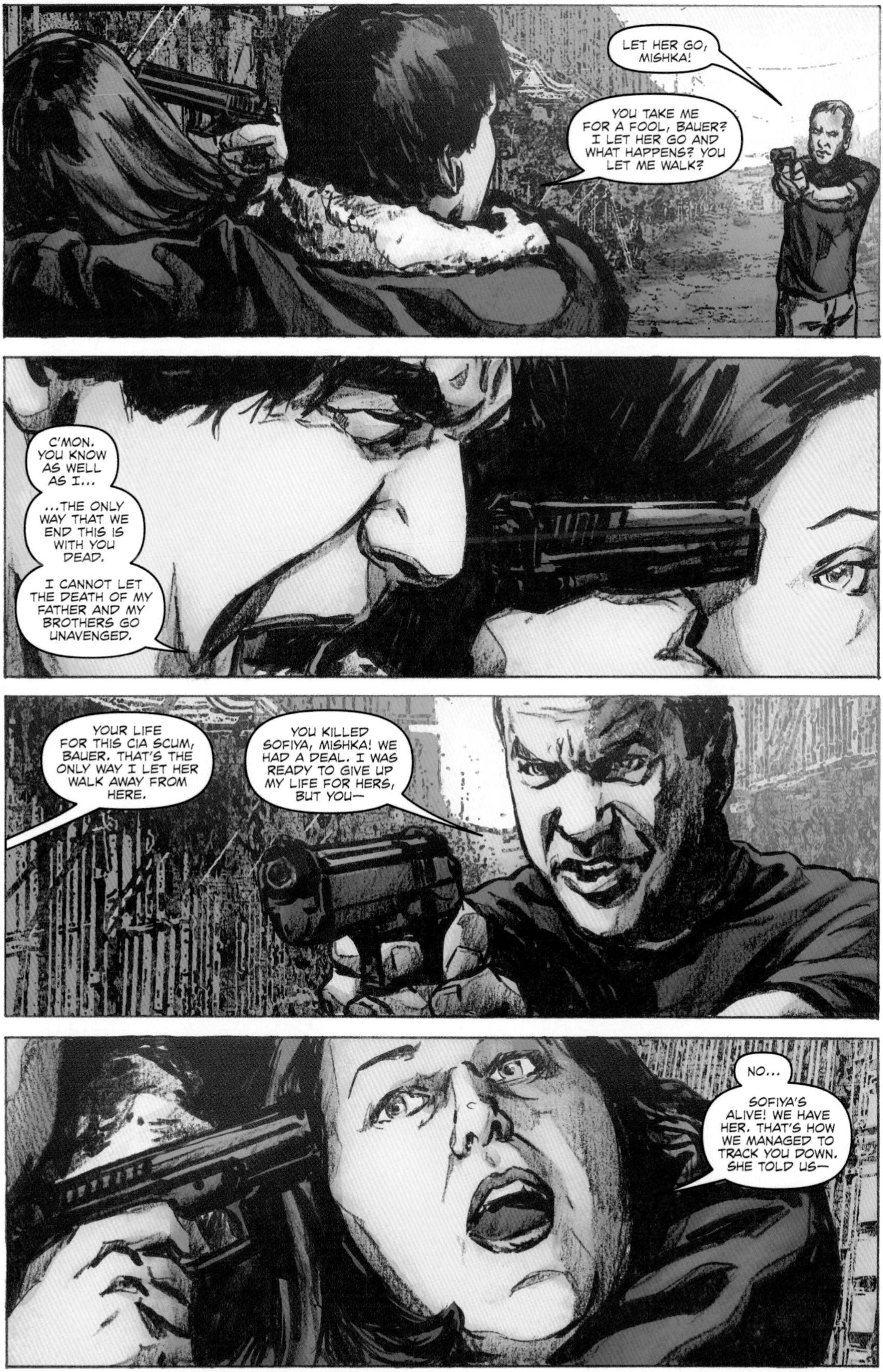

LET HER GO, MISHKA!
YOU TAKE ME FOR A FOOL, BAUER? I LET HER GO AND WHAT HAPPENS? YOU LET ME WALK?
C'MON. YOU KNOW AS WELL AS I...
...THE ONLY WAY THAT WE END THIS IS WITH YOU DEAD.
I CANNOT LET THE DEATH OF MY FATHER AND MY BROTHERS GO UNAVENGED.
YOUR LIFE FOR THIS CIA SCUM, BAUER. THAT'S THE ONLY WAY I LET HER WALK AWAY FROM HERE.
YOU KILLED SOFIYA, MISHKA! WE HAD A DEAL. I WAS READY TO GIVE UP MY LIFE FOR HERS, BUT YOU—
NO...
SOFIYA'S ALIVE! WE HAVE HER. THAT'S HOW WE MANAGED TO TRACK YOU DOWN. SHE TOLD US—

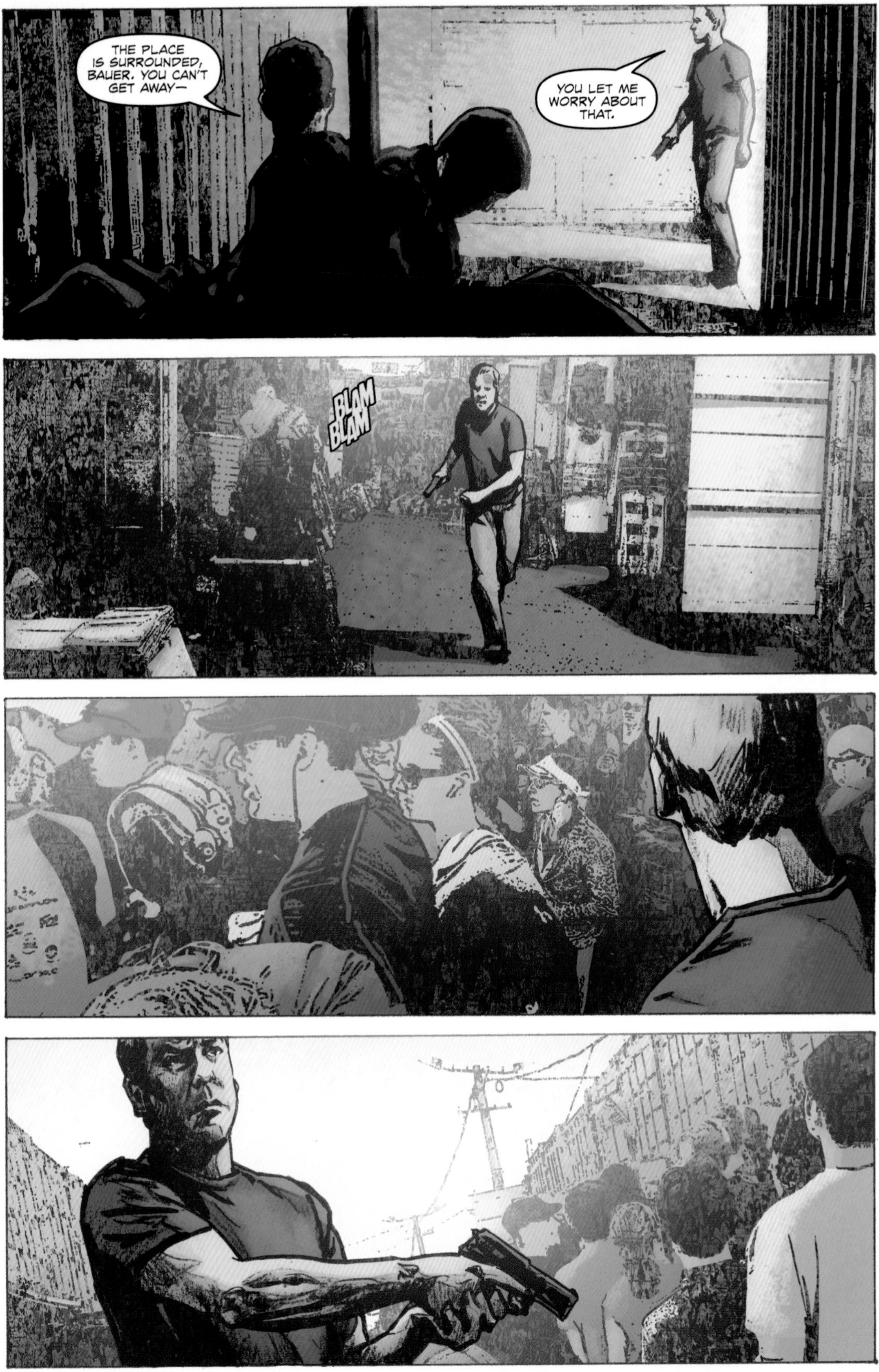
THE PLACE IS SURROUNDED, BAUER. YOU CAN'T GET AWAY—
YOU LET ME WORRY ABOUT THAT.
BLAM BLAM

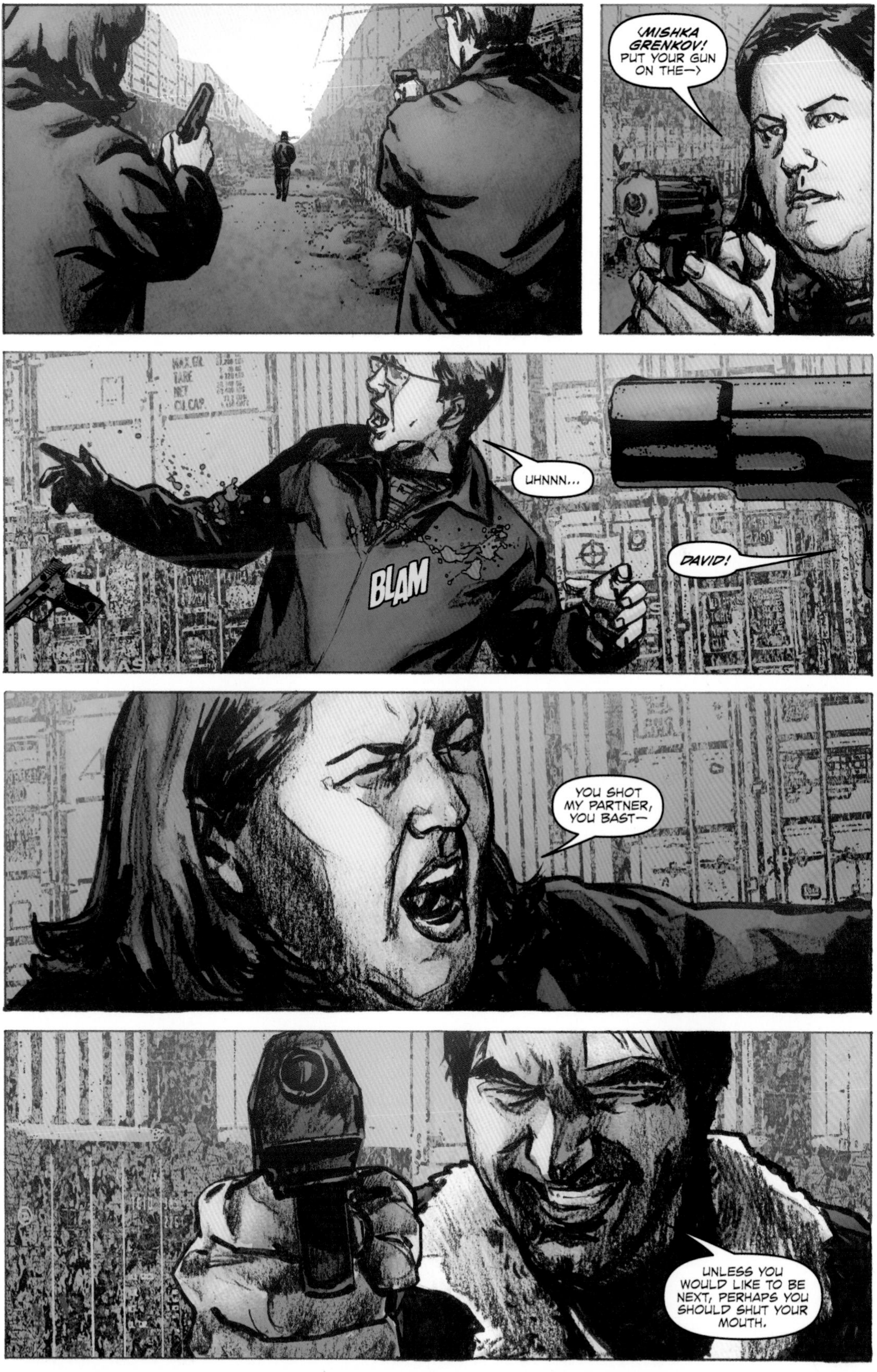
‹MISHKA GRENKOV! PUT YOUR GUN ON THE—›
UHNNN...
BLAM
DAVID!
YOU SHOT MY PARTNER, YOU BAST—
UNLESS YOU WOULD LIKE TO BE NEXT, PERHAPS YOU SHOULD SHUT YOUR MOUTH.

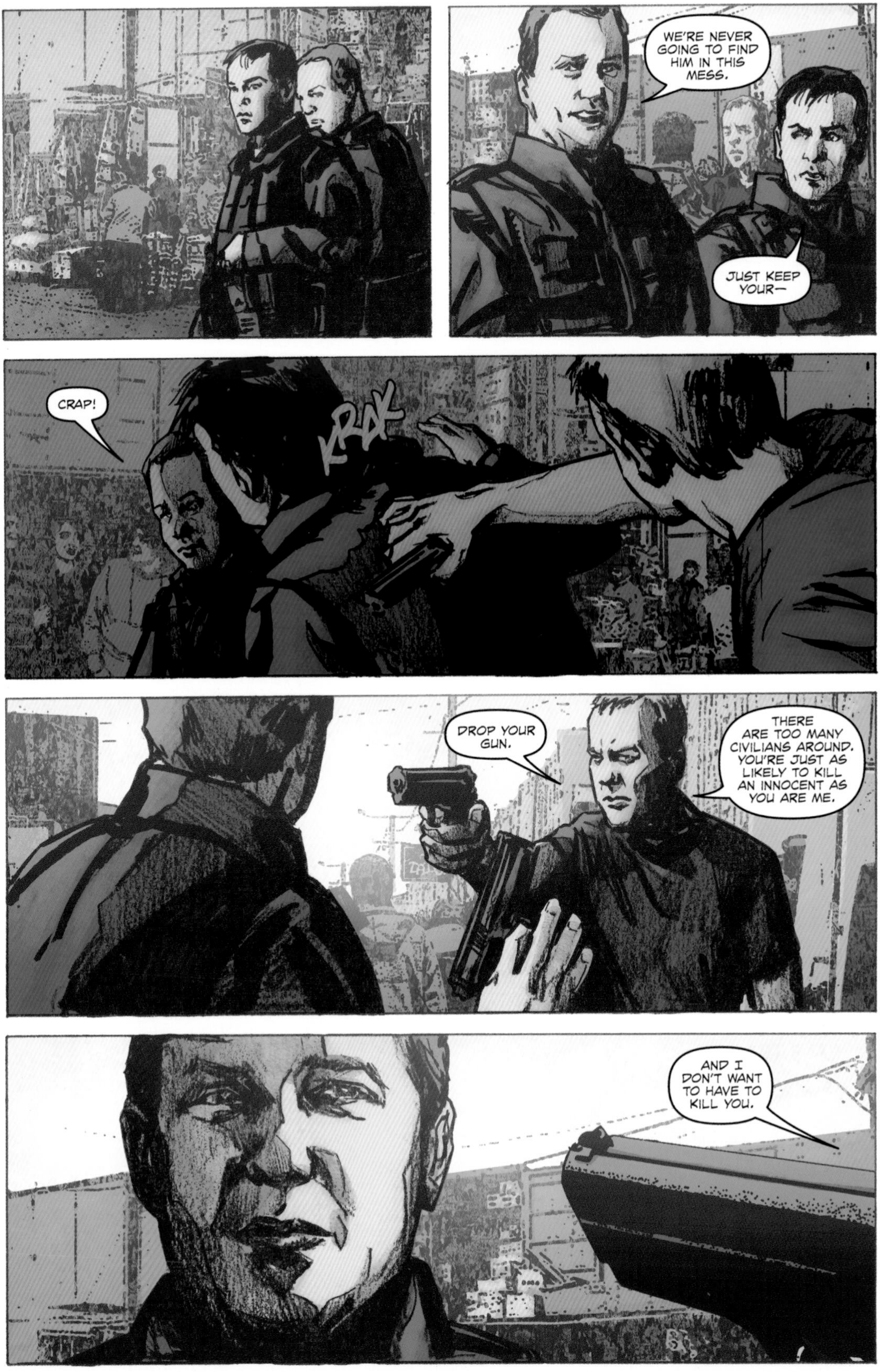

WE'RE NEVER GOING TO FIND HIM IN THIS MESS.
JUST KEEP YOUR—
CRAP!
KRAK
DROP YOUR GUN.
THERE ARE TOO MANY CIVILIANS AROUND. YOU'RE JUST AS LIKELY TO KILL AN INNOCENT AS YOU ARE ME.
AND I DON'T WANT TO HAVE TO KILL YOU.

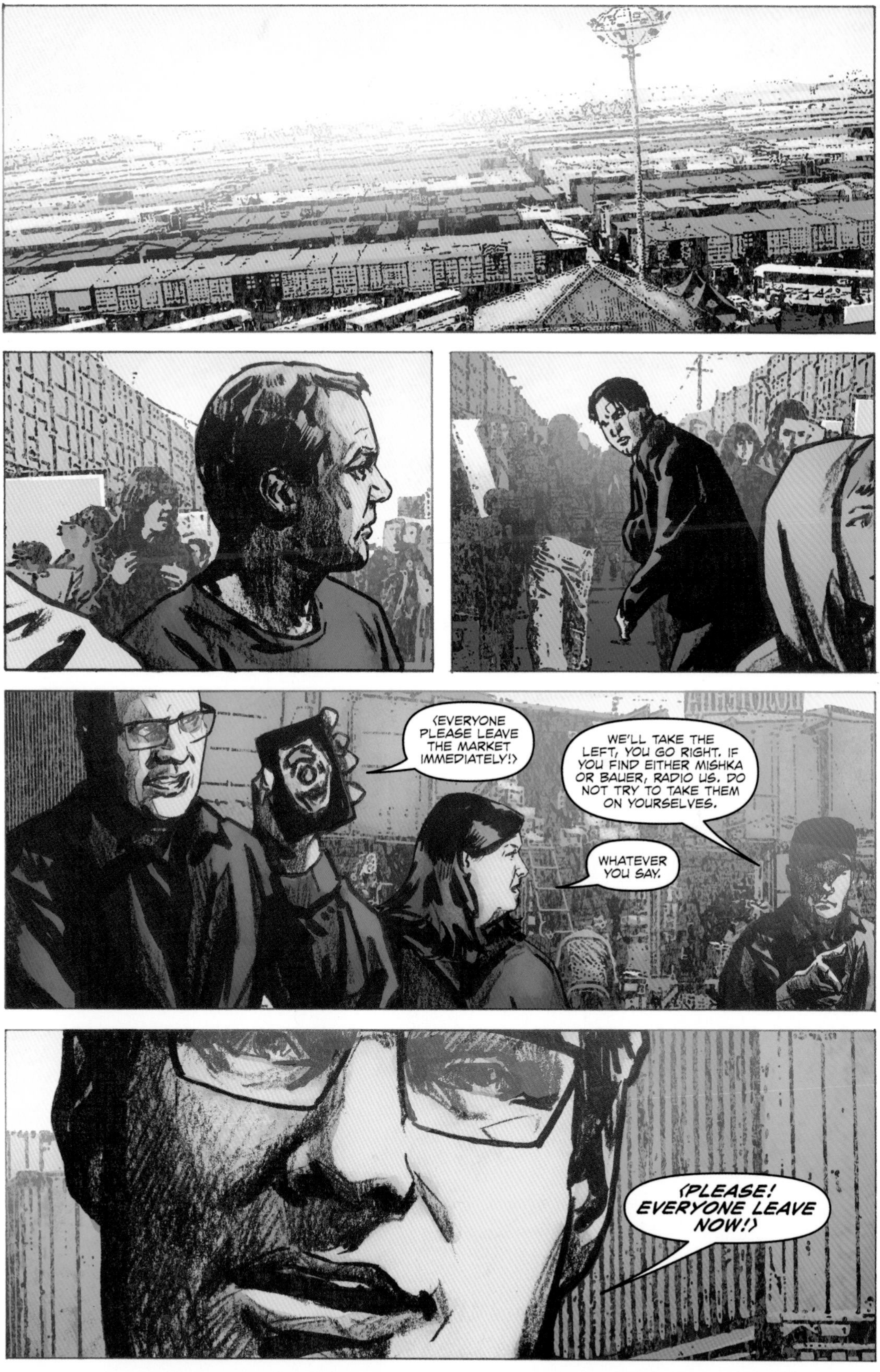
‹EVERYONE PLEASE LEAVE THE MARKET IMMEDIATELY!›
WE'LL TAKE THE LEFT, YOU GO RIGHT. IF YOU FIND EITHER MISHKA OR BAUER, RADIO US. DO NOT TRY TO TAKE THEM ON YOURSELVES.
WHATEVER YOU SAY.
‹PLEASE! EVERYONE LEAVE NOW!›

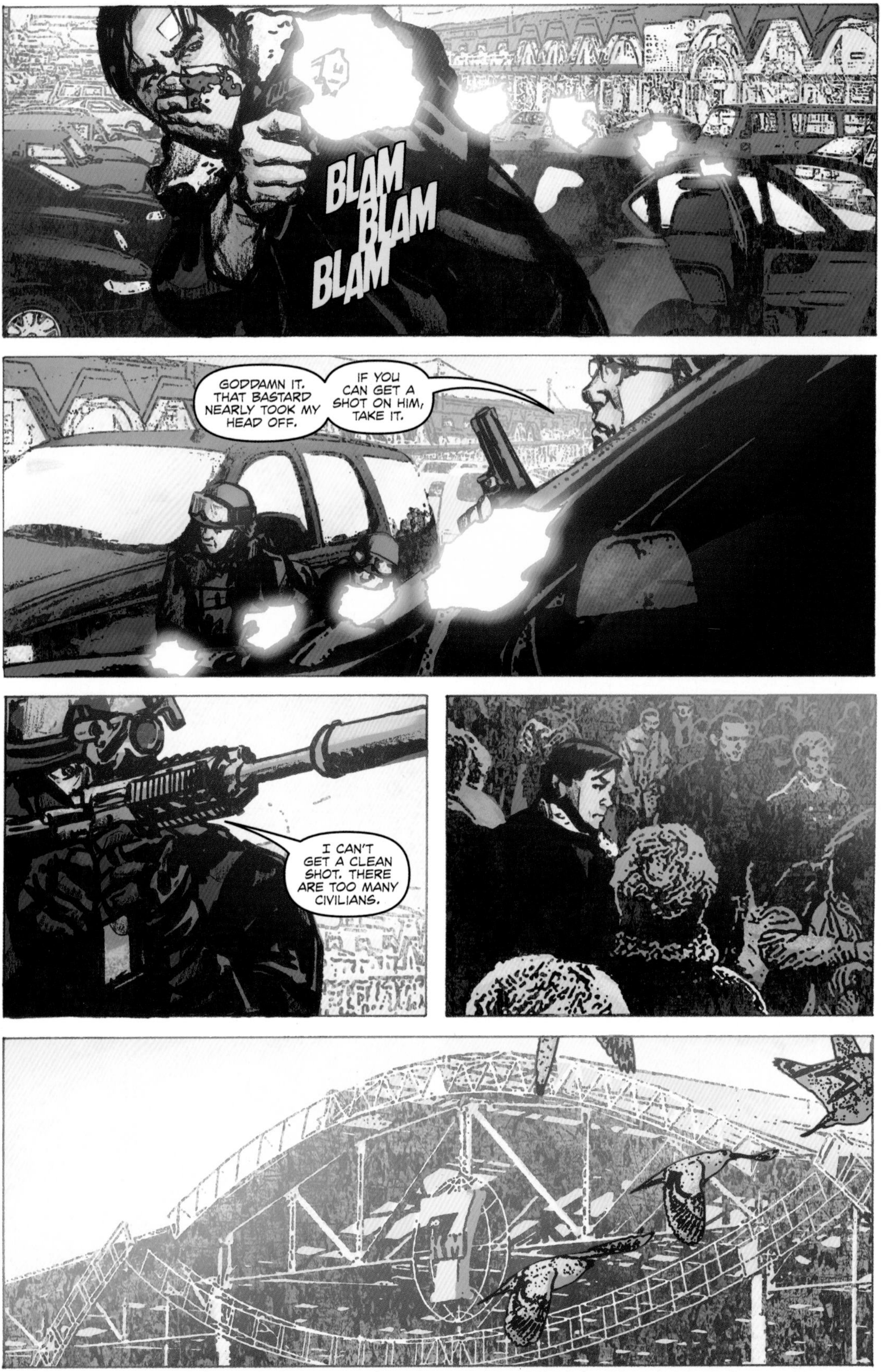
BLAM BLAM BLAM
GODDAMN IT. THAT BASTARD NEARLY TOOK MY HEAD OFF.
IF YOU CAN GET A SHOT ON HIM, TAKE IT.
I CAN'T GET A CLEAN SHOT. THERE ARE TOO MANY CIVILIANS.

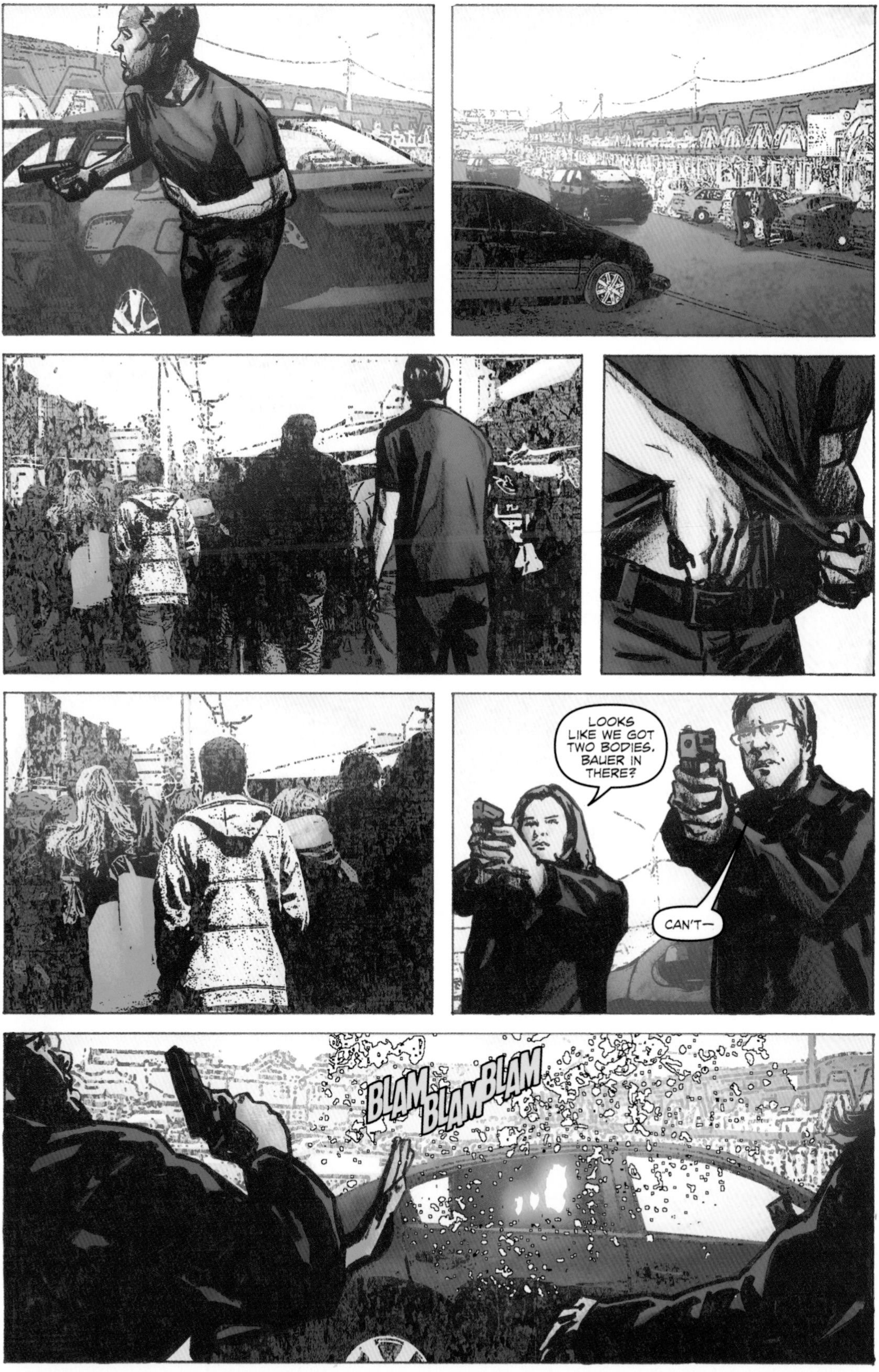
LOOKS LIKE WE GOT TWO BODIES. BAUER IN THERE?
CAN'T—
BLAM BLAM BLAM

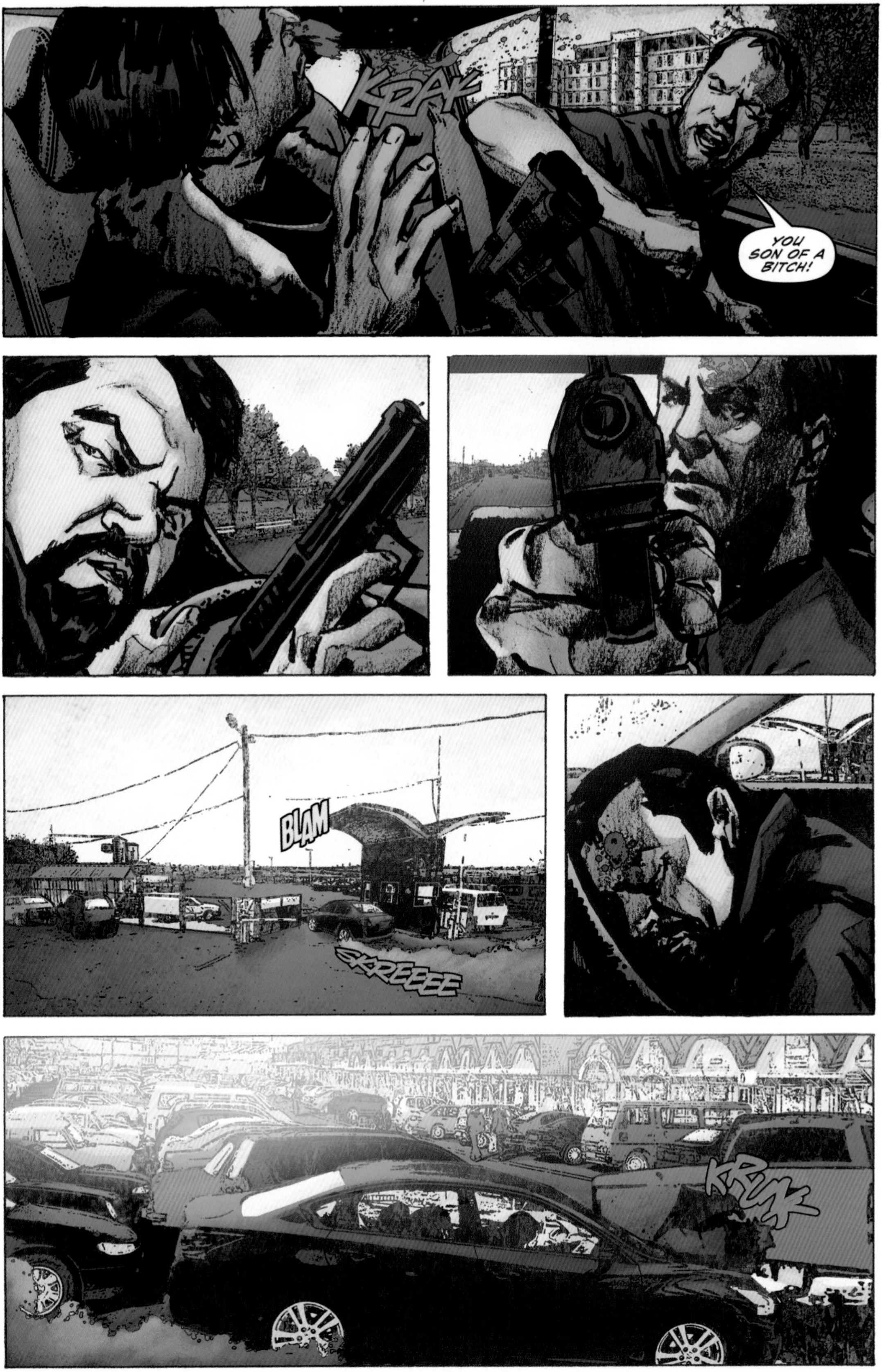
KRAK
YOU SON OF A BITCH!
BLAM
SKREEEE
KRUNK

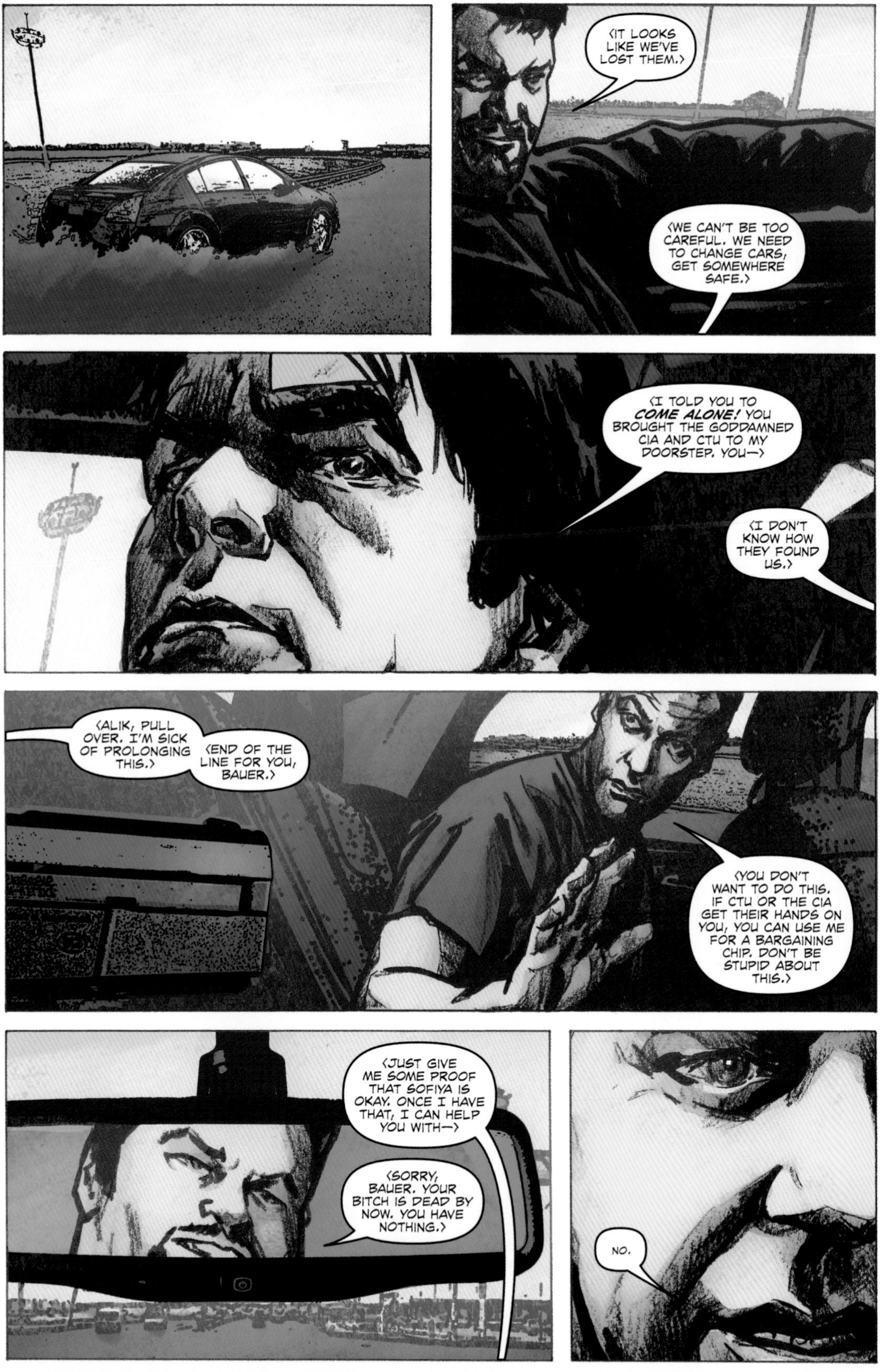

‹IT LOOKS LIKE WE'VE LOST THEM.›
‹WE CAN'T BE TOO CAREFUL. WE NEED TO CHANGE CARS, GET SOMEWHERE SAFE.›
‹I TOLD YOU TO **COME ALONE!** YOU BROUGHT THE GODDAMNED CIA AND CTU TO MY DOORSTEP. YOU—›
‹I DON'T KNOW HOW THEY FOUND US.›
‹ALIK, PULL OVER. I'M SICK OF PROLONGING THIS.›
‹END OF THE LINE FOR YOU, BAUER.›
‹YOU DON'T WANT TO DO THIS. IF CTU OR THE CIA GET THEIR HANDS ON YOU, YOU CAN USE ME FOR A BARGAINING CHIP. DON'T BE STUPID ABOUT THIS.›
‹JUST GIVE ME SOME PROOF THAT SOFIYA IS OKAY. ONCE I HAVE THAT, I CAN HELP YOU WITH—›
‹SORRY, BAUER. YOUR BITCH IS DEAD BY NOW. YOU HAVE NOTHING.›
NO.

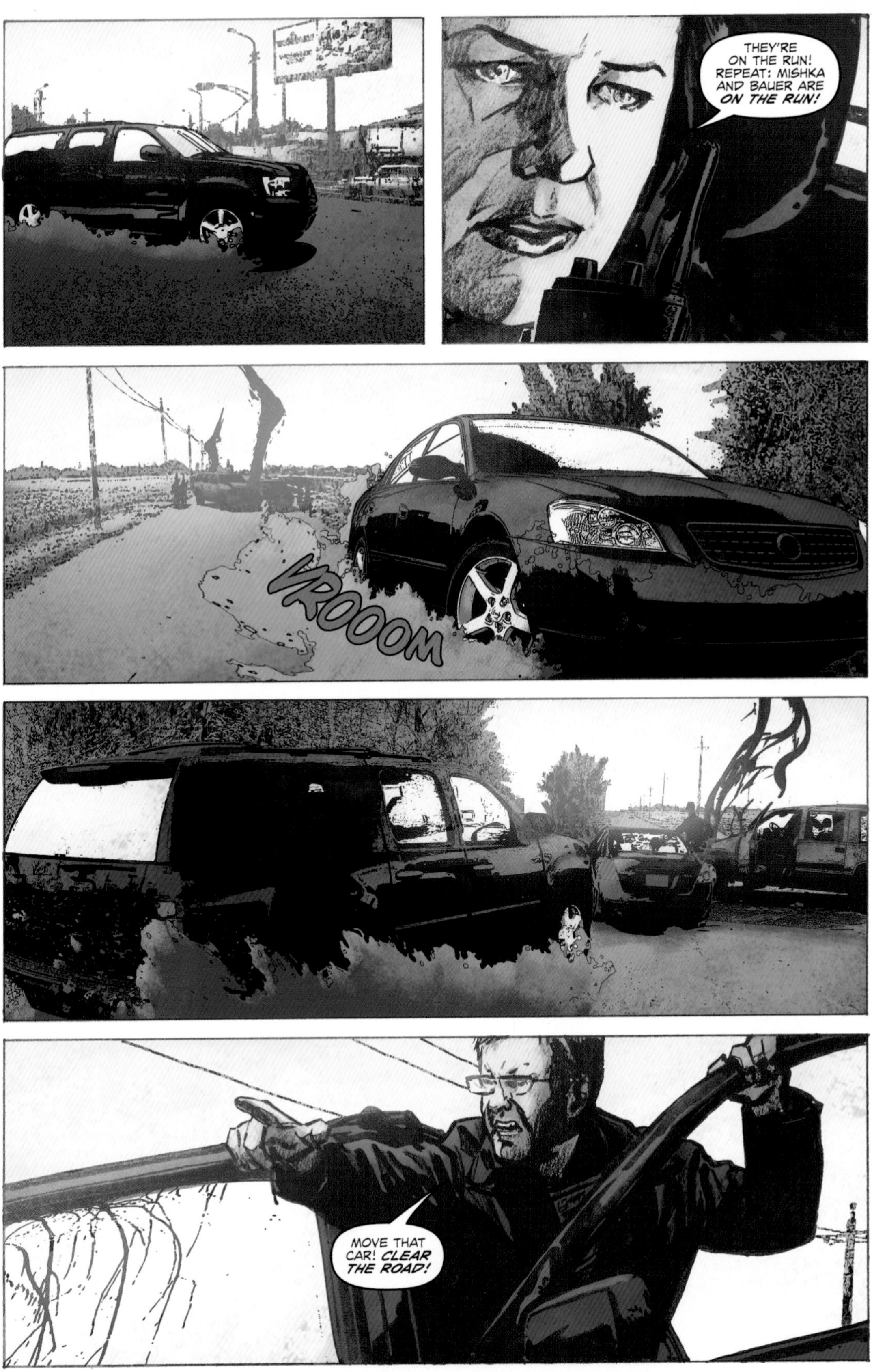
THEY'RE ON THE RUN! REPEAT: MISHKA AND BAUER ARE ON THE RUN!
VROOOM
MOVE THAT CAR! CLEAR THE ROAD!

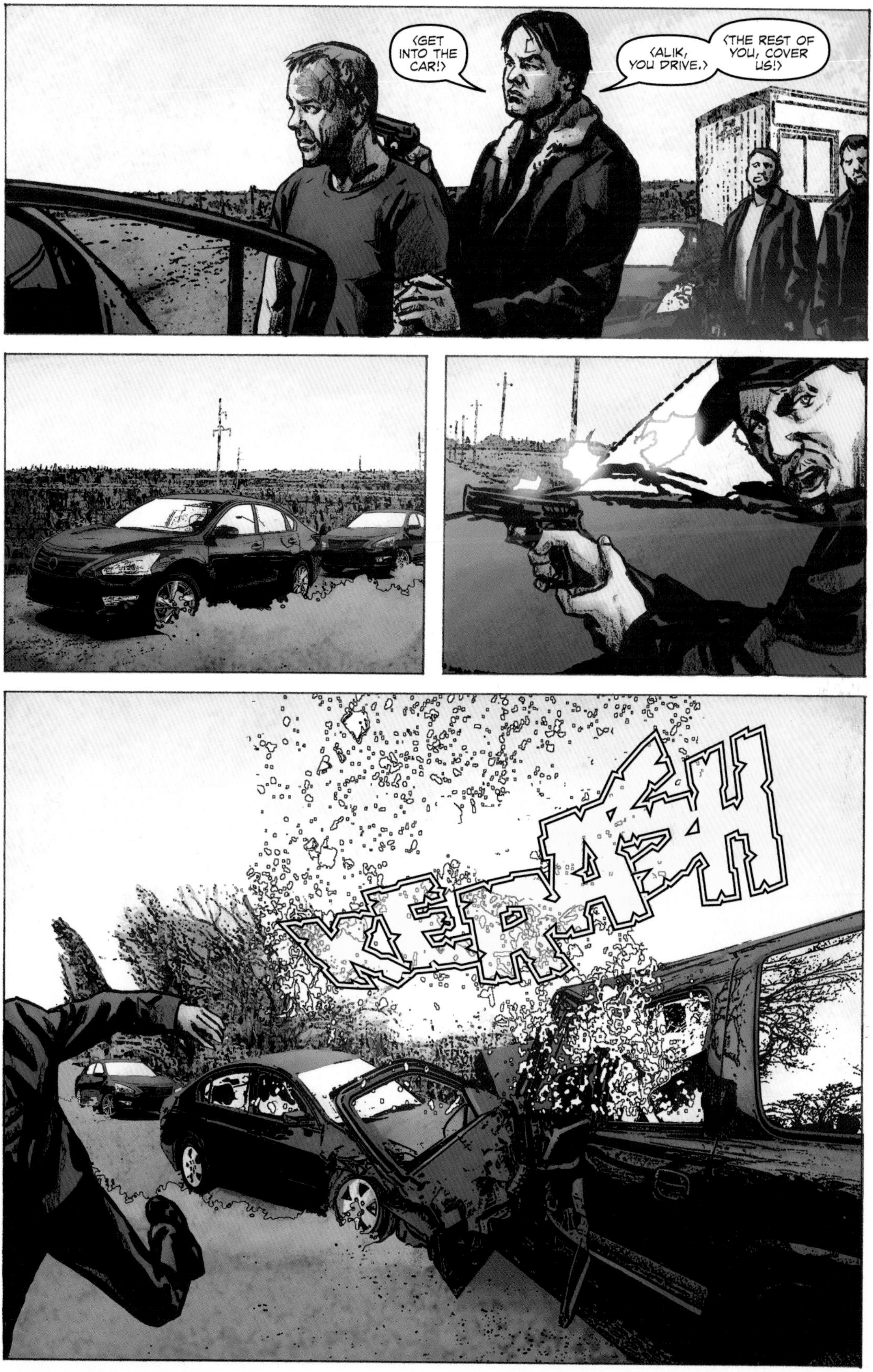

‹GET INTO THE CAR!›
‹ALIK, YOU DRIVE.›
‹THE REST OF YOU, COVER US!›

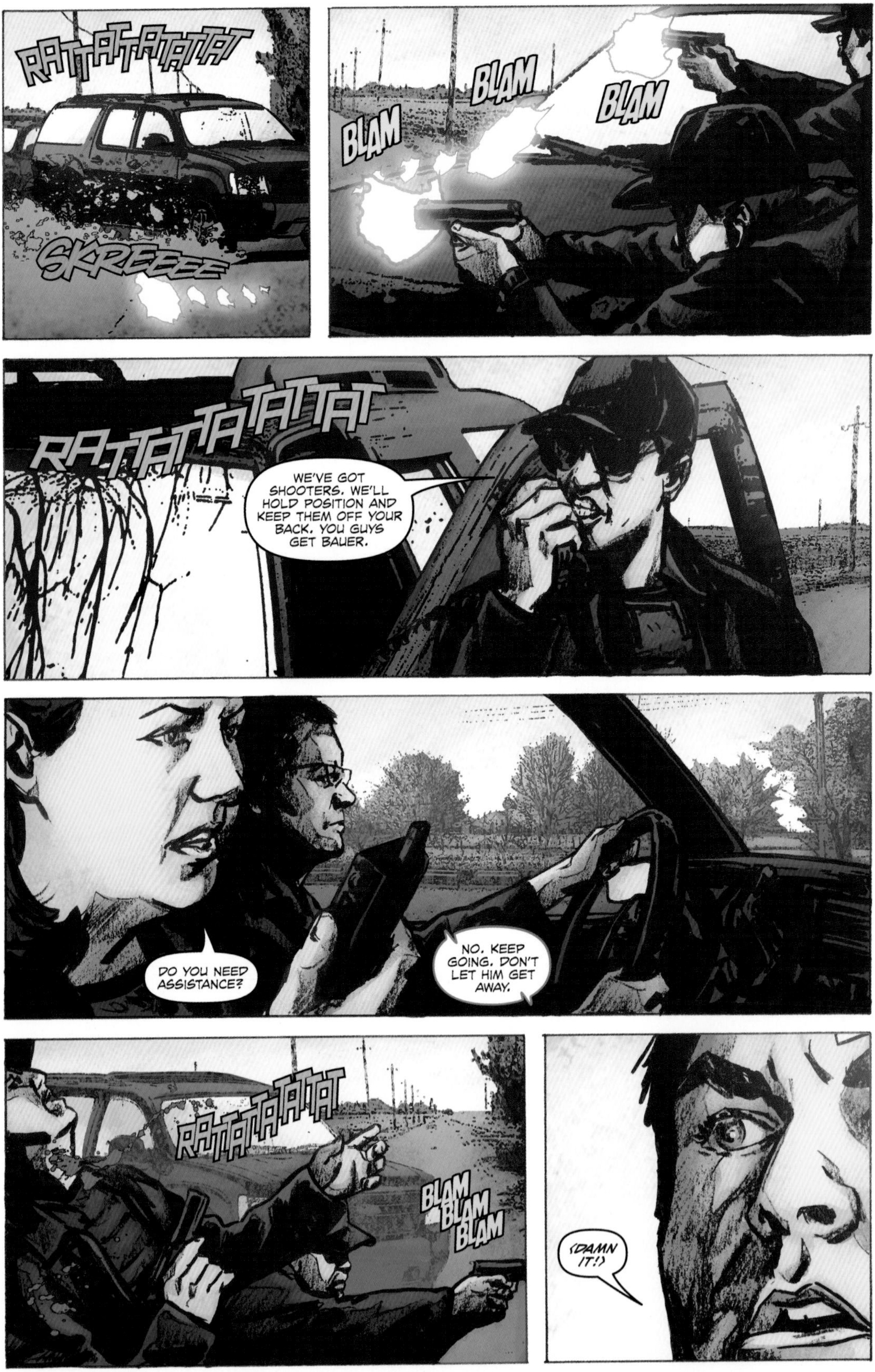
RATTATTATATTAT
SKREEEEE
BLAM
BLAM
BLAM
RATTATTATATTAT
WE'VE GOT SHOOTERS. WE'LL HOLD POSITION AND KEEP THEM OFF YOUR BACK. YOU GUYS GET BAUER.
DO YOU NEED ASSISTANCE?
NO. KEEP GOING. DON'T LET HIM GET AWAY.
RATTATTATATTAT
BLAM BLAM BLAM
‹DAMN IT!›

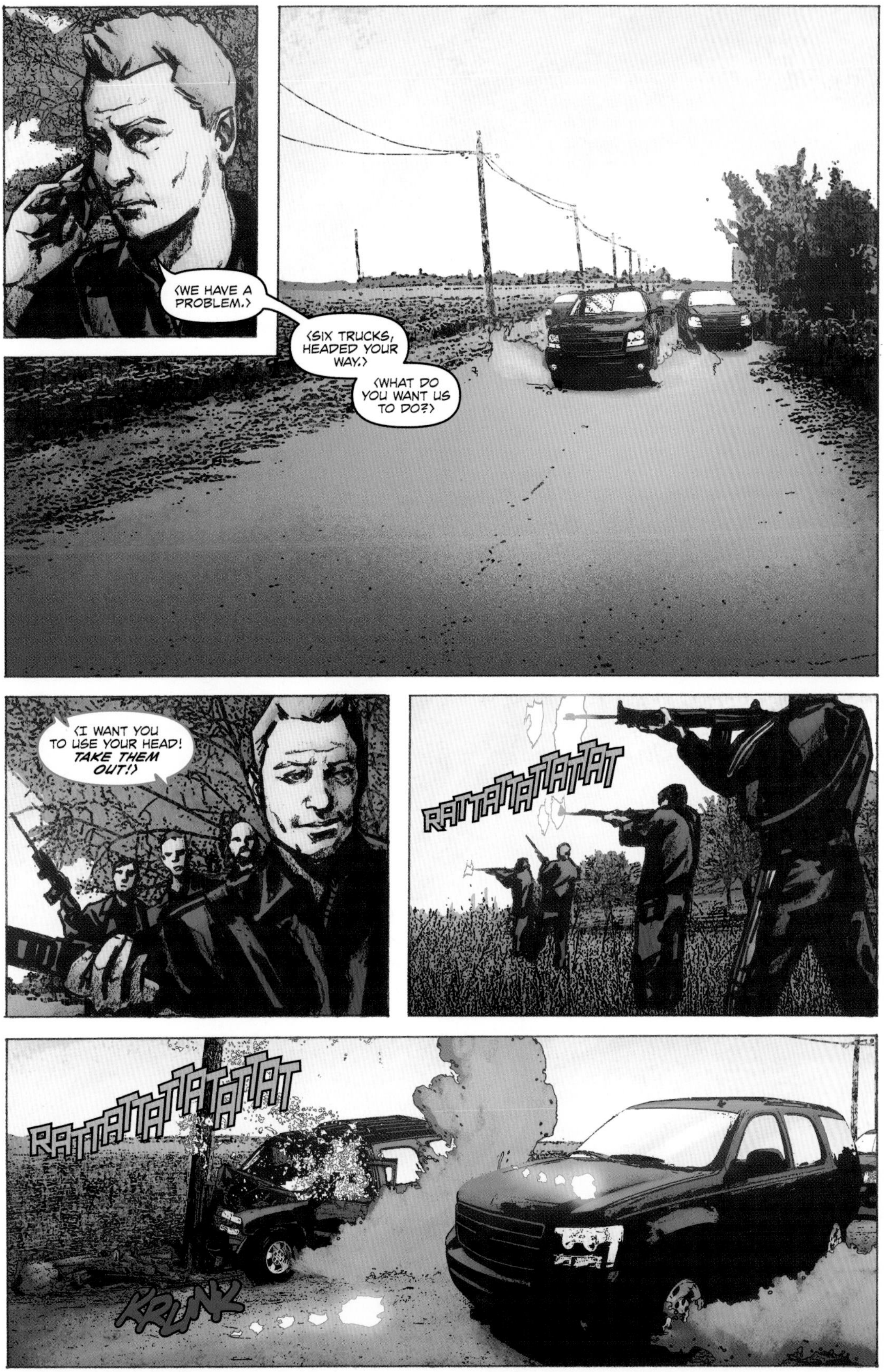

‹WE HAVE A PROBLEM.›
‹SIX TRUCKS, HEADED YOUR WAY.›
‹WHAT DO YOU WANT US TO DO?›
‹I WANT YOU TO USE YOUR HEAD! *TAKE THEM OUT!*›
RATTATTATTATTAT
RATTATTATTATTATTAT
KRUNK

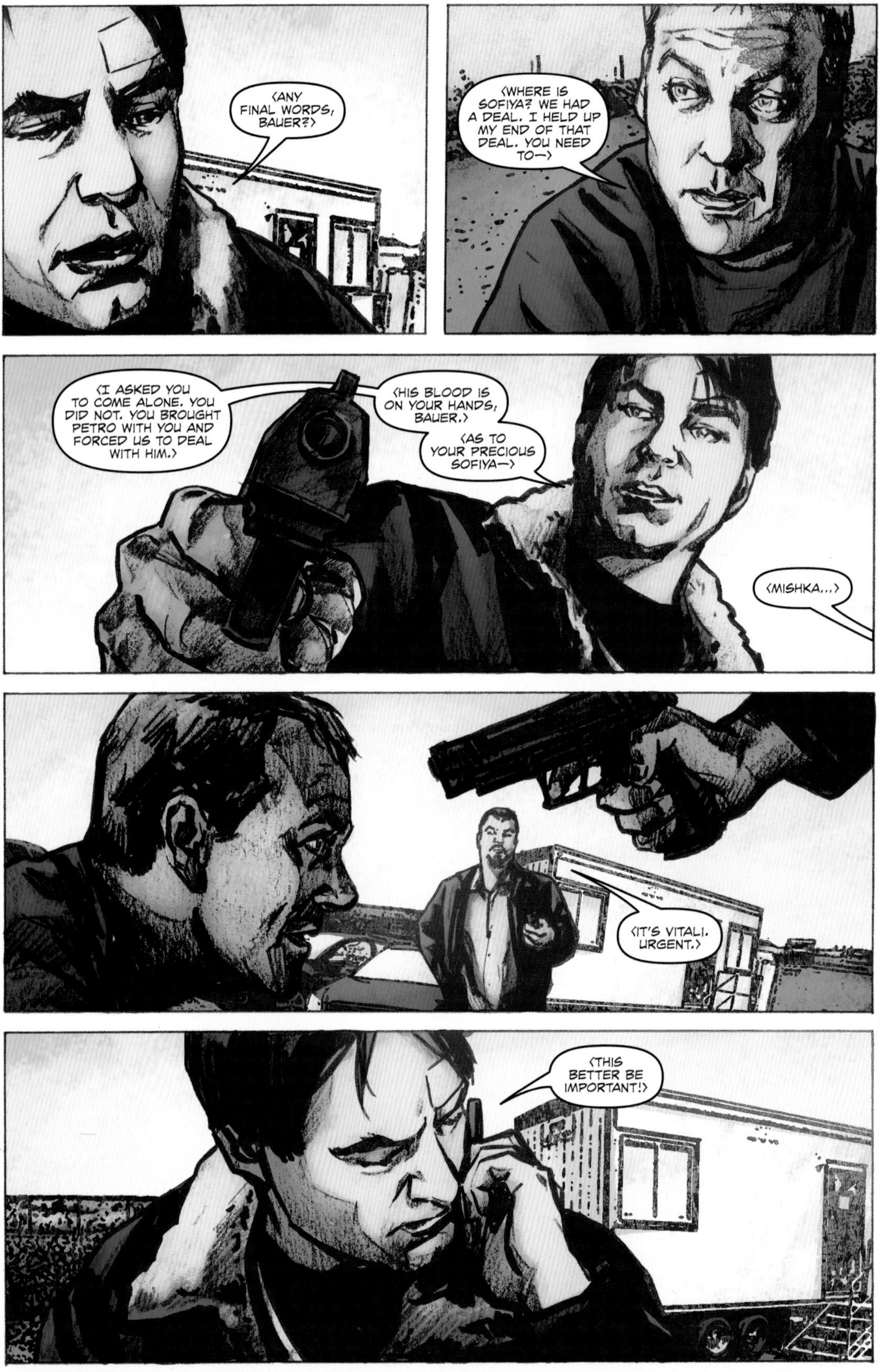
<ANY FINAL WORDS, BAUER?>
<WHERE IS SOFIYA? WE HAD A DEAL. I HELD UP MY END OF THAT DEAL. YOU NEED TO—>
<I ASKED YOU TO COME ALONE. YOU DID NOT. YOU BROUGHT PETRO WITH YOU AND FORCED US TO DEAL WITH HIM.>
<HIS BLOOD IS ON YOUR HANDS, BAUER.>
<AS TO YOUR PRECIOUS SOFIYA—>
<MISHKA...>
<IT'S VITALI. URGENT.>
<THIS BETTER BE IMPORTANT!>

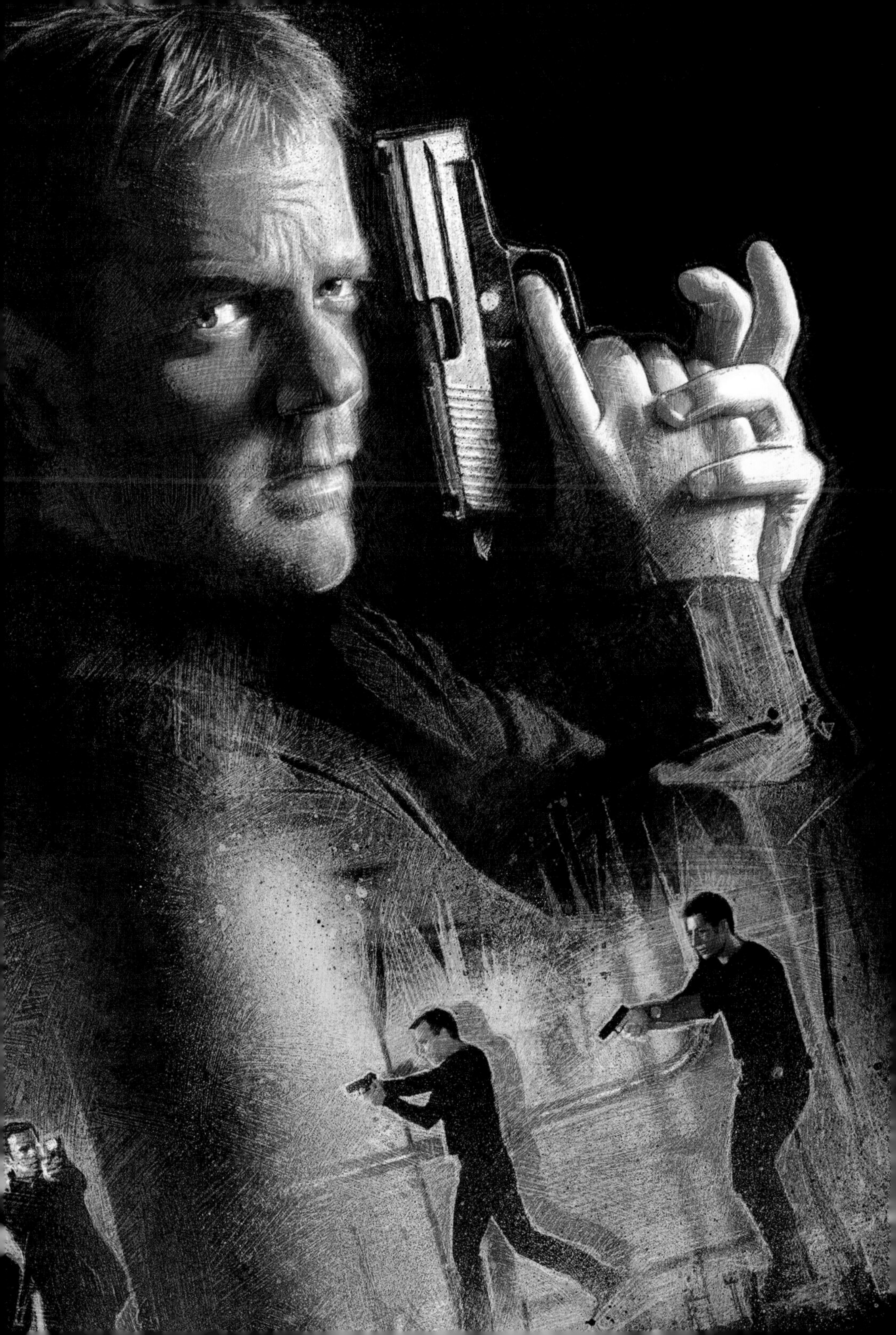

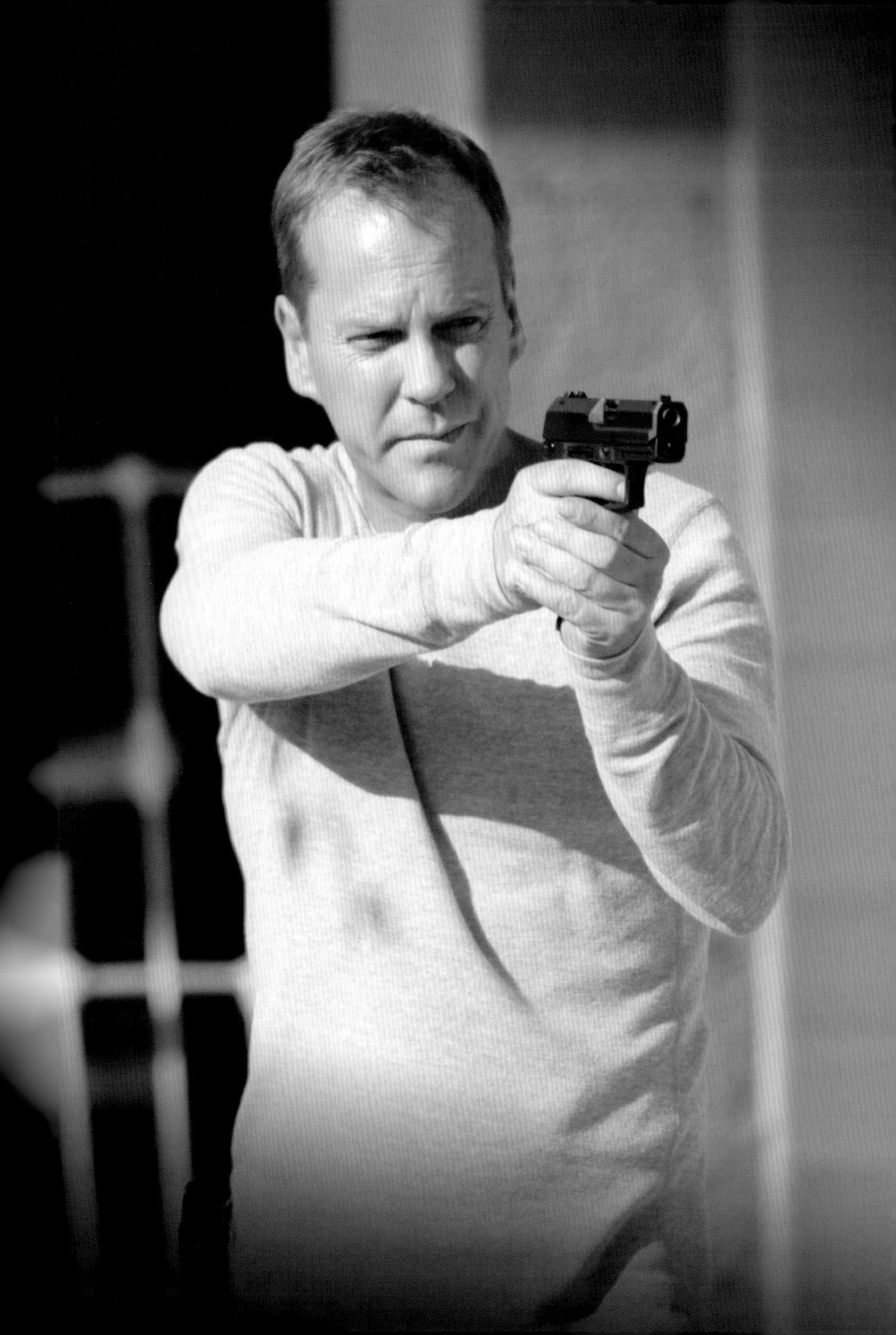

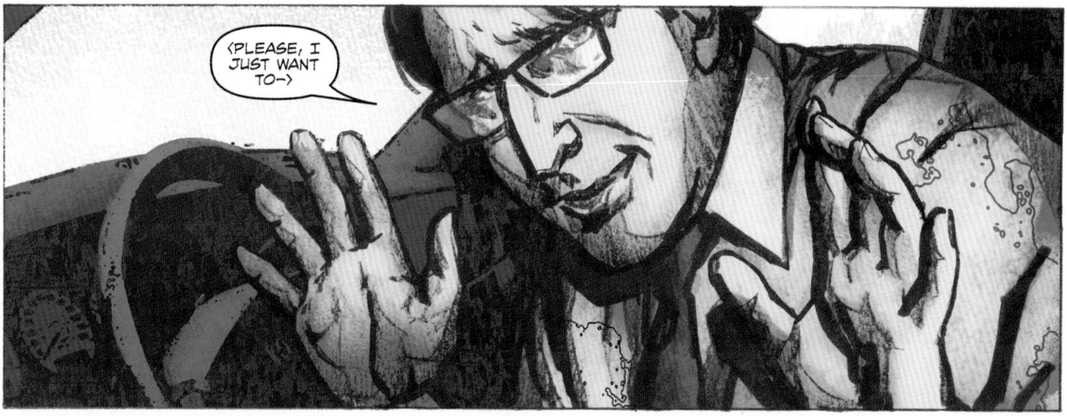
‹PLEASE, I JUST WANT TO-›

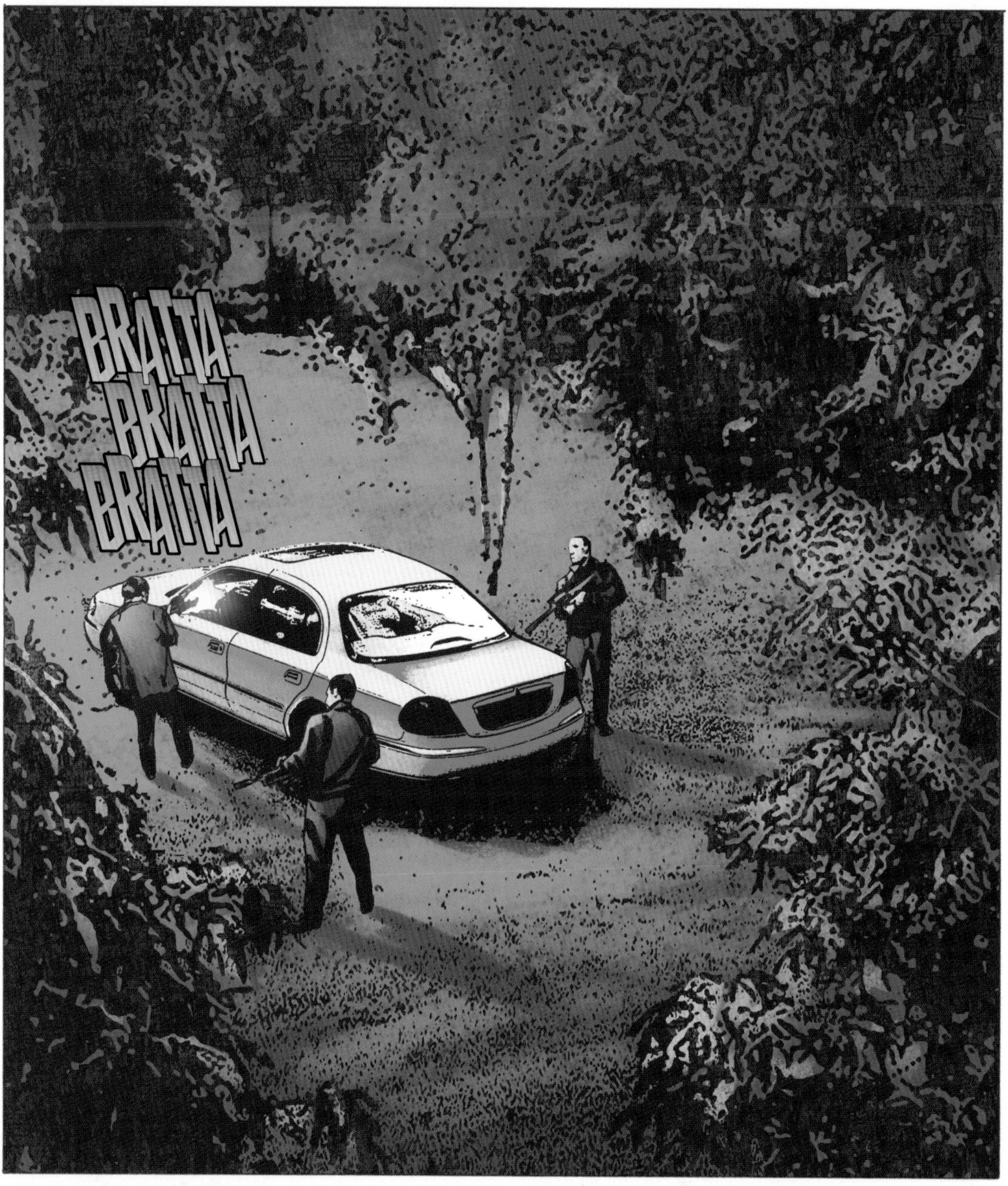
BRATTA
BRATTA
BRATTA

("APPARENTLY I'M NOT THE ONLY ONE TO BREAK HIS PROMISE.")

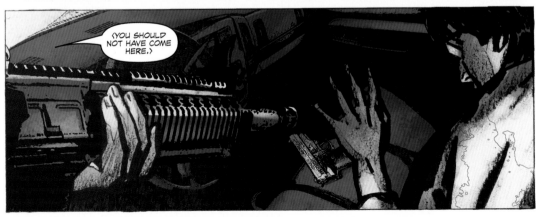

〈YOU SHOULD NOT HAVE COME HERE.〉

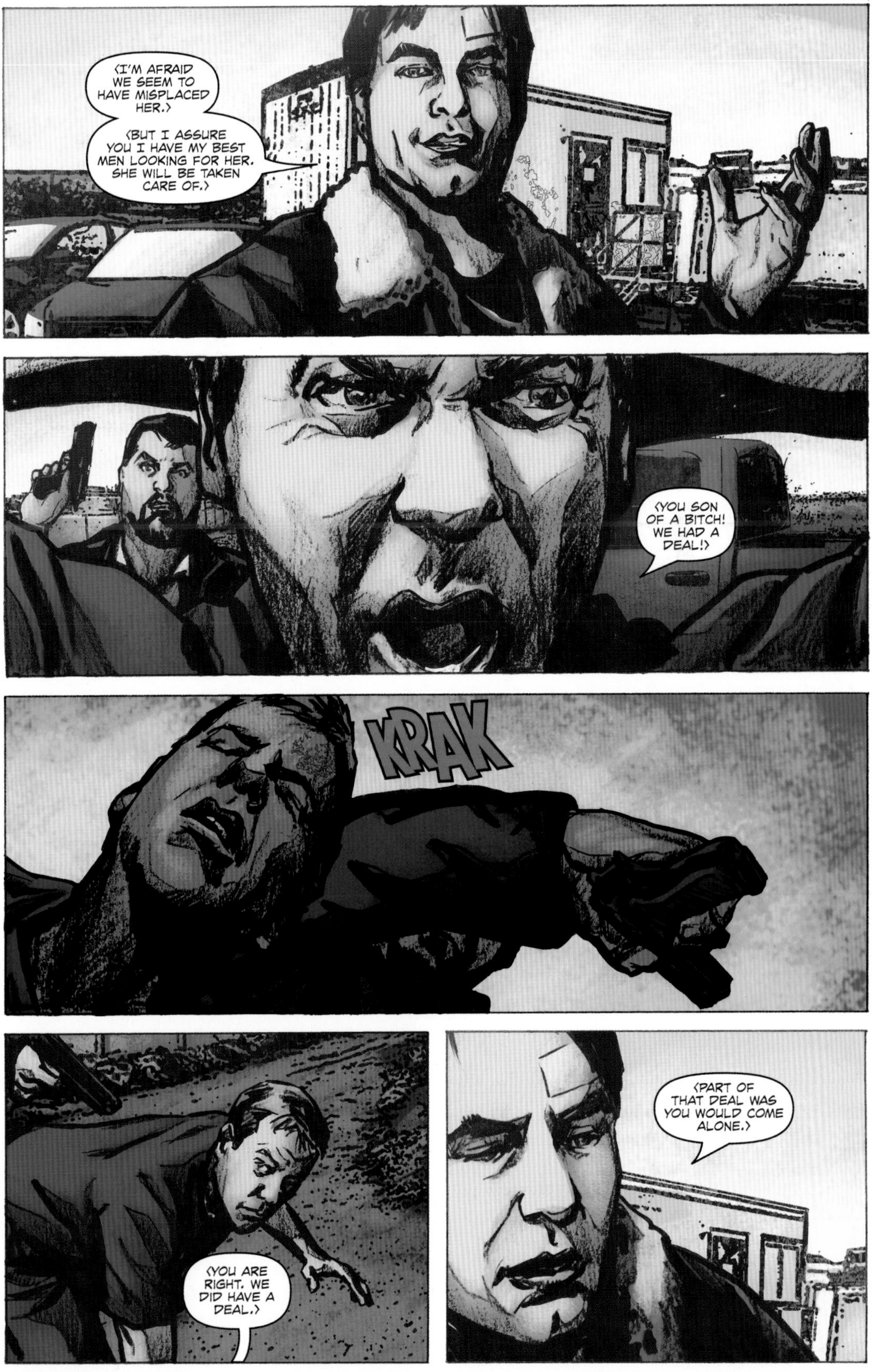
<I'M AFRAID WE SEEM TO HAVE MISPLACED HER.>
<BUT I ASSURE YOU I HAVE MY BEST MEN LOOKING FOR HER. SHE WILL BE TAKEN CARE OF.>
<YOU SON OF A BITCH! WE HAD A DEAL!>
KRAK
<YOU ARE RIGHT. WE DID HAVE A DEAL.>
<PART OF THAT DEAL WAS YOU WOULD COME ALONE.>

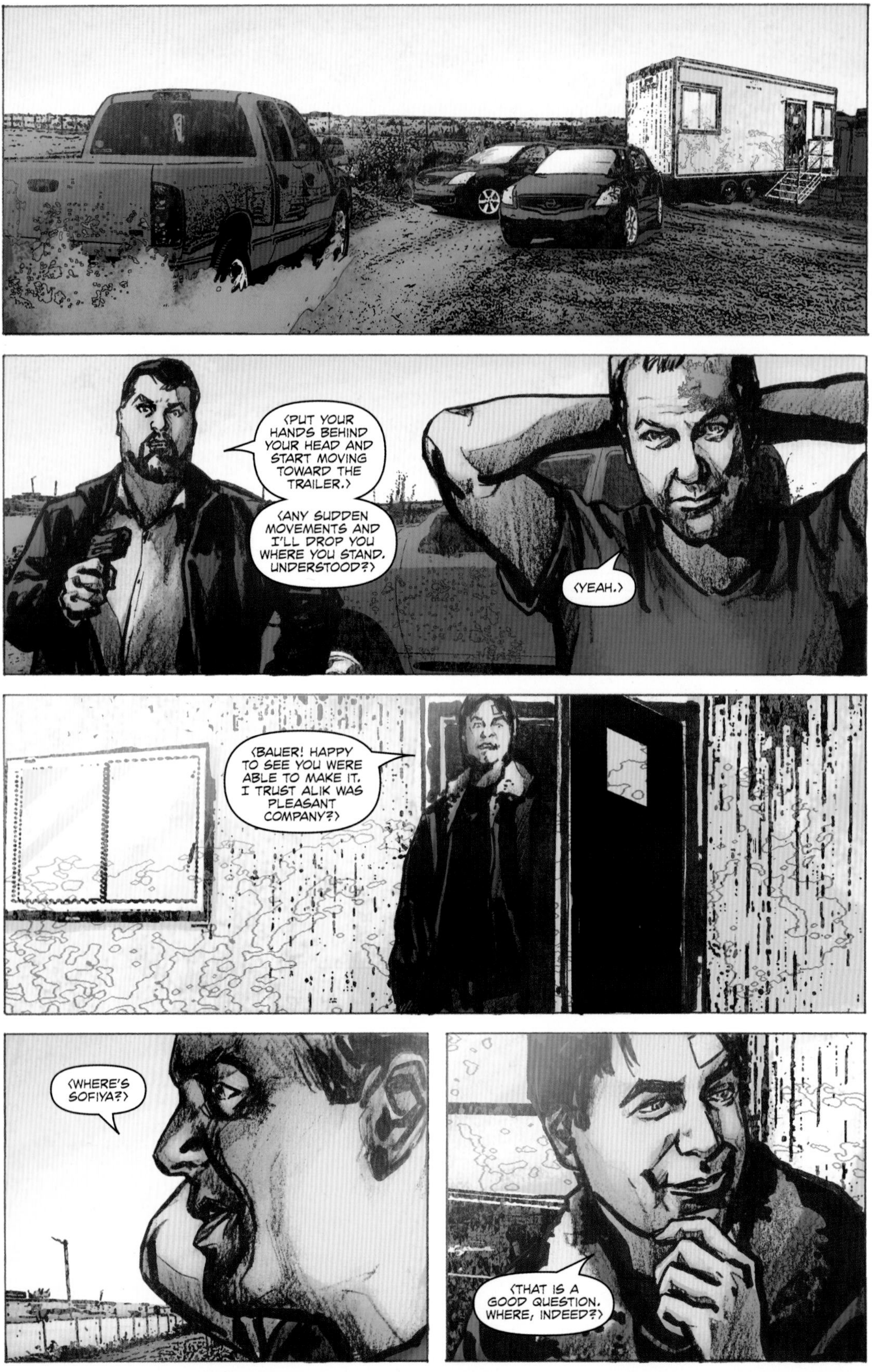
<PUT YOUR HANDS BEHIND YOUR HEAD AND START MOVING TOWARD THE TRAILER.>
<ANY SUDDEN MOVEMENTS AND I'LL DROP YOU WHERE YOU STAND. UNDERSTOOD?>
<YEAH.>
<BAUER! HAPPY TO SEE YOU WERE ABLE TO MAKE IT. I TRUST ALIK WAS PLEASANT COMPANY?>
<WHERE'S SOFIYA?>
<THAT IS A GOOD QUESTION. WHERE, INDEED?>

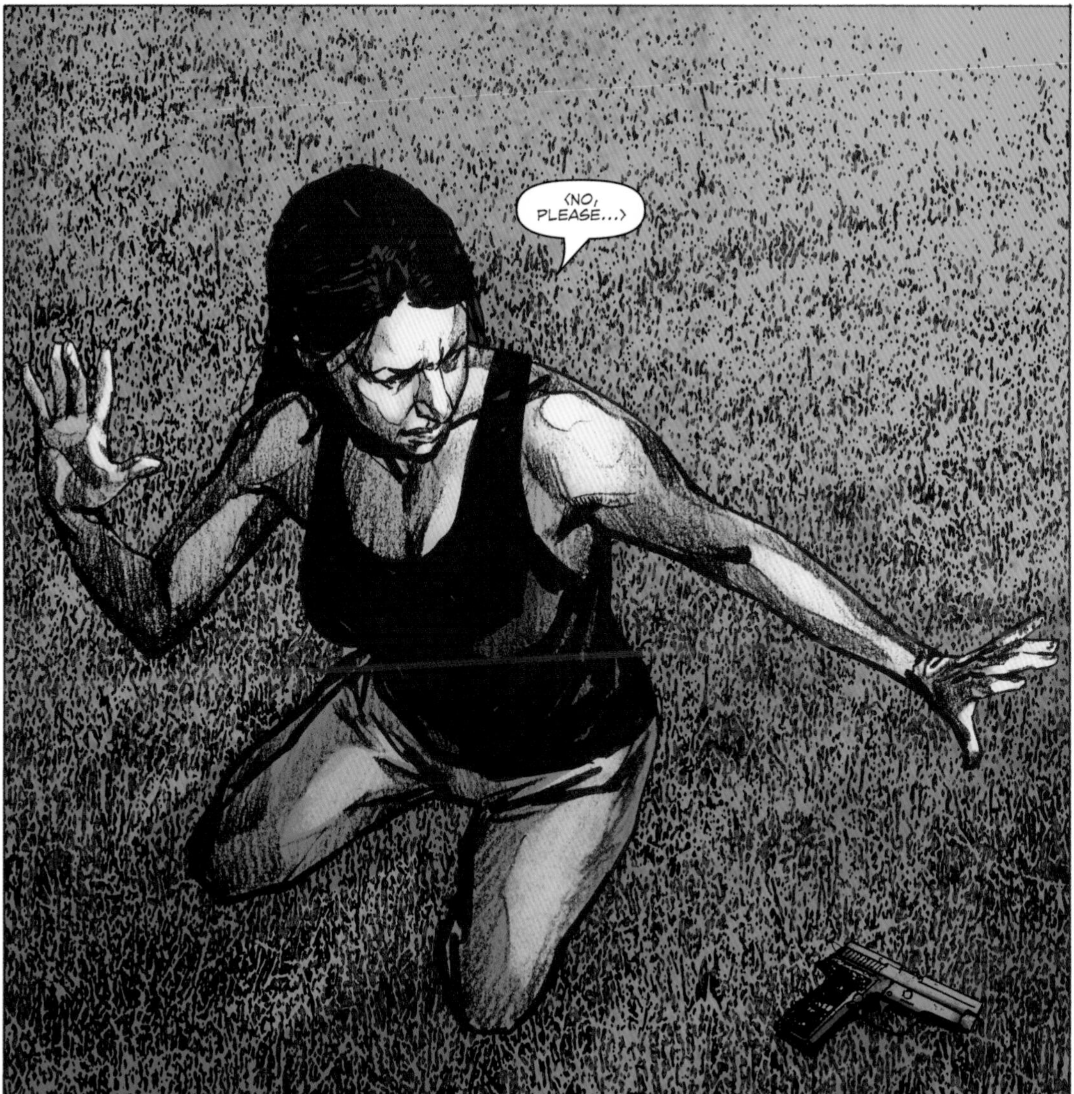
‹NO, PLEASE...›

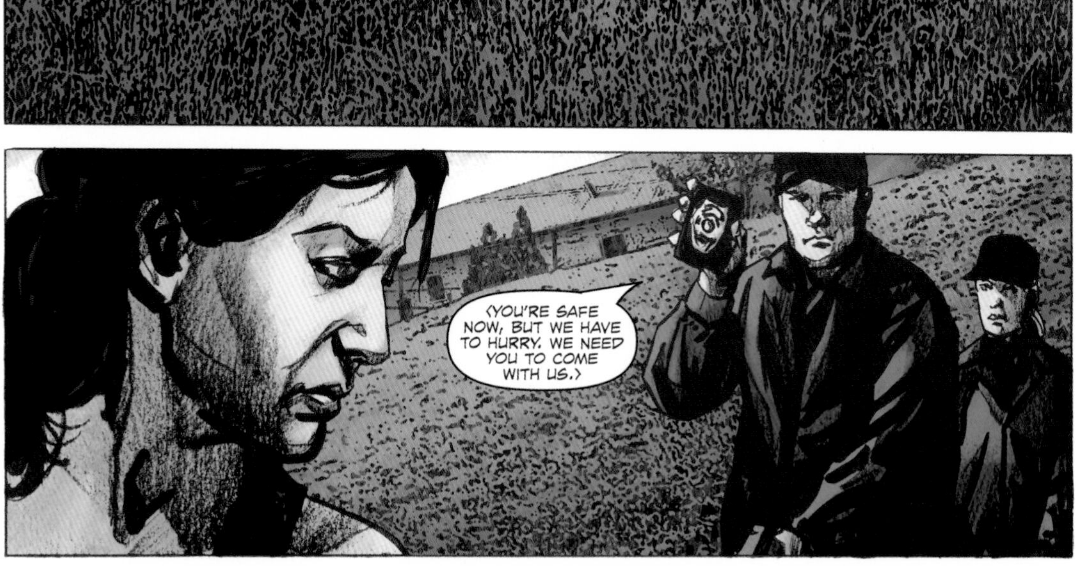
‹YOU'RE SAFE NOW, BUT WE HAVE TO HURRY. WE NEED YOU TO COME WITH US.›

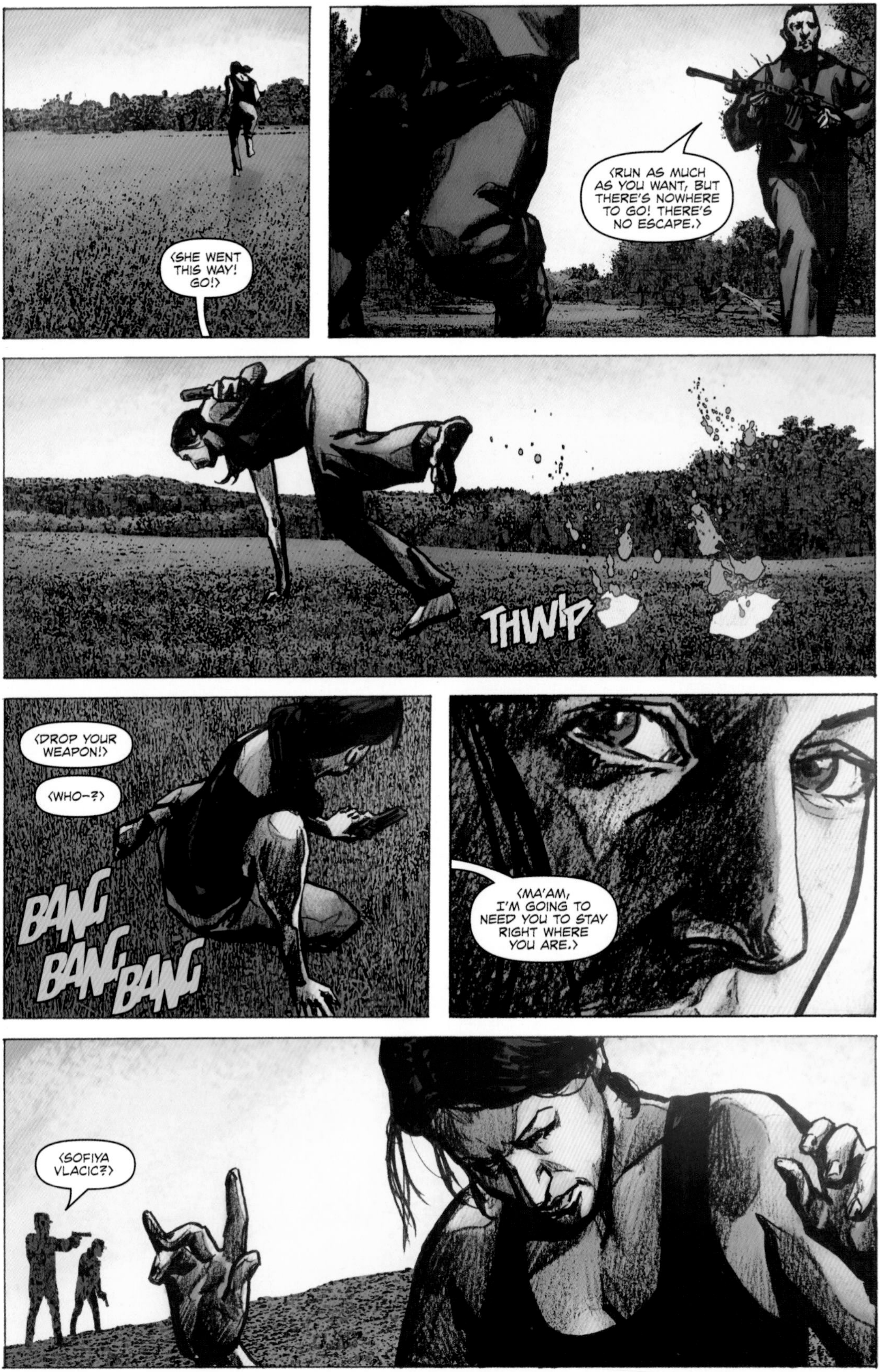

<SHE WENT THIS WAY! GO!>
<RUN AS MUCH AS YOU WANT, BUT THERE'S NOWHERE TO GO! THERE'S NO ESCAPE.>
THWIP
<DROP YOUR WEAPON!>
<WHO-?>
BANG BANG BANG
<MA'AM, I'M GOING TO NEED YOU TO STAY RIGHT WHERE YOU ARE.>
<SOFIYA VLACIC?>

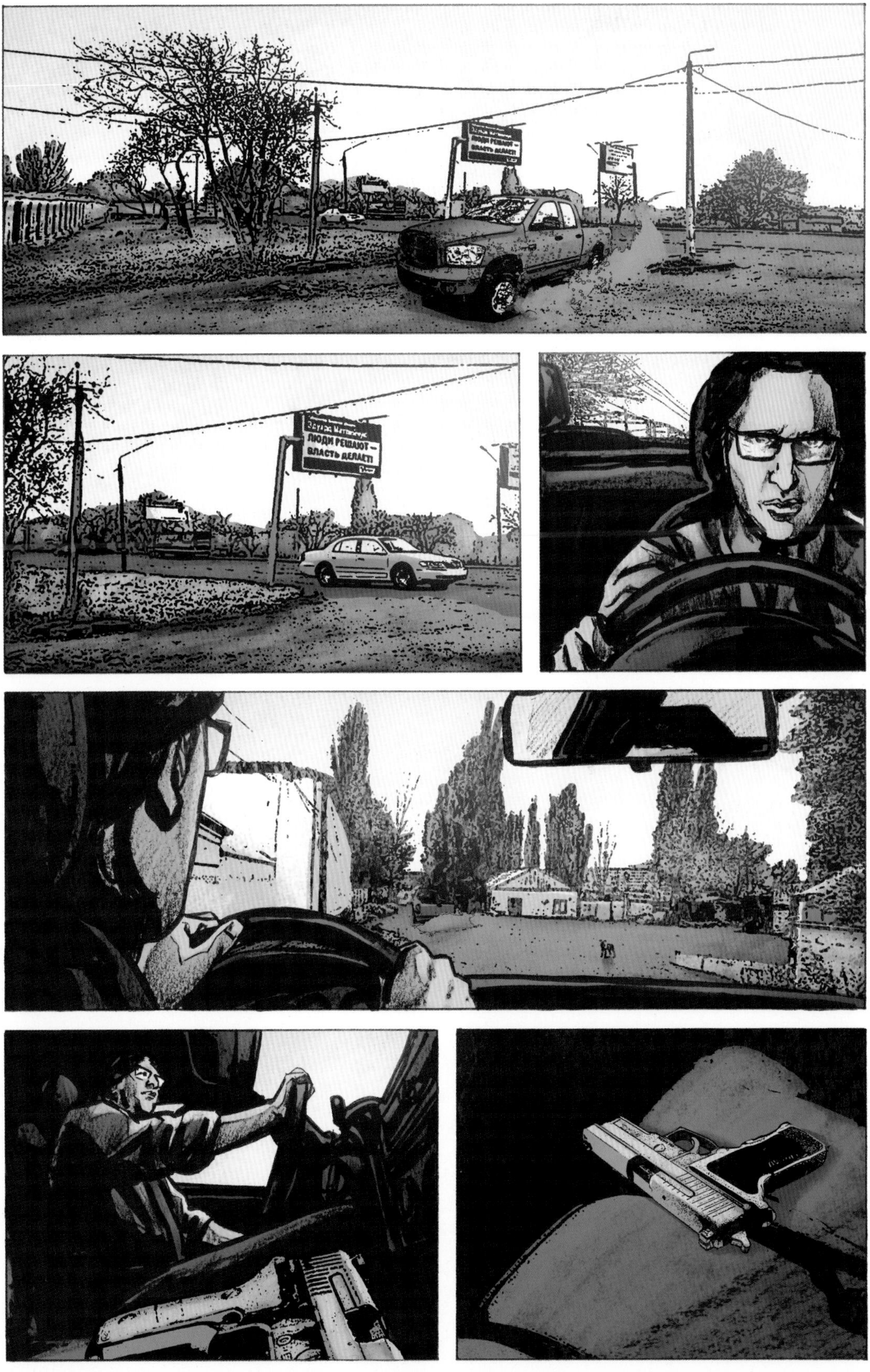
ЛЮДИ РЕШАЮТ —
ВЛАСТЬ ДЕЛАЕТ!

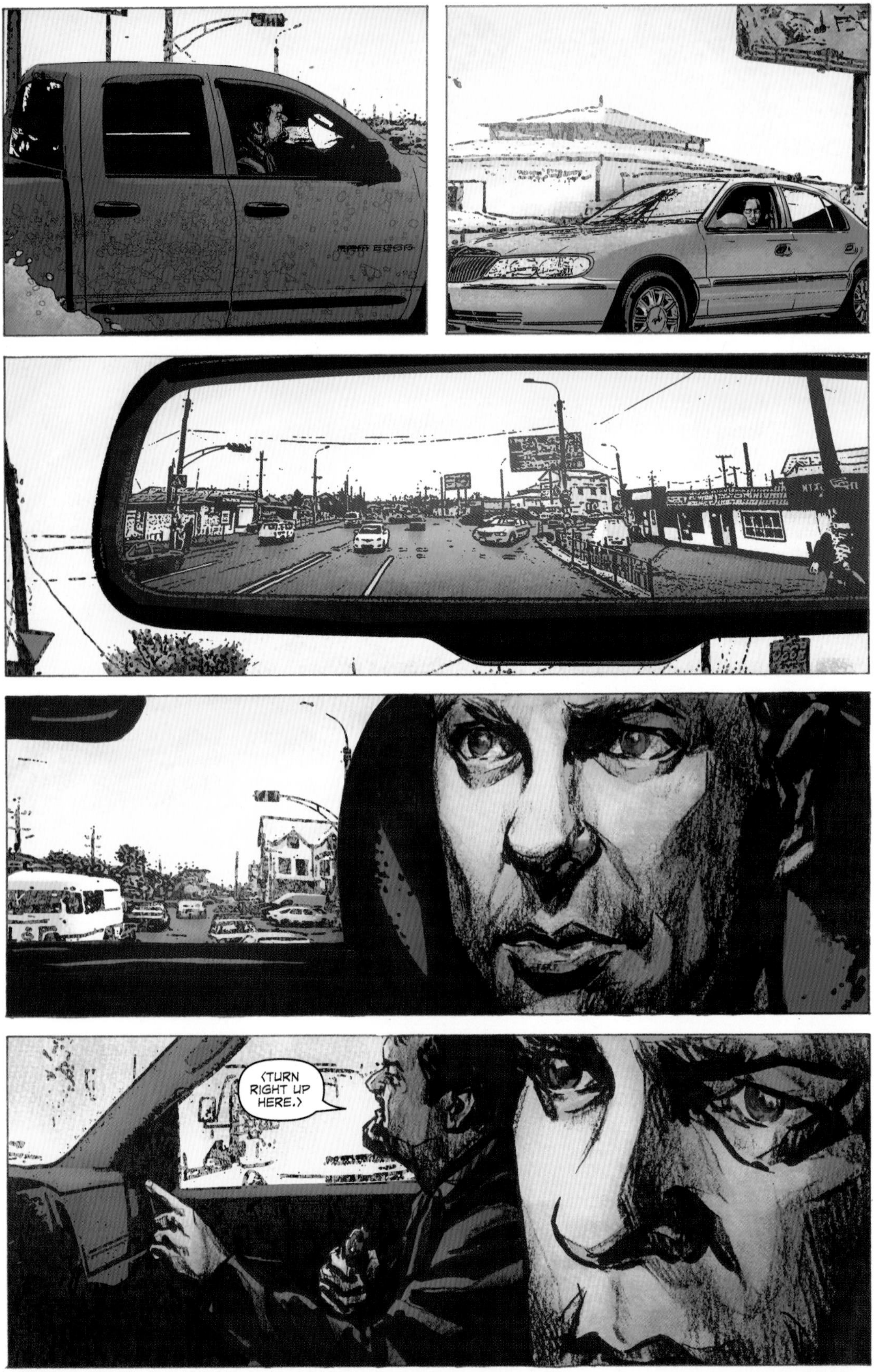
‹TURN RIGHT UP HERE.›

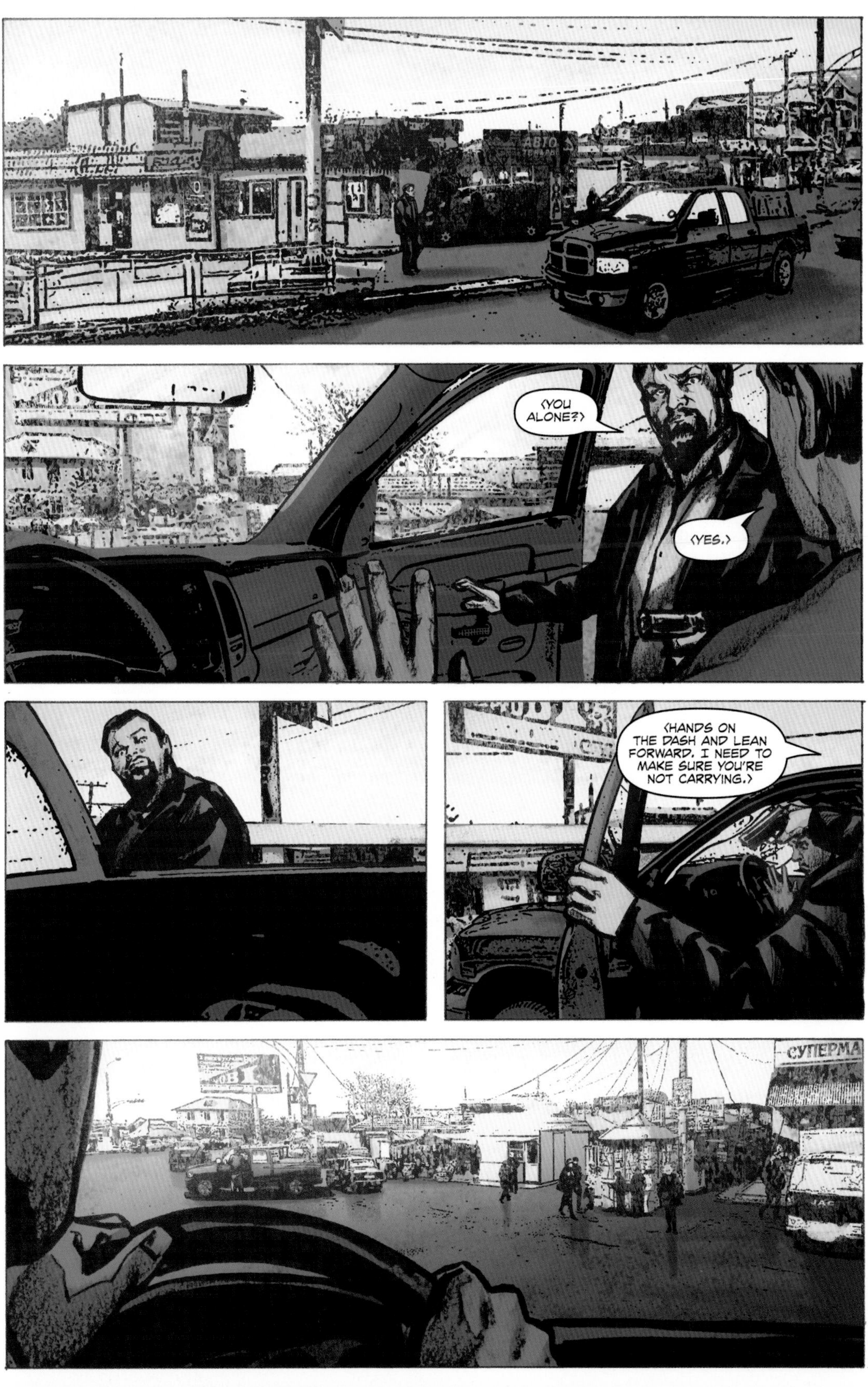
‹YOU ALONE?›
‹YES.›
‹HANDS ON THE DASH AND LEAN FORWARD. I NEED TO MAKE SURE YOU'RE NOT CARRYING.›
СУПЕРМА

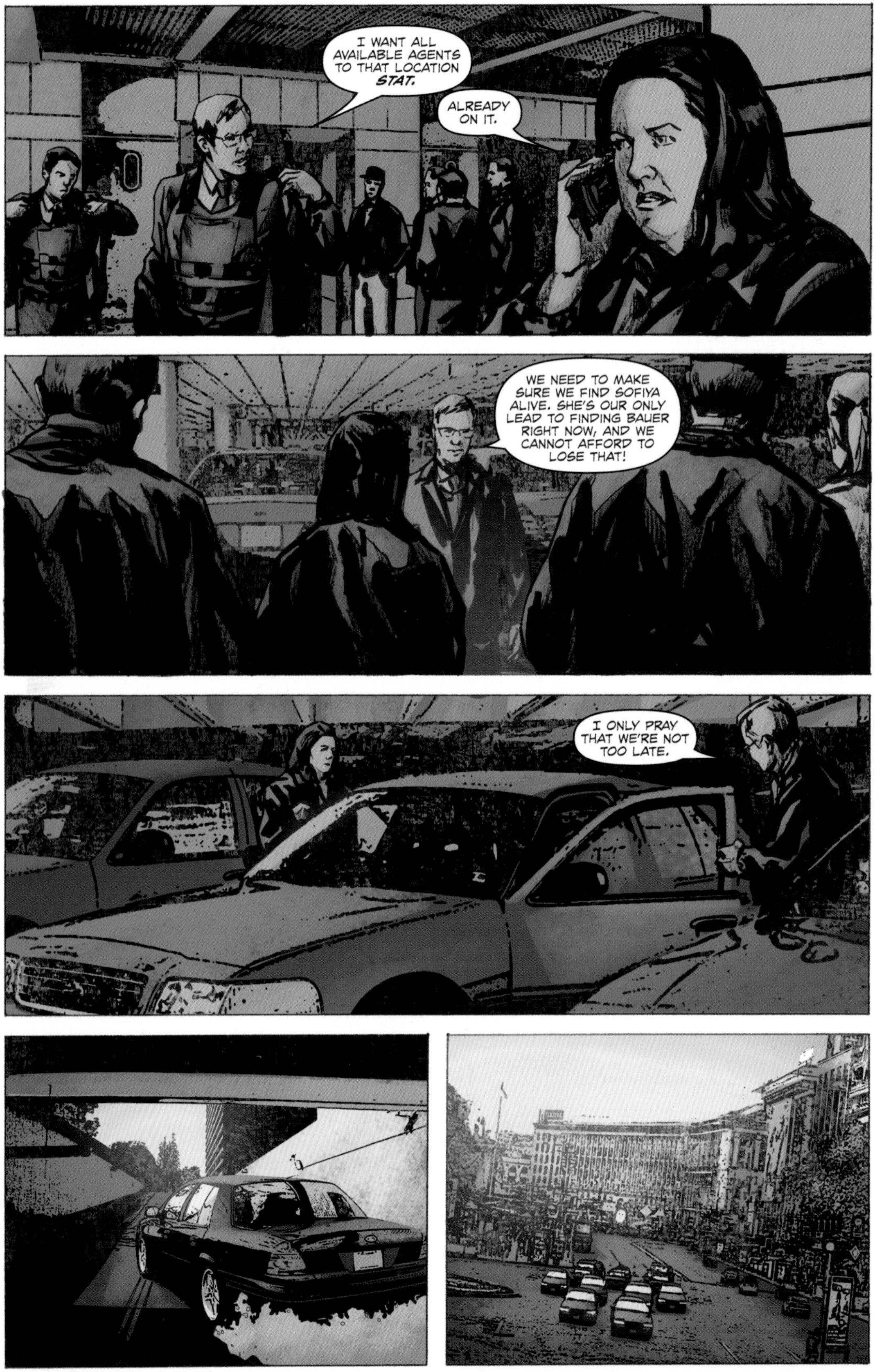
I WANT ALL AVAILABLE AGENTS TO THAT LOCATION STAT.
ALREADY ON IT.
WE NEED TO MAKE SURE WE FIND SOFIYA ALIVE. SHE'S OUR ONLY LEAD TO FINDING BAUER RIGHT NOW, AND WE CANNOT AFFORD TO LOSE THAT!
I ONLY PRAY THAT WE'RE NOT TOO LATE.

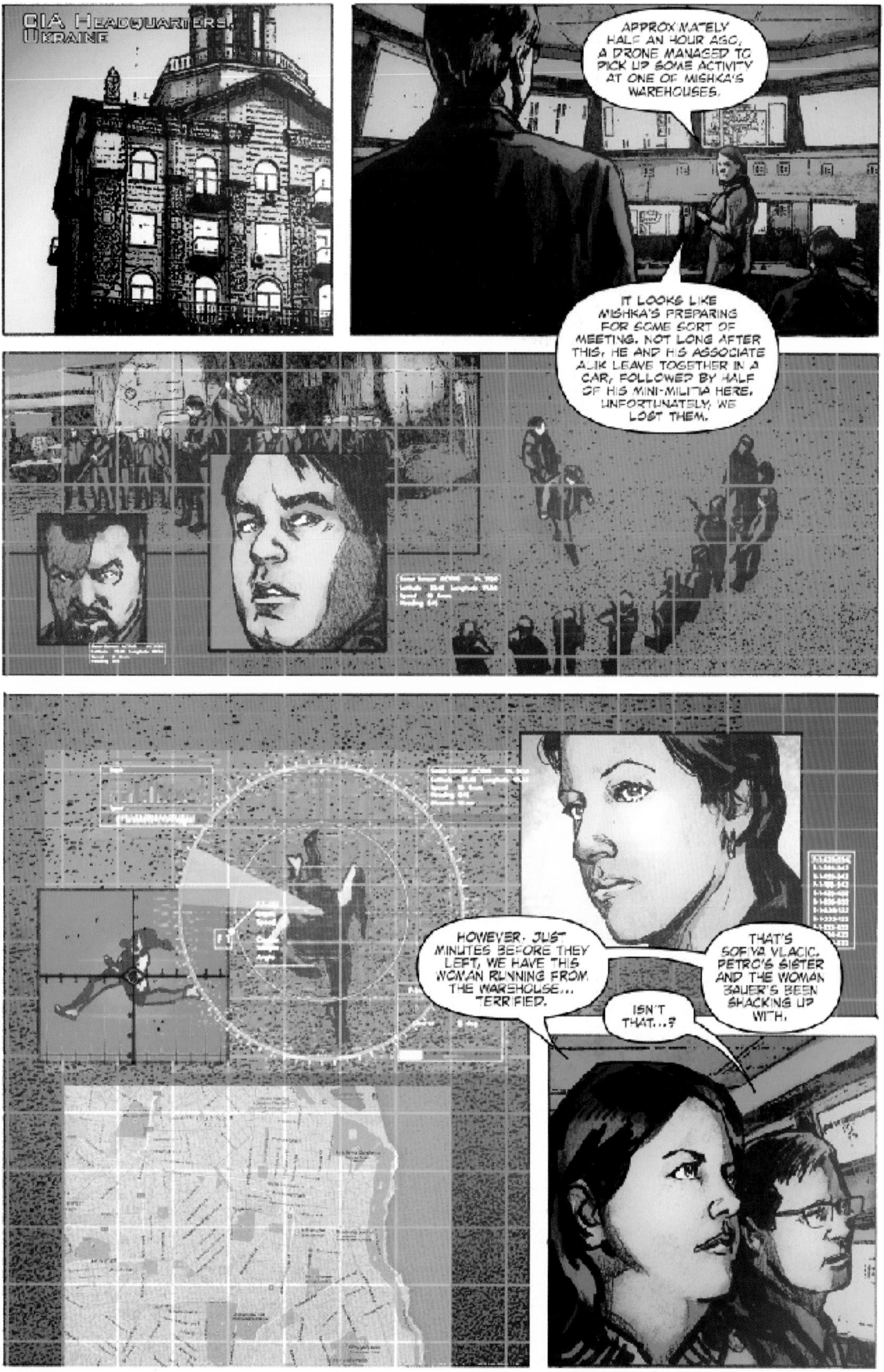
CIA Headquarters, Ukraine
APPROXIMATELY HALF AN HOUR AGO, A DRONE MANAGED TO PICK UP SOME ACTIVITY AT ONE OF MISHKA'S WAREHOUSES.
IT LOOKS LIKE MISHKA'S PREPARING FOR SOME SORT OF MEETING. NOT LONG AFTER THIS, HE AND HIS ASSOCIATE ALIK LEAVE TOGETHER IN A CAR, FOLLOWED BY HALF OF HIS MINI-MILITIA HERE. UNFORTUNATELY, WE LOST THEM.
HOWEVER, JUST MINUTES BEFORE THEY LEFT, WE HAVE THIS WOMAN RUNNING FROM THE WAREHOUSE... TERRIFIED.
ISN'T THAT...?
THAT'S SOFIYA VLACIC. PETRO'S SISTER AND THE WOMAN BAUER'S BEEN SHACKING UP WITH.

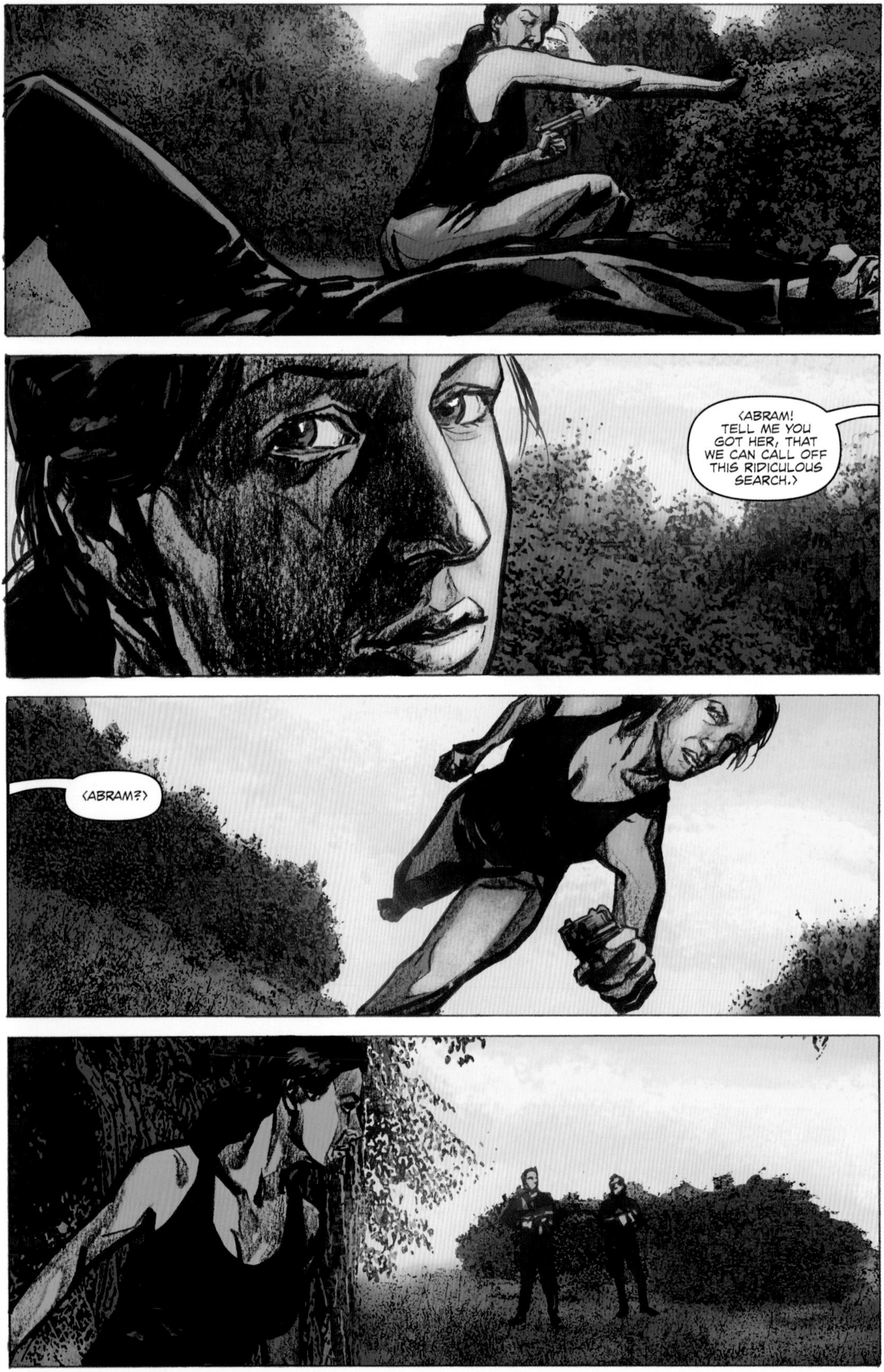

‹ABRAM! TELL ME YOU GOT HER, THAT WE CAN CALL OFF THIS RIDICULOUS SEARCH.›
‹ABRAM?›

EH?

‹IT'S NO USE. COME ON OUT FROM THERE, AND WE'LL GO EASIER ON YOU.›

‹PLEASE... JUST... DON'T. JUST LEAVE ME... I DON'T WANT TO...›

‹OF COURSE YOU DON'T WANT TO SHOOT ANYONE. JUST COME ON OUT FROM THERE, AND WE CAN TALK THIS—›

‹GET AWAY!›

BANG

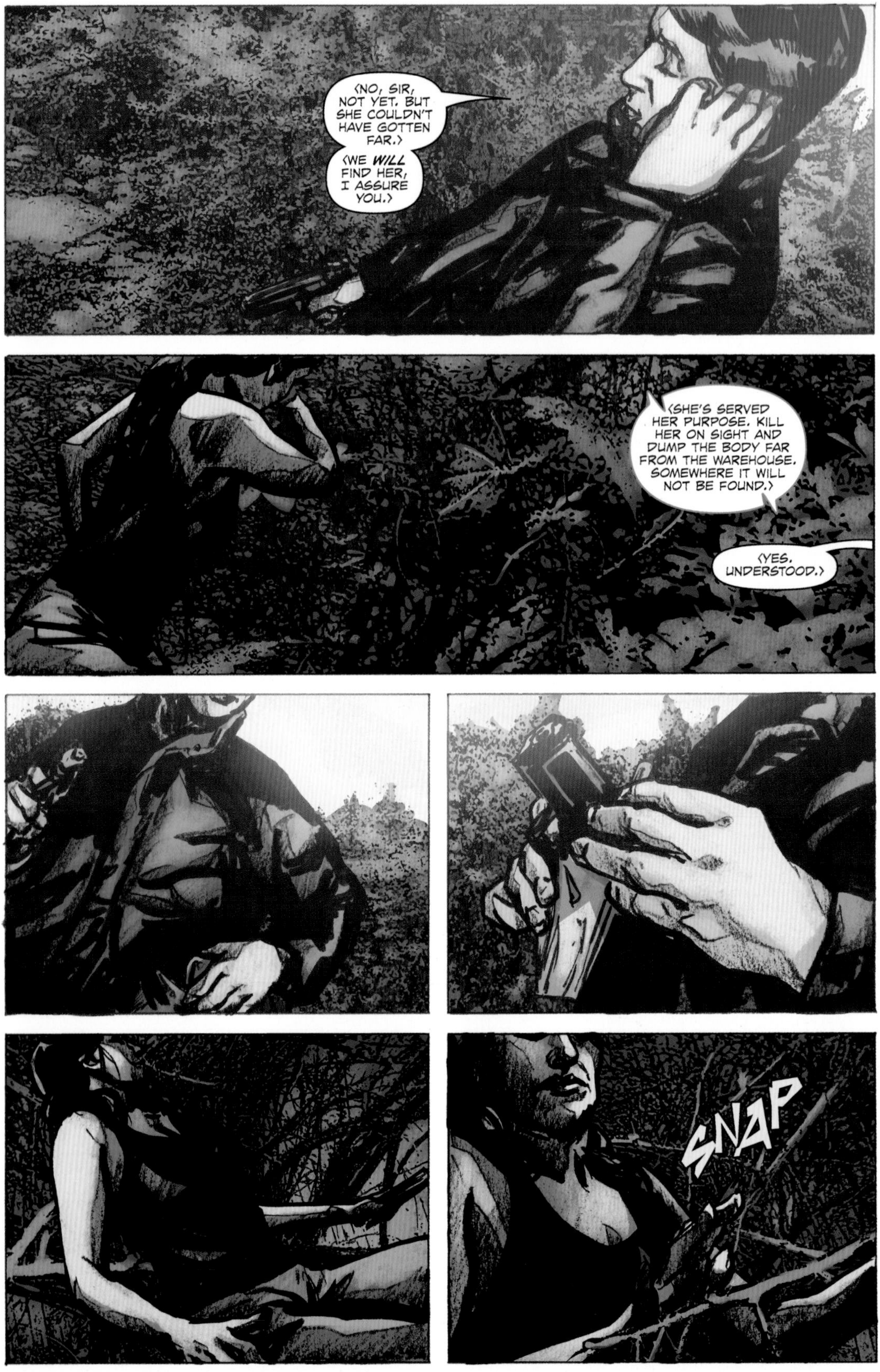

‹NO, SIR, NOT YET. BUT SHE COULDN'T HAVE GOTTEN FAR.›
‹WE WILL FIND HER, I ASSURE YOU.›
‹SHE'S SERVED HER PURPOSE. KILL HER ON SIGHT AND DUMP THE BODY FAR FROM THE WAREHOUSE. SOMEWHERE IT WILL NOT BE FOUND.›
‹YES. UNDERSTOOD.›
SNAP

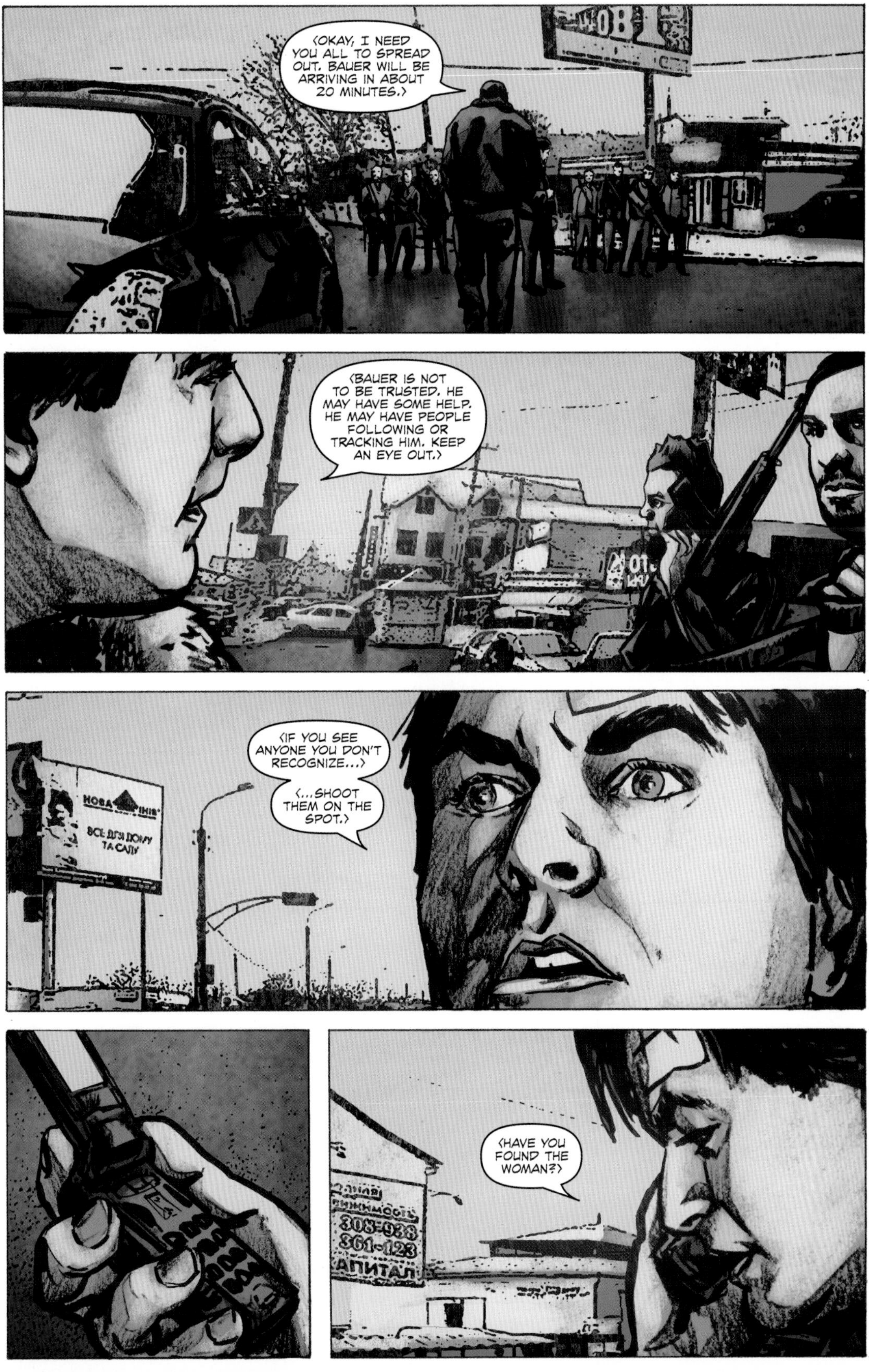
‹OKAY, I NEED YOU ALL TO SPREAD OUT. BAUER WILL BE ARRIVING IN ABOUT 20 MINUTES.›
‹BAUER IS NOT TO BE TRUSTED. HE MAY HAVE SOME HELP. HE MAY HAVE PEOPLE FOLLOWING OR TRACKING HIM. KEEP AN EYE OUT.›
‹IF YOU SEE ANYONE YOU DON'T RECOGNIZE...›
‹...SHOOT THEM ON THE SPOT.›
308-938
361-123
‹HAVE YOU FOUND THE WOMAN?›

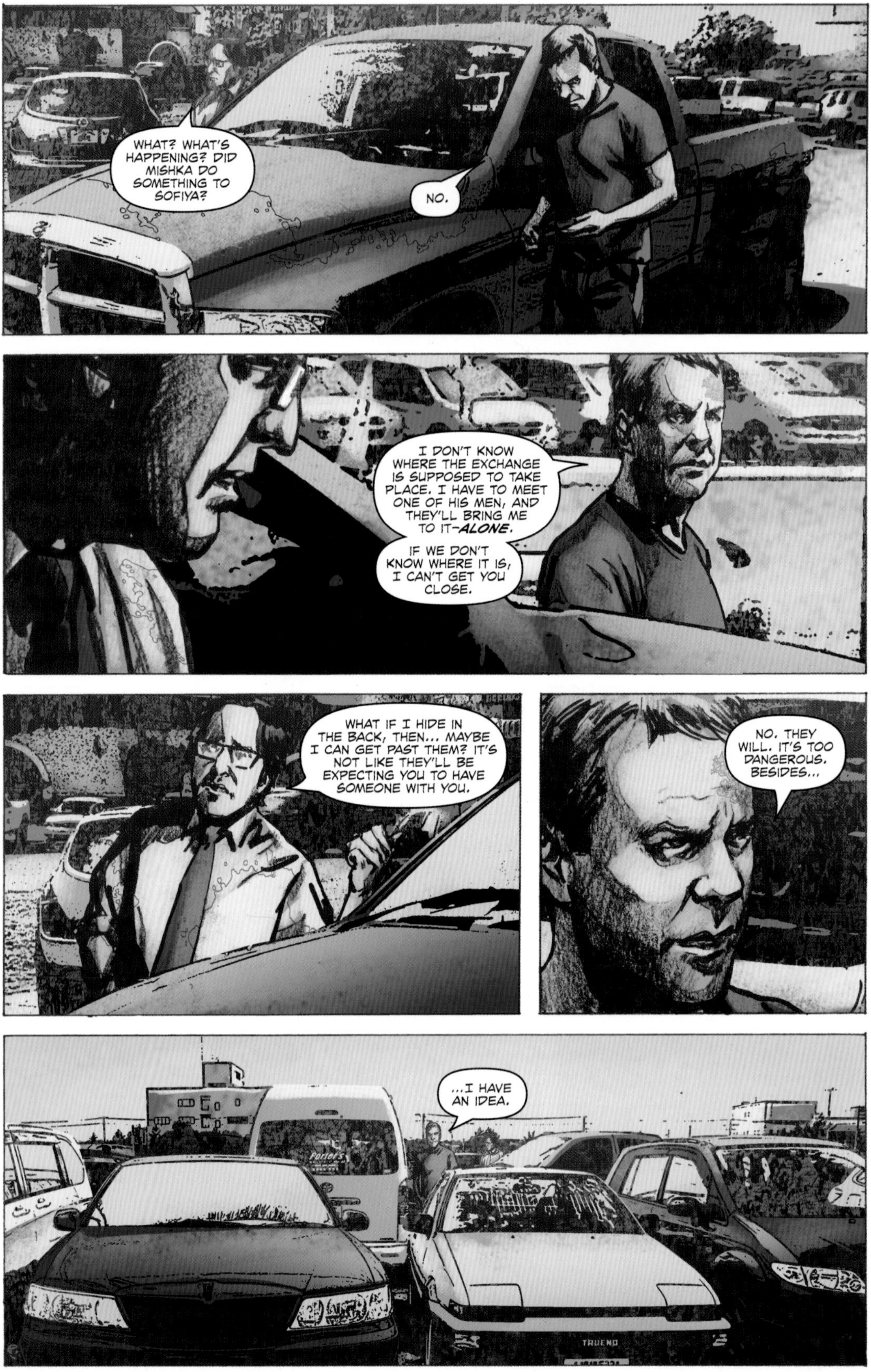
WHAT? WHAT'S HAPPENING? DID MISHKA DO SOMETHING TO SOFIYA?
NO.
I DON'T KNOW WHERE THE EXCHANGE IS SUPPOSED TO TAKE PLACE. I HAVE TO MEET ONE OF HIS MEN, AND THEY'LL BRING ME TO IT–*ALONE.*
IF WE DON'T KNOW WHERE IT IS, I CAN'T GET YOU CLOSE.
WHAT IF I HIDE IN THE BACK, THEN... MAYBE I CAN GET PAST THEM? IT'S NOT LIKE THEY'LL BE EXPECTING YOU TO HAVE SOMEONE WITH YOU.
NO. THEY WILL. IT'S TOO DANGEROUS. BESIDES...
...I HAVE AN IDEA.

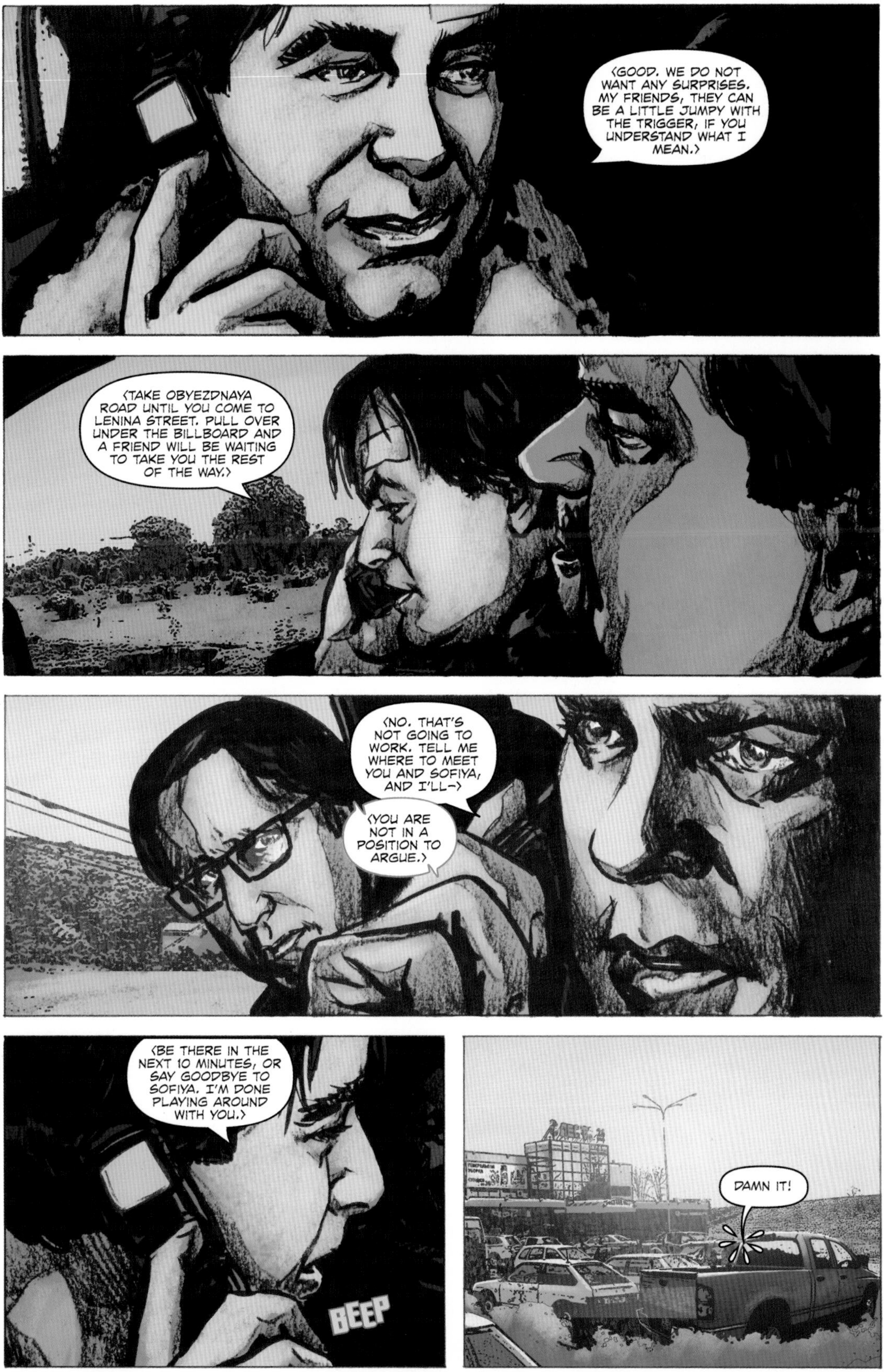
<GOOD. WE DO NOT WANT ANY SURPRISES. MY FRIENDS, THEY CAN BE A LITTLE JUMPY WITH THE TRIGGER, IF YOU UNDERSTAND WHAT I MEAN.>
<TAKE OBYEZDNAYA ROAD UNTIL YOU COME TO LENINA STREET. PULL OVER UNDER THE BILLBOARD AND A FRIEND WILL BE WAITING TO TAKE YOU THE REST OF THE WAY.>
<NO. THAT'S NOT GOING TO WORK. TELL ME WHERE TO MEET YOU AND SOFIYA, AND I'LL-->
<YOU ARE NOT IN A POSITION TO ARGUE.>
<BE THERE IN THE NEXT 10 MINUTES, OR SAY GOODBYE TO SOFIYA. I'M DONE PLAYING AROUND WITH YOU.>
BEEP
DAMN IT!

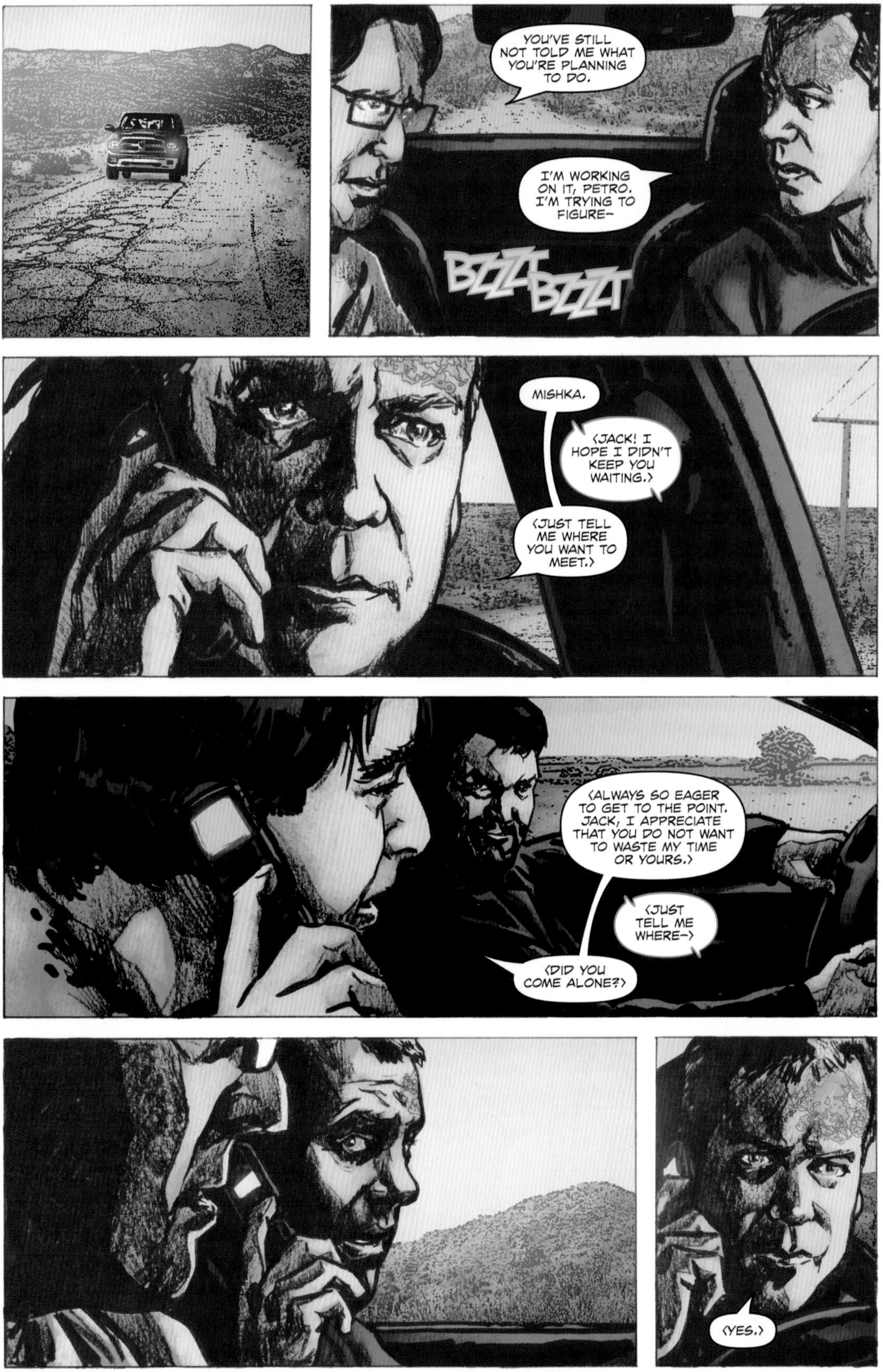
YOU'VE STILL NOT TOLD ME WHAT YOU'RE PLANNING TO DO.
I'M WORKING ON IT, PETRO. I'M TRYING TO FIGURE—
BZZZT BZZZT
MISHKA.
‹JACK! I HOPE I DIDN'T KEEP YOU WAITING.›
‹JUST TELL ME WHERE YOU WANT TO MEET.›
‹ALWAYS SO EAGER TO GET TO THE POINT. JACK, I APPRECIATE THAT YOU DO NOT WANT TO WASTE MY TIME OR YOURS.›
‹JUST TELL ME WHERE—›
‹DID YOU COME ALONE?›
‹YES.›

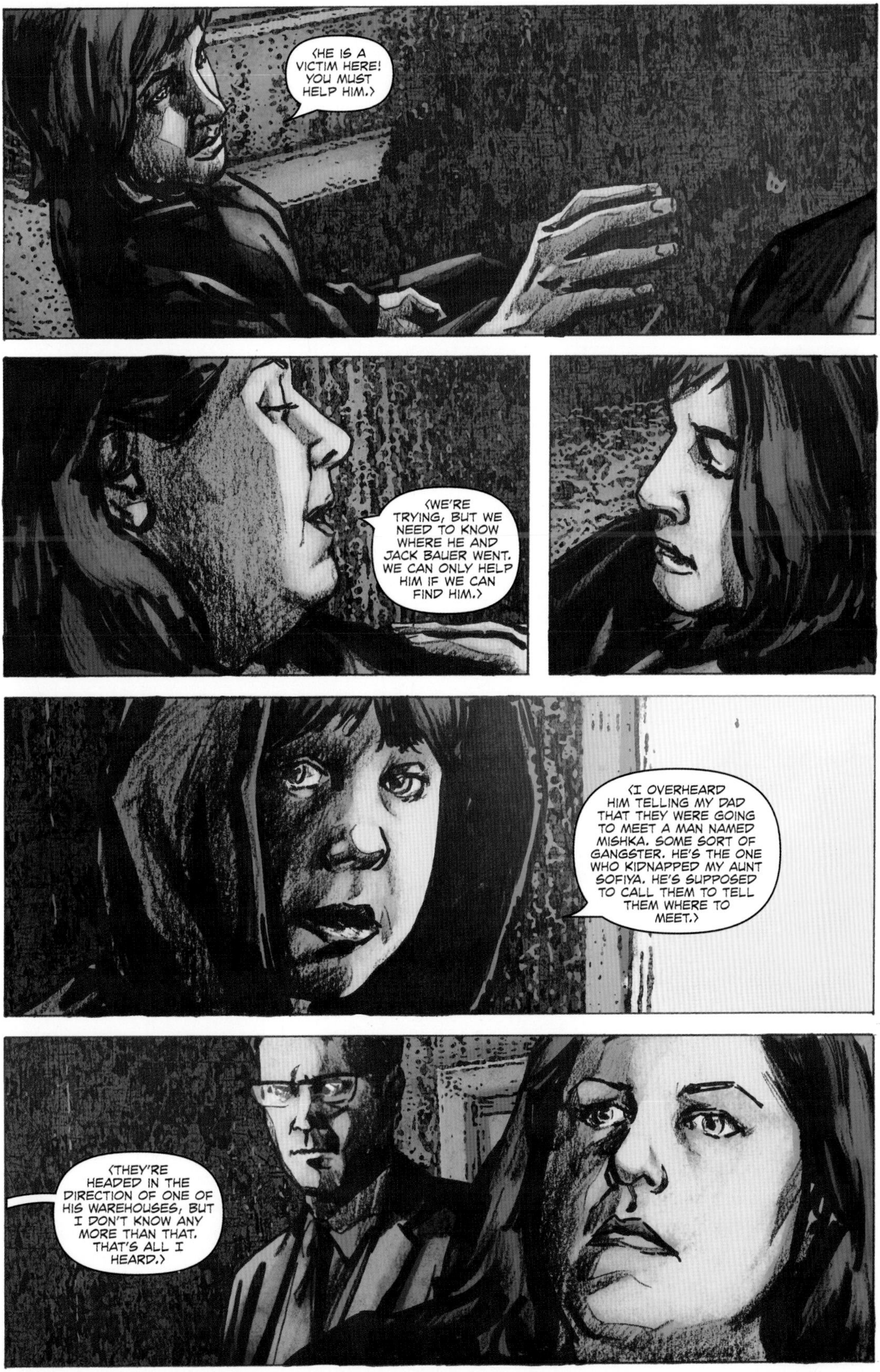

‹HE IS A VICTIM HERE! YOU MUST HELP HIM.›
‹WE'RE TRYING, BUT WE NEED TO KNOW WHERE HE AND JACK BAUER WENT. WE CAN ONLY HELP HIM IF WE CAN FIND HIM.›
‹I OVERHEARD HIM TELLING MY DAD THAT THEY WERE GOING TO MEET A MAN NAMED MISHKA. SOME SORT OF GANGSTER. HE'S THE ONE WHO KIDNAPPED MY AUNT SOFIYA. HE'S SUPPOSED TO CALL THEM TO TELL THEM WHERE TO MEET.›
‹THEY'RE HEADED IN THE DIRECTION OF ONE OF HIS WAREHOUSES, BUT I DON'T KNOW ANY MORE THAN THAT. THAT'S ALL I HEARD.›

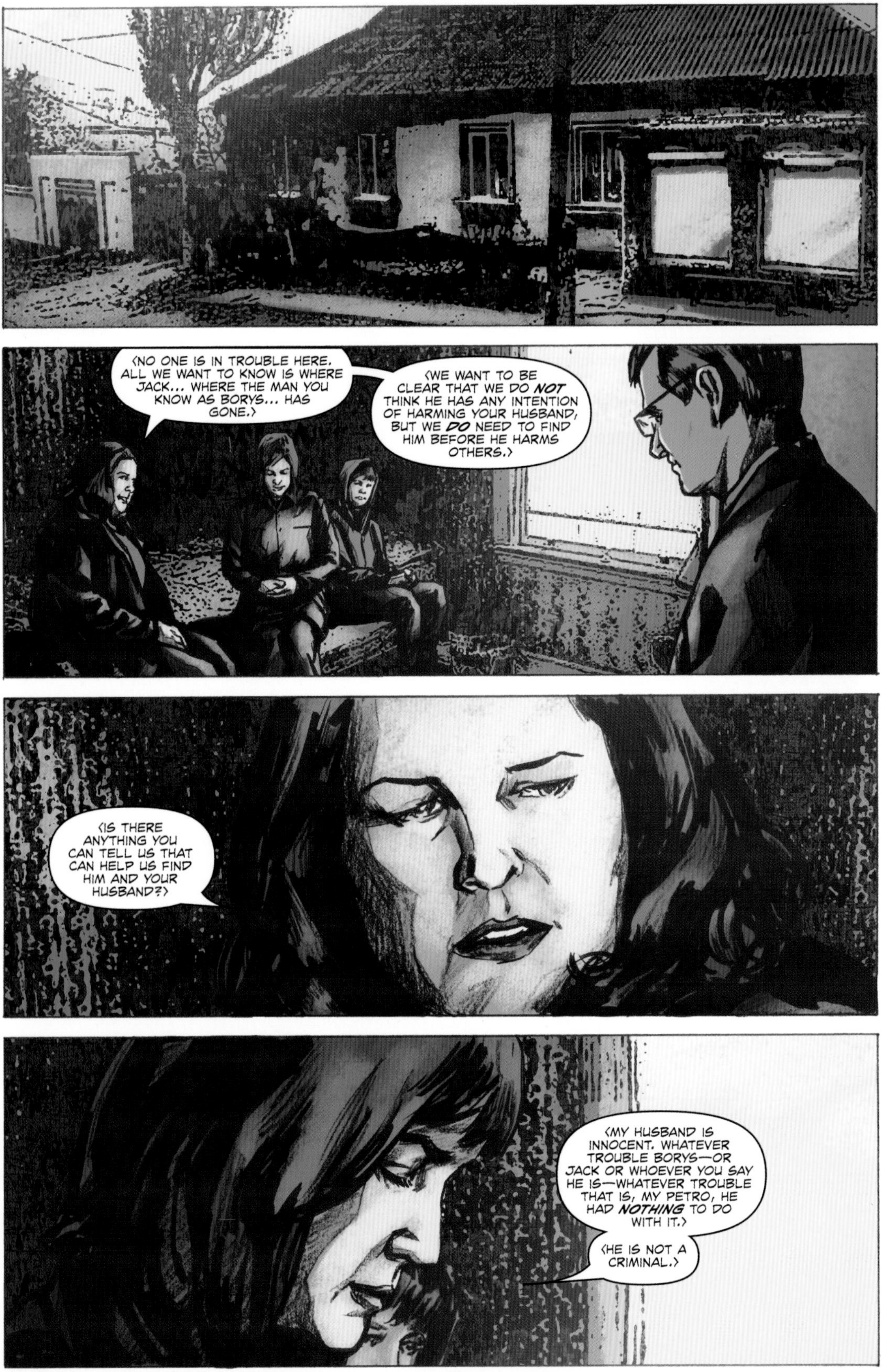
‹NO ONE IS IN TROUBLE HERE. ALL WE WANT TO KNOW IS WHERE JACK... WHERE THE MAN YOU KNOW AS BORYS... HAS GONE.›
‹WE WANT TO BE CLEAR THAT WE DO NOT THINK HE HAS ANY INTENTION OF HARMING YOUR HUSBAND, BUT WE DO NEED TO FIND HIM BEFORE HE HARMS OTHERS.›
‹IS THERE ANYTHING YOU CAN TELL US THAT CAN HELP US FIND HIM AND YOUR HUSBAND?›
‹MY HUSBAND IS INNOCENT. WHATEVER TROUBLE BORYS—OR JACK OR WHOEVER YOU SAY HE IS—WHATEVER TROUBLE THAT IS, MY PETRO, HE HAD NOTHING TO DO WITH IT.›
‹HE IS NOT A CRIMINAL.›

4 Art by Davide Furnó

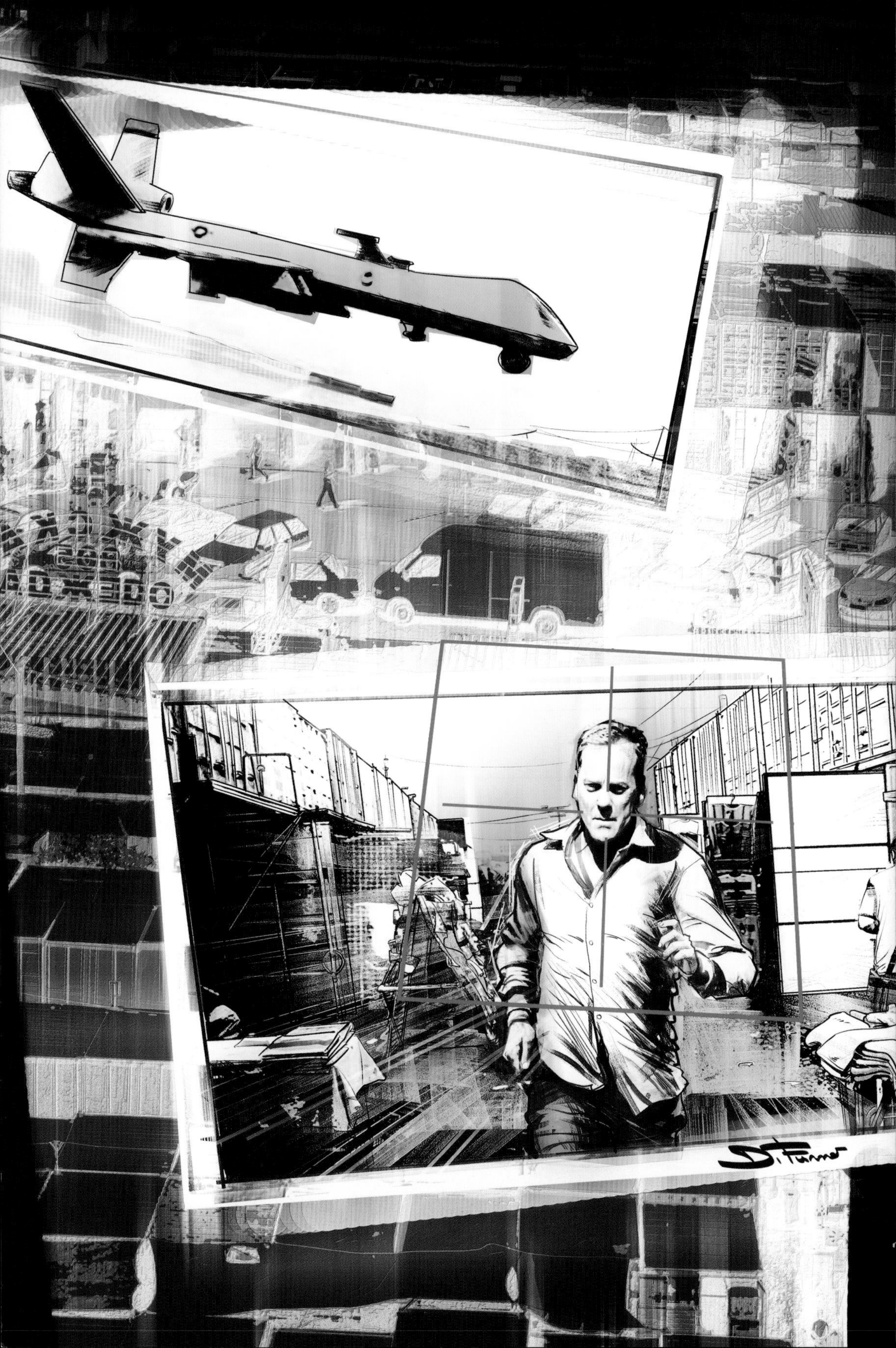

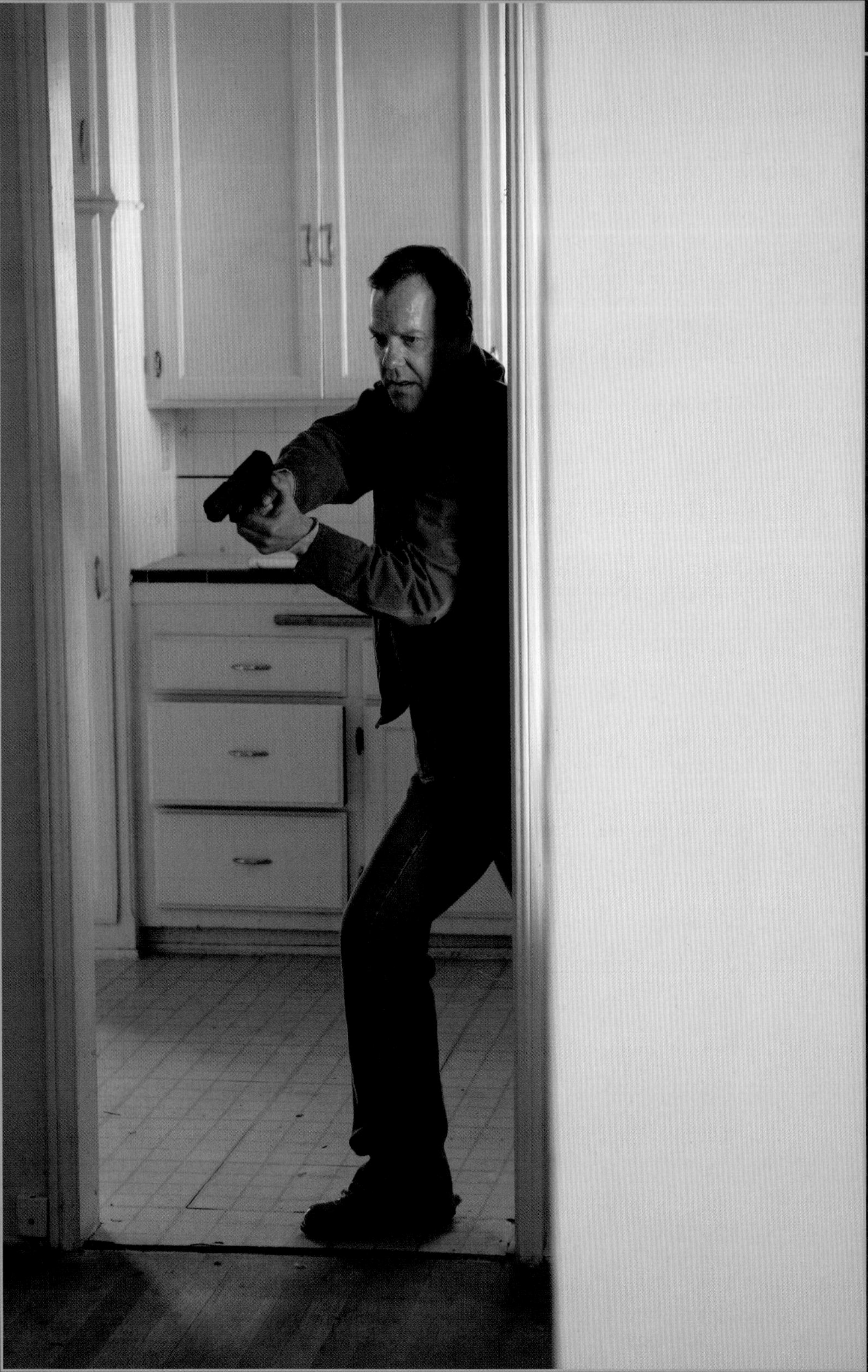

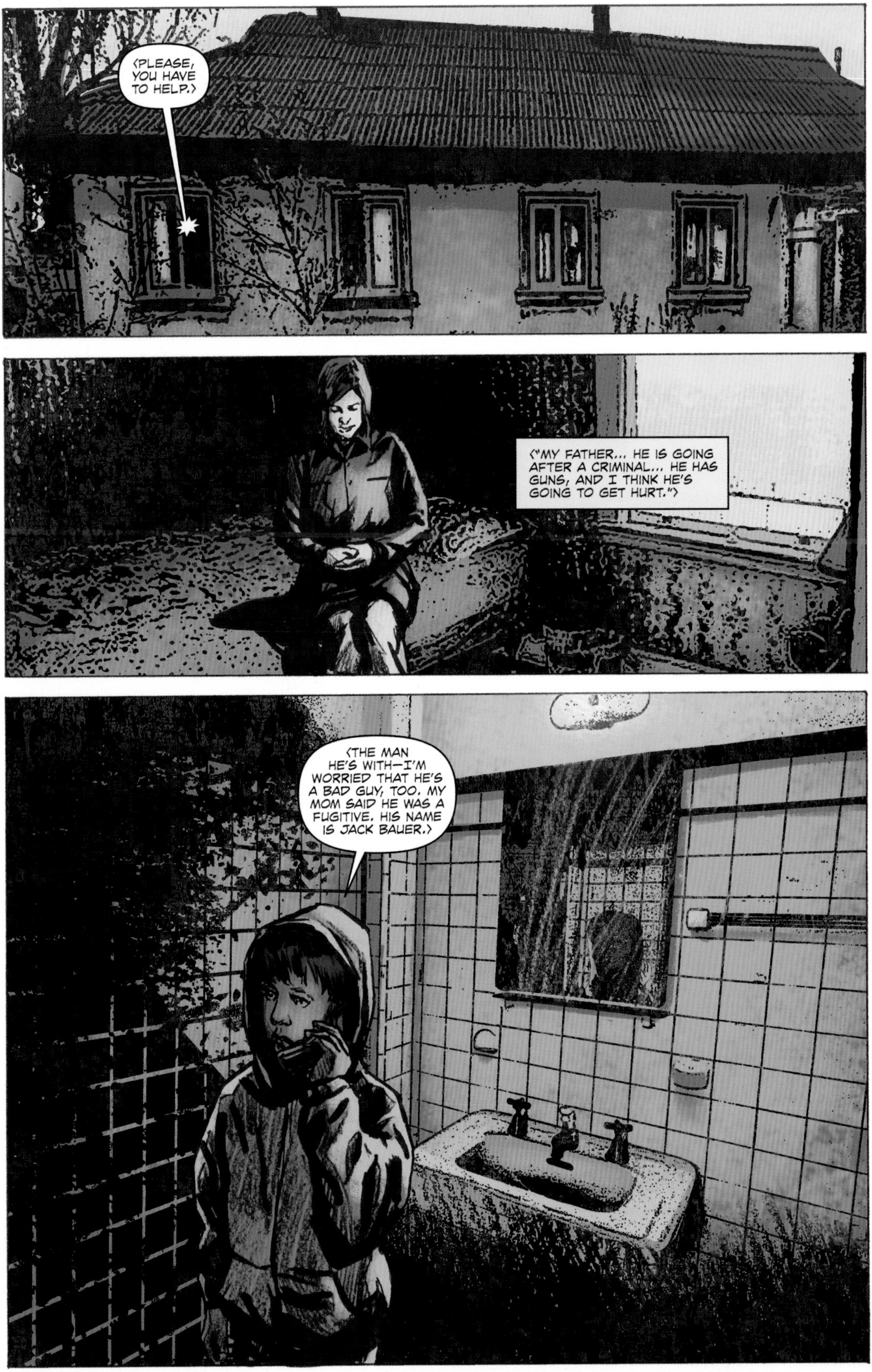
‹PLEASE, YOU HAVE TO HELP.›
‹"MY FATHER... HE IS GOING AFTER A CRIMINAL... HE HAS GUNS, AND I THINK HE'S GOING TO GET HURT."›
‹THE MAN HE'S WITH—I'M WORRIED THAT HE'S A BAD GUY, TOO. MY MOM SAID HE WAS A FUGITIVE. HIS NAME IS JACK BAUER.›

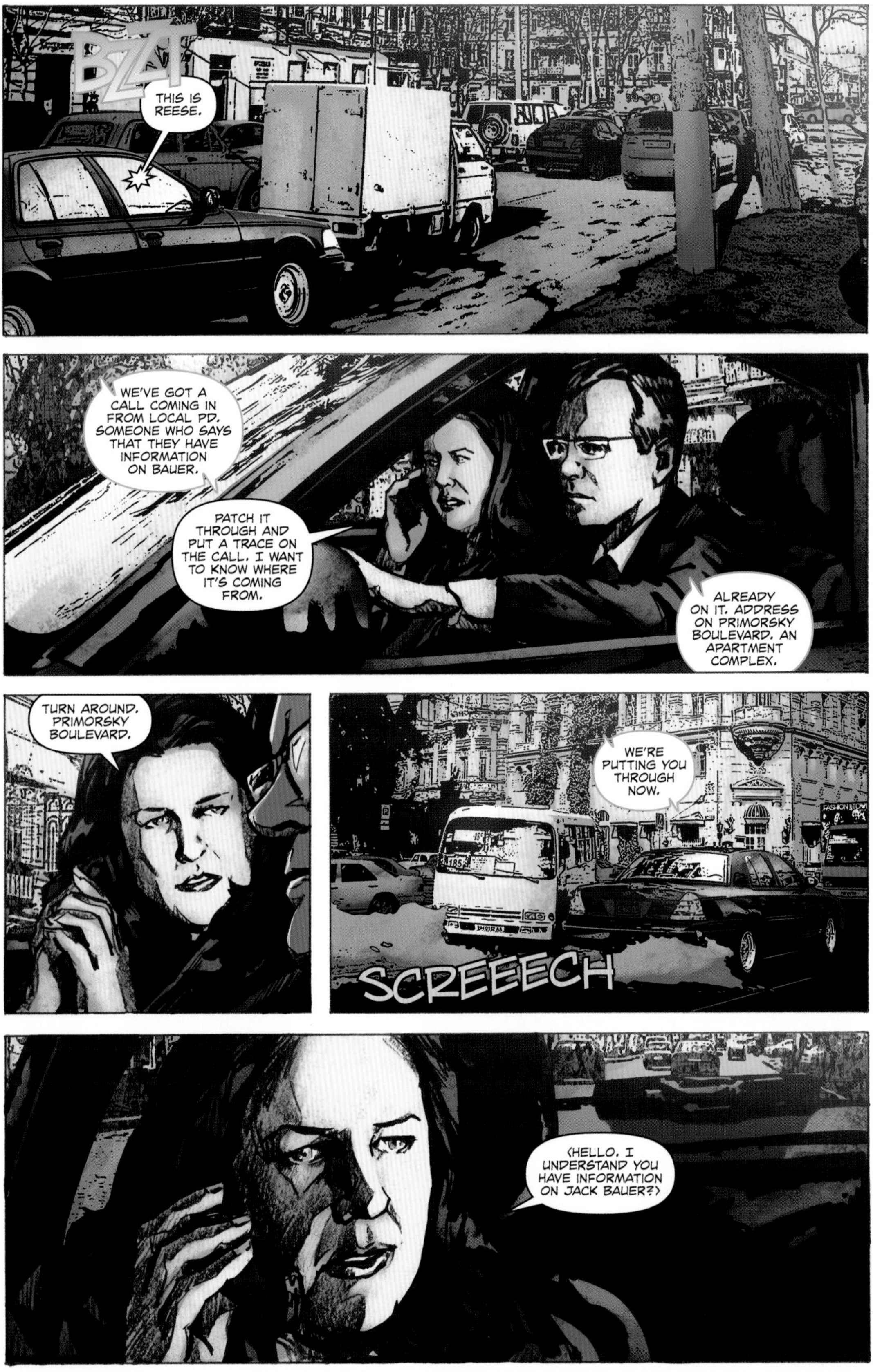
BZZT
THIS IS REESE.
WE'VE GOT A CALL COMING IN FROM LOCAL PD. SOMEONE WHO SAYS THAT THEY HAVE INFORMATION ON BAUER.
PATCH IT THROUGH AND PUT A TRACE ON THE CALL. I WANT TO KNOW WHERE IT'S COMING FROM.
ALREADY ON IT. ADDRESS ON PRIMORSKY BOULEVARD. AN APARTMENT COMPLEX.
TURN AROUND. PRIMORSKY BOULEVARD.
WE'RE PUTTING YOU THROUGH NOW.
SCREEECH
⟨HELLO. I UNDERSTAND YOU HAVE INFORMATION ON JACK BAUER?⟩

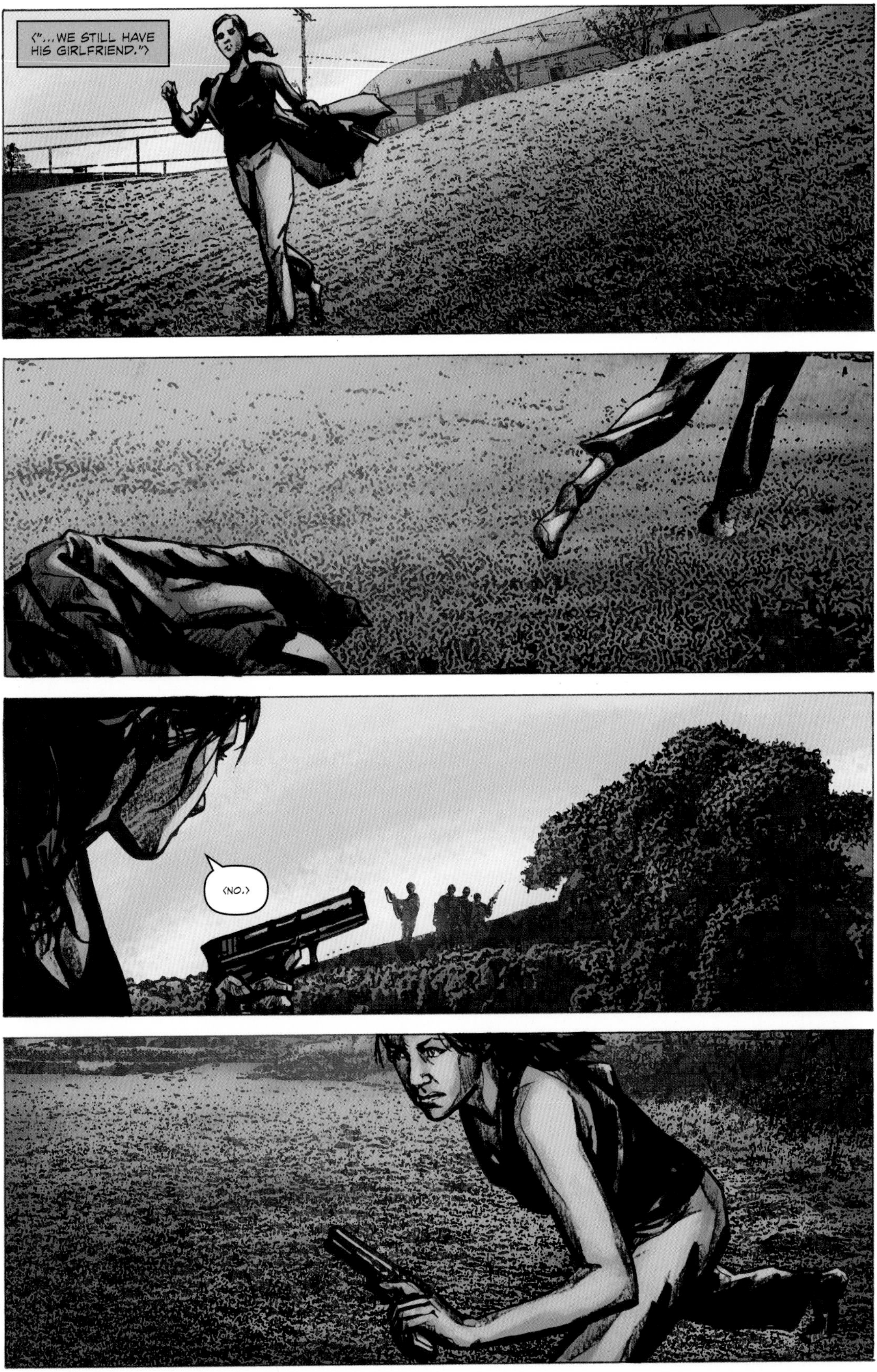
<"...WE STILL HAVE HIS GIRLFRIEND.">
<NO.>

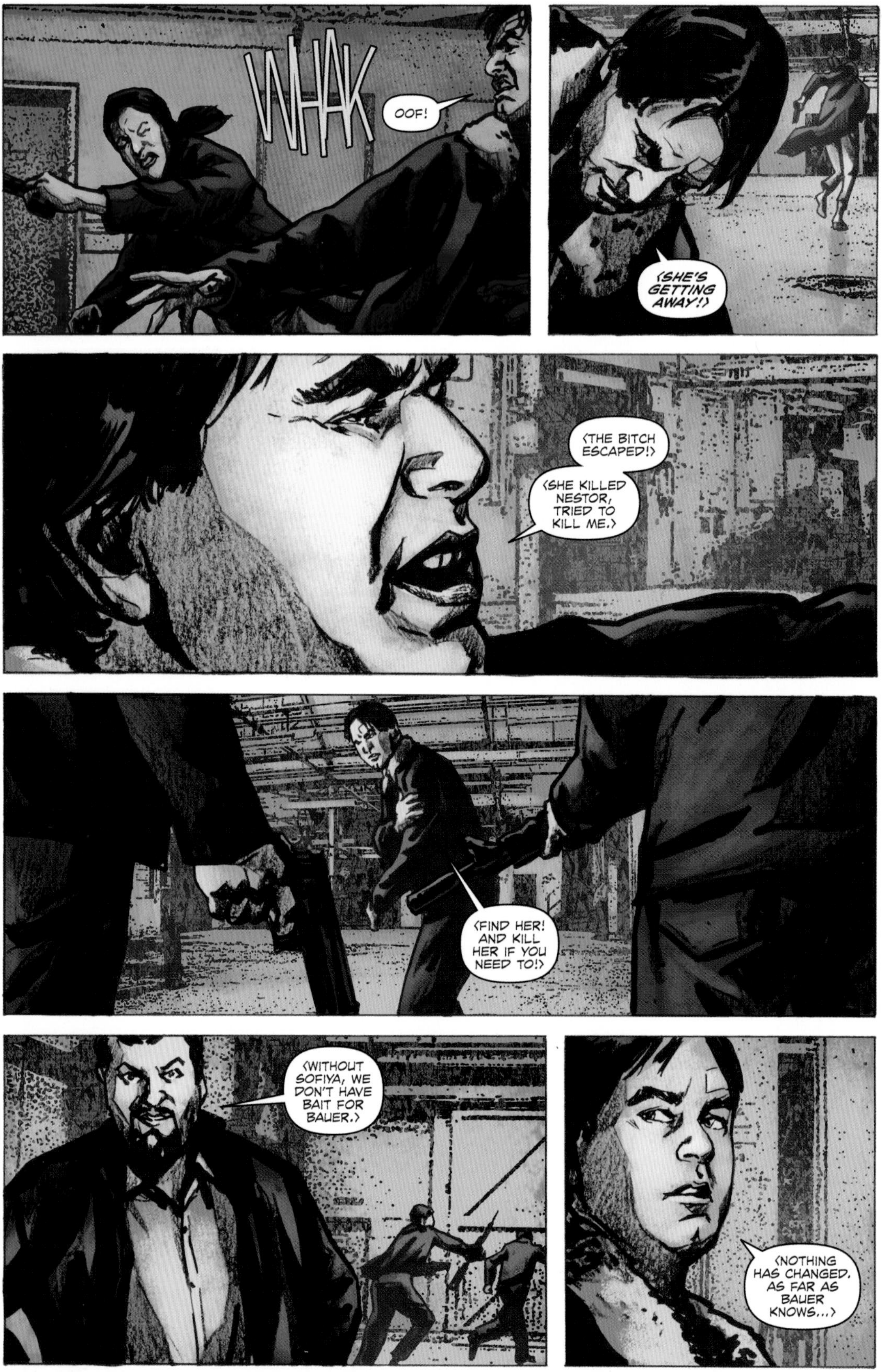
WHAK
OOF!
‹SHE'S GETTING AWAY!›
‹THE BITCH ESCAPED!›
‹SHE KILLED NESTOR, TRIED TO KILL ME.›
‹FIND HER! AND KILL HER IF YOU NEED TO!›
‹WITHOUT SOFIYA, WE DON'T HAVE BAIT FOR BAUER.›
‹NOTHING HAS CHANGED. AS FAR AS BAUER KNOWS...›

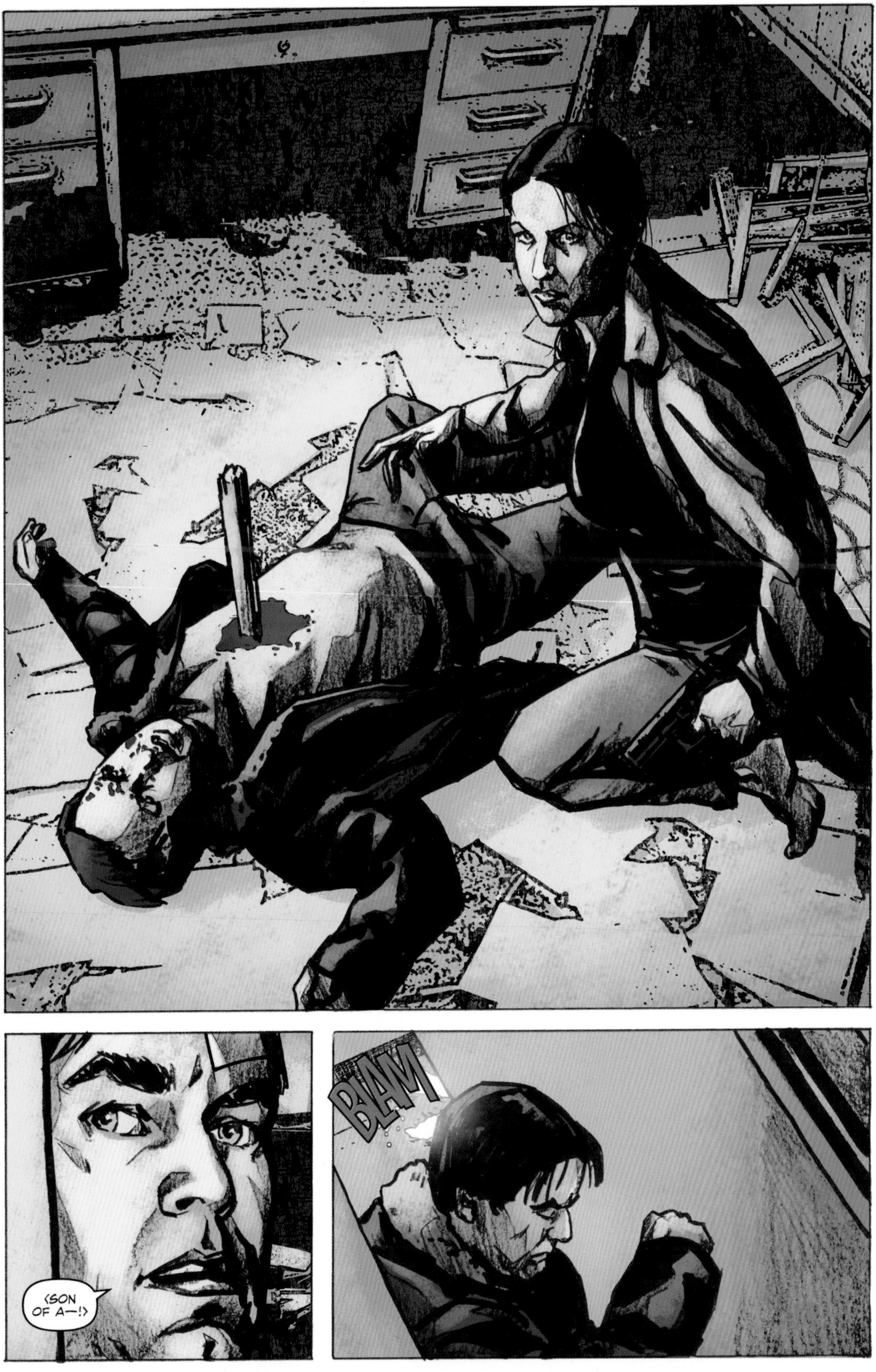
‹SON OF A—!›
BLAM

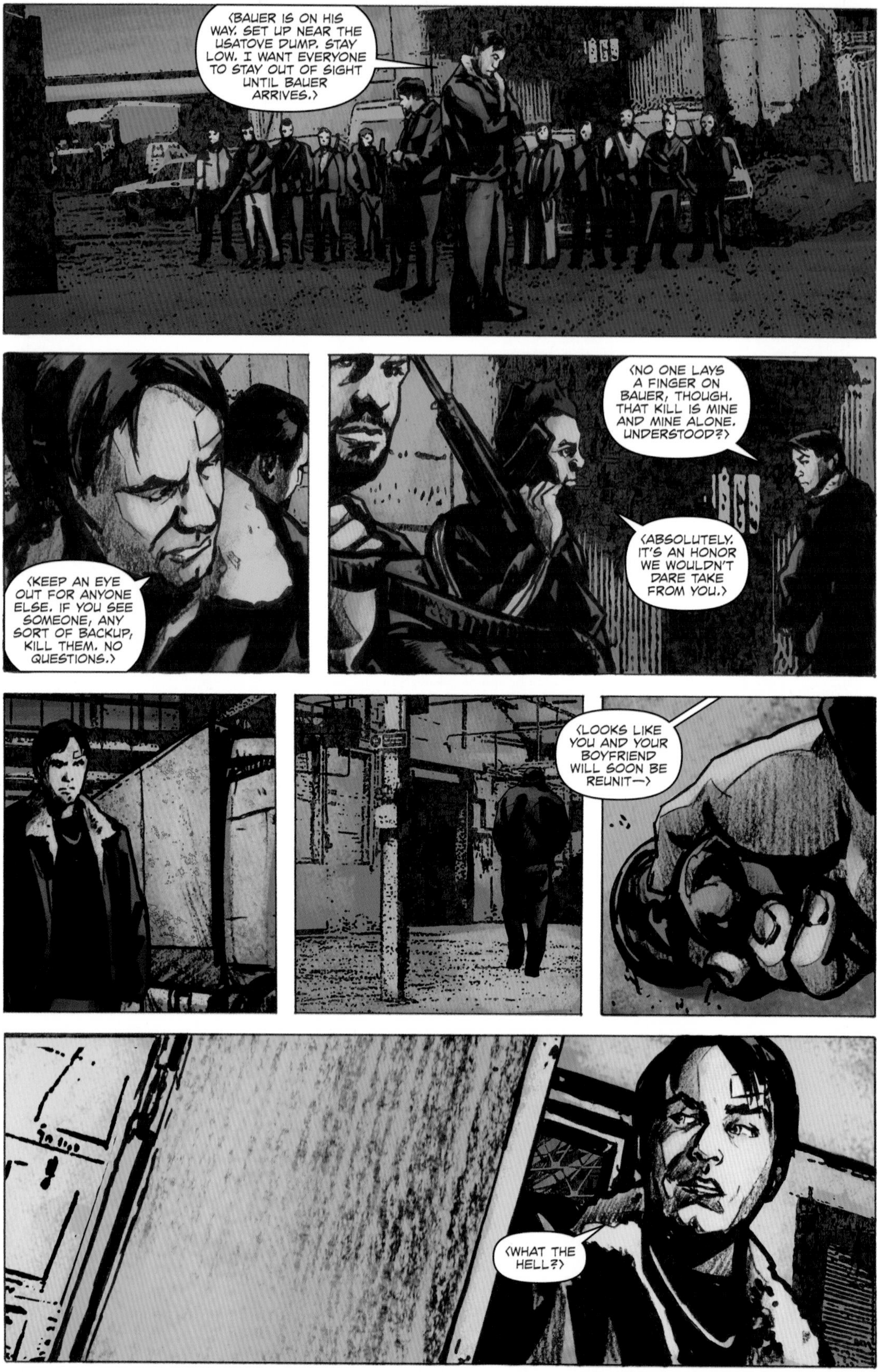
‹BAUER IS ON HIS WAY. SET UP NEAR THE USATOVE DUMP. STAY LOW. I WANT EVERYONE TO STAY OUT OF SIGHT UNTIL BAUER ARRIVES.›
‹KEEP AN EYE OUT FOR ANYONE ELSE. IF YOU SEE SOMEONE, ANY SORT OF BACKUP, KILL THEM. NO QUESTIONS.›
‹NO ONE LAYS A FINGER ON BAUER, THOUGH. THAT KILL IS MINE AND MINE ALONE. UNDERSTOOD?›
‹ABSOLUTELY. IT'S AN HONOR WE WOULDN'T DARE TAKE FROM YOU.›
‹LOOKS LIKE YOU AND YOUR BOYFRIEND WILL SOON BE REUNIT—›
‹WHAT THE HELL?›

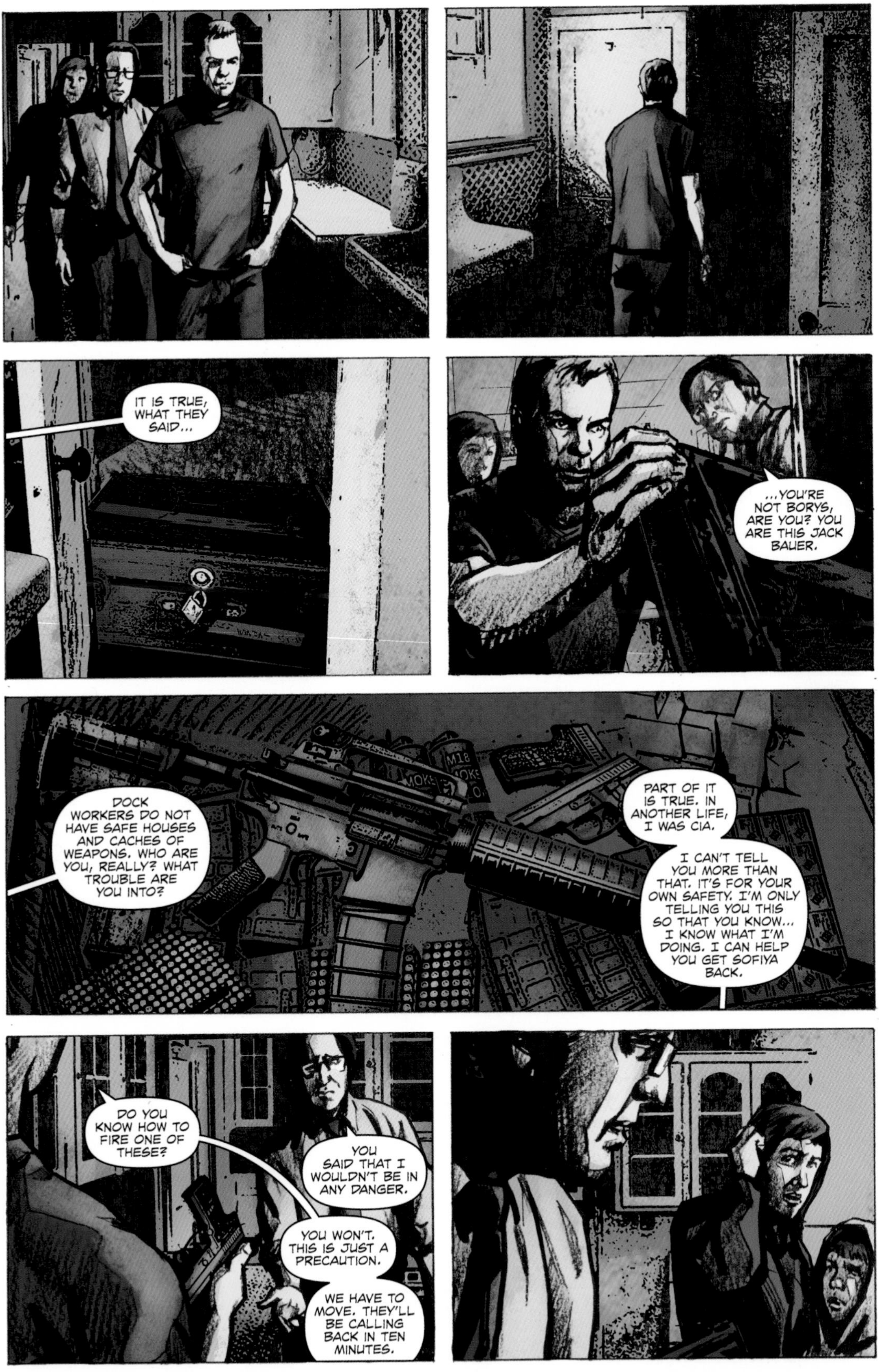
IT IS TRUE, WHAT THEY SAID...
...YOU'RE NOT BORYS, ARE YOU? YOU ARE THIS JACK BAUER.
DOCK WORKERS DO NOT HAVE SAFE HOUSES AND CACHES OF WEAPONS. WHO ARE YOU, REALLY? WHAT TROUBLE ARE YOU INTO?
PART OF IT IS TRUE. IN ANOTHER LIFE, I WAS CIA.
I CAN'T TELL YOU MORE THAN THAT. IT'S FOR YOUR OWN SAFETY. I'M ONLY TELLING YOU THIS SO THAT YOU KNOW... I KNOW WHAT I'M DOING. I CAN HELP YOU GET SOFIYA BACK.
DO YOU KNOW HOW TO FIRE ONE OF THESE?
YOU SAID THAT I WOULDN'T BE IN ANY DANGER.
YOU WON'T. THIS IS JUST A PRECAUTION.
WE HAVE TO MOVE. THEY'LL BE CALLING BACK IN TEN MINUTES.

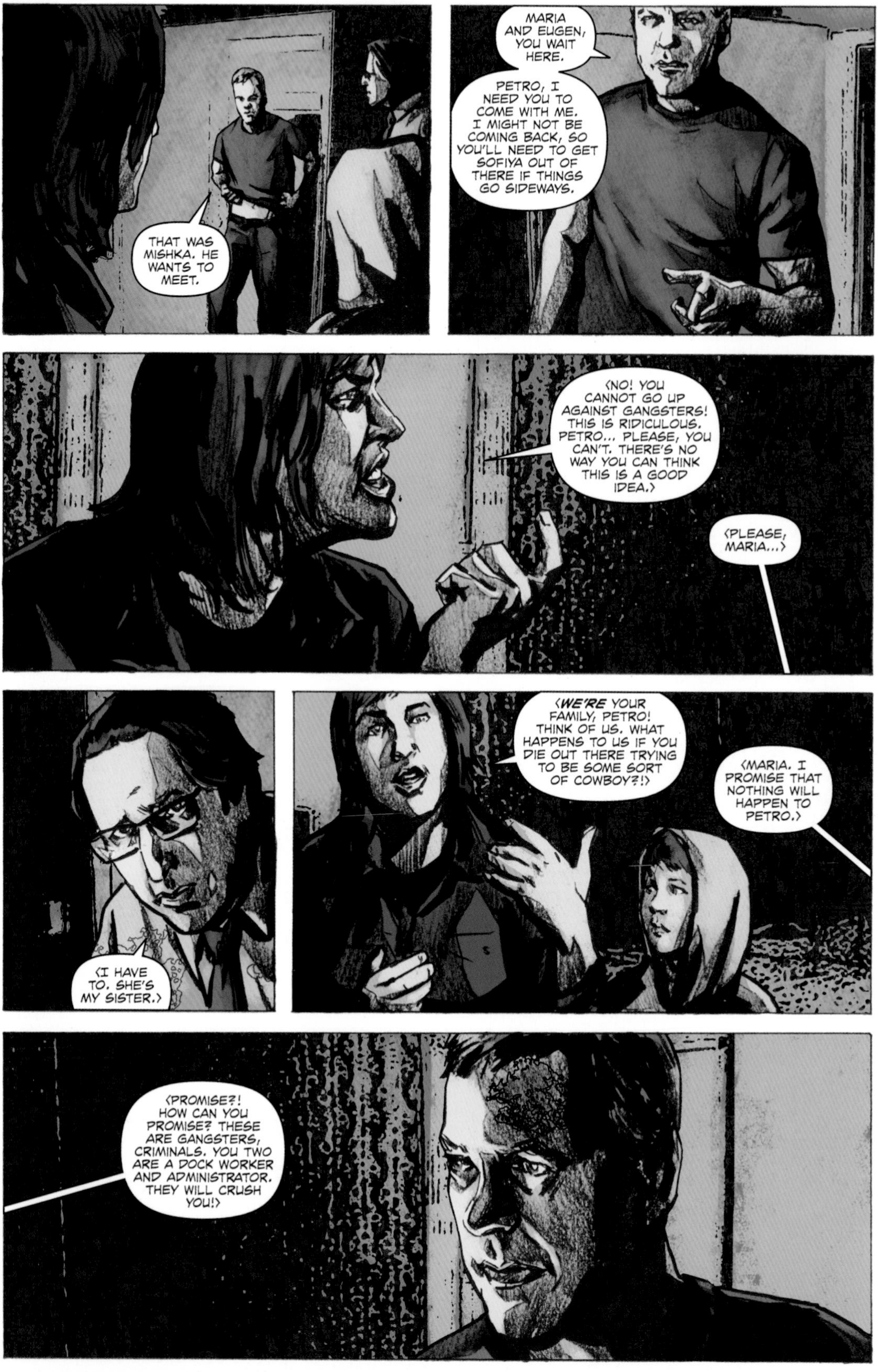

THAT WAS MISHKA. HE WANTS TO MEET.
MARIA AND EUGEN, YOU WAIT HERE.
PETRO, I NEED YOU TO COME WITH ME. I MIGHT NOT BE COMING BACK, SO YOU'LL NEED TO GET SOFIYA OUT OF THERE IF THINGS GO SIDEWAYS.
‹NO! YOU CANNOT GO UP AGAINST GANGSTERS! THIS IS RIDICULOUS. PETRO... PLEASE, YOU CAN'T. THERE'S NO WAY YOU CAN THINK THIS IS A GOOD IDEA.›
‹PLEASE, MARIA...›
‹I HAVE TO. SHE'S MY SISTER.›
‹***WE'RE*** YOUR FAMILY, PETRO! THINK OF US. WHAT HAPPENS TO US IF YOU DIE OUT THERE TRYING TO BE SOME SORT OF COWBOY?!›
‹MARIA. I PROMISE THAT NOTHING WILL HAPPEN TO PETRO.›
‹PROMISE?! HOW CAN YOU PROMISE? THESE ARE GANGSTERS, CRIMINALS. YOU TWO ARE A DOCK WORKER AND ADMINISTRATOR. THEY WILL CRUSH YOU!›

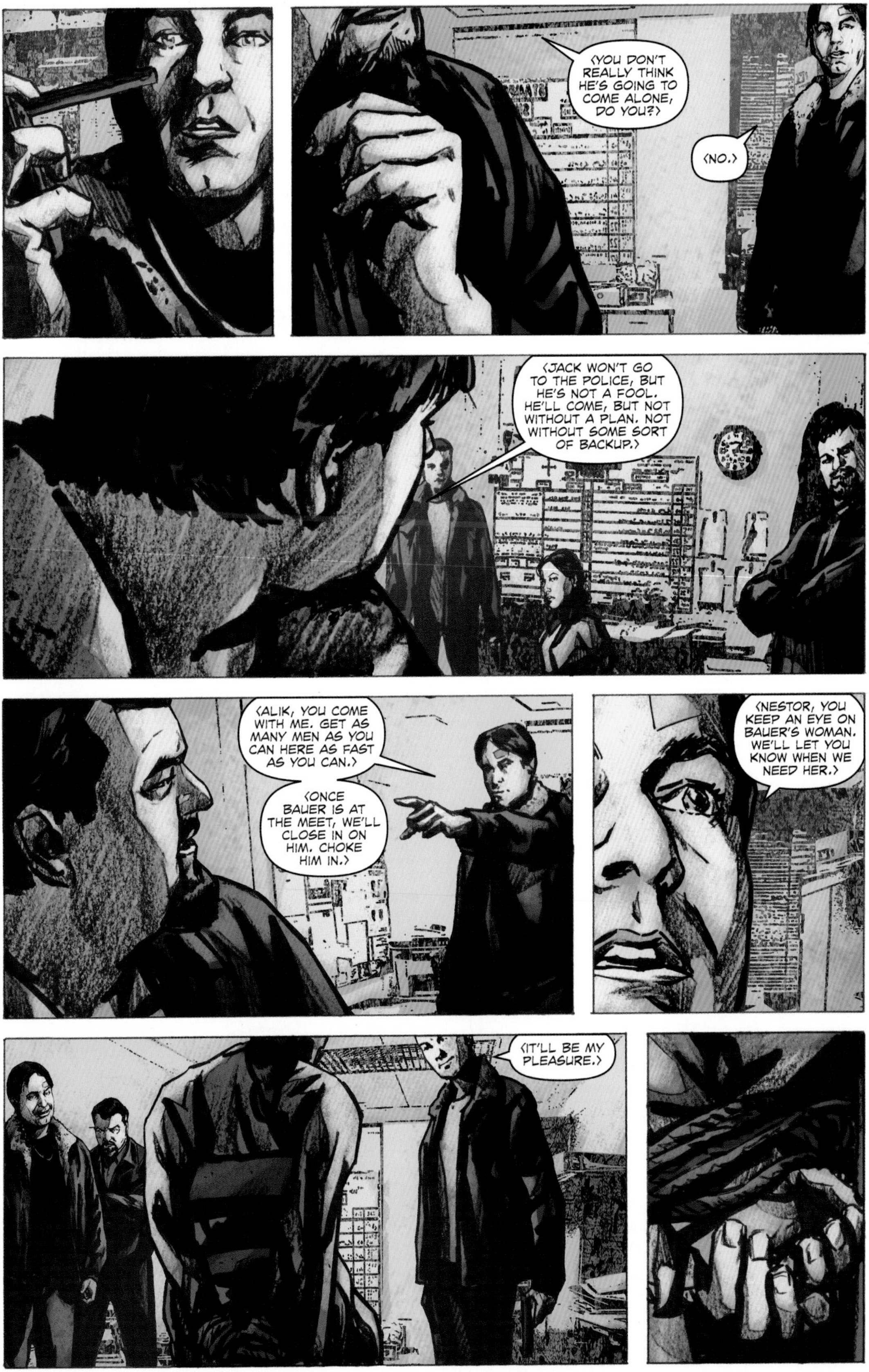

<YOU DON'T REALLY THINK HE'S GOING TO COME ALONE, DO YOU?>
<NO.>
<JACK WON'T GO TO THE POLICE, BUT HE'S NOT A FOOL. HE'LL COME, BUT NOT WITHOUT A PLAN. NOT WITHOUT SOME SORT OF BACKUP.>
<ALIK, YOU COME WITH ME. GET AS MANY MEN AS YOU CAN HERE AS FAST AS YOU CAN.>
<ONCE BAUER IS AT THE MEET, WE'LL CLOSE IN ON HIM. CHOKE HIM IN.>
<NESTOR, YOU KEEP AN EYE ON BAUER'S WOMAN. WE'LL LET YOU KNOW WHEN WE NEED HER.>
<IT'LL BE MY PLEASURE.>

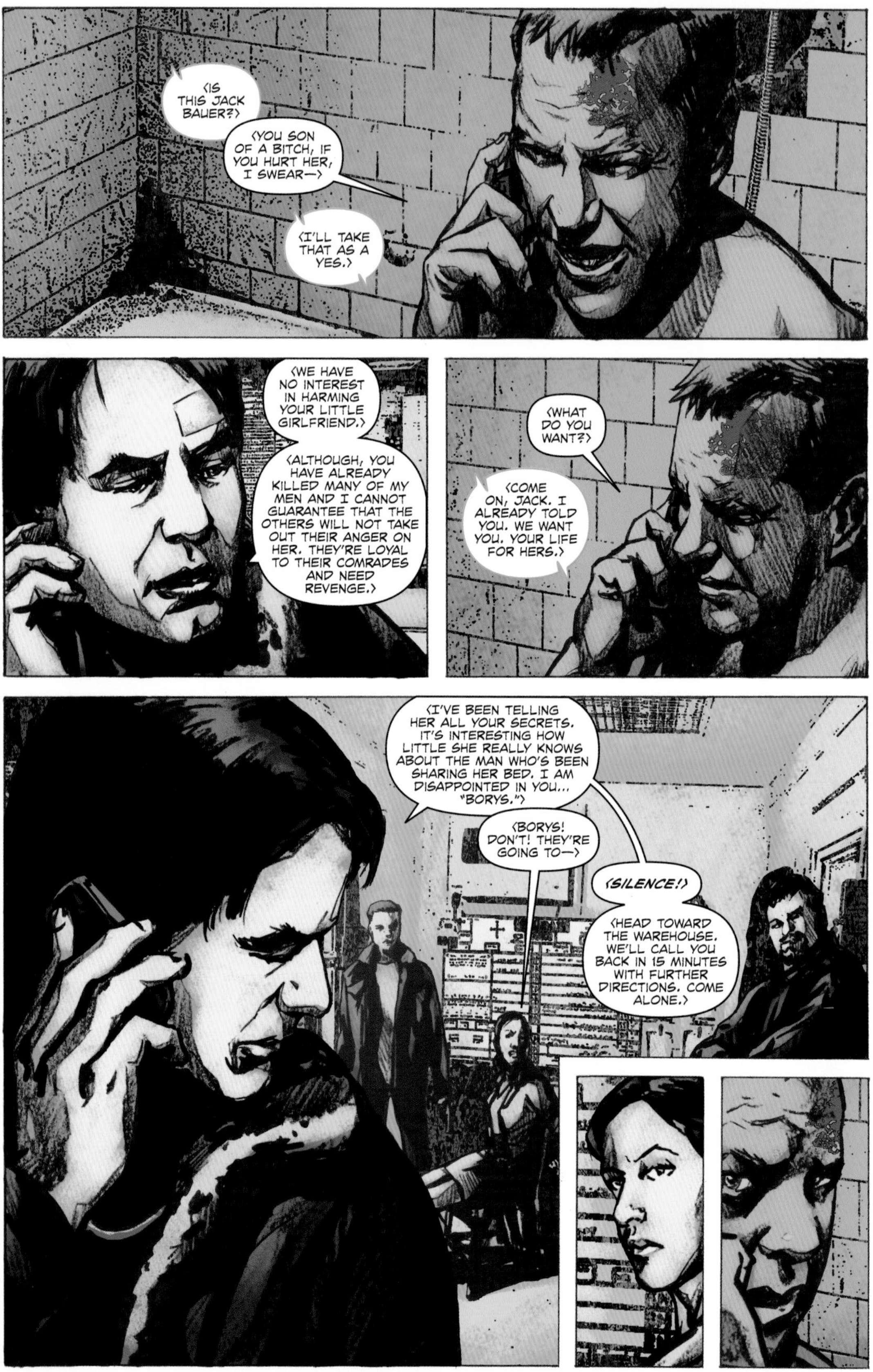
‹IS THIS JACK BAUER?›
‹YOU SON OF A BITCH, IF YOU HURT HER, I SWEAR—›
‹I'LL TAKE THAT AS A YES.›
‹WE HAVE NO INTEREST IN HARMING YOUR LITTLE GIRLFRIEND.›
‹ALTHOUGH, YOU HAVE ALREADY KILLED MANY OF MY MEN AND I CANNOT GUARANTEE THAT THE OTHERS WILL NOT TAKE OUT THEIR ANGER ON HER. THEY'RE LOYAL TO THEIR COMRADES AND NEED REVENGE.›
‹WHAT DO YOU WANT?›
‹COME ON, JACK. I ALREADY TOLD YOU. WE WANT YOU. YOUR LIFE FOR HERS.›
‹I'VE BEEN TELLING HER ALL YOUR SECRETS. IT'S INTERESTING HOW LITTLE SHE REALLY KNOWS ABOUT THE MAN WHO'S BEEN SHARING HER BED. I AM DISAPPOINTED IN YOU... "BORYS."›
‹BORYS! DON'T! THEY'RE GOING TO—›
‹SILENCE!›
‹HEAD TOWARD THE WAREHOUSE. WE'LL CALL YOU BACK IN 15 MINUTES WITH FURTHER DIRECTIONS. COME ALONE.›

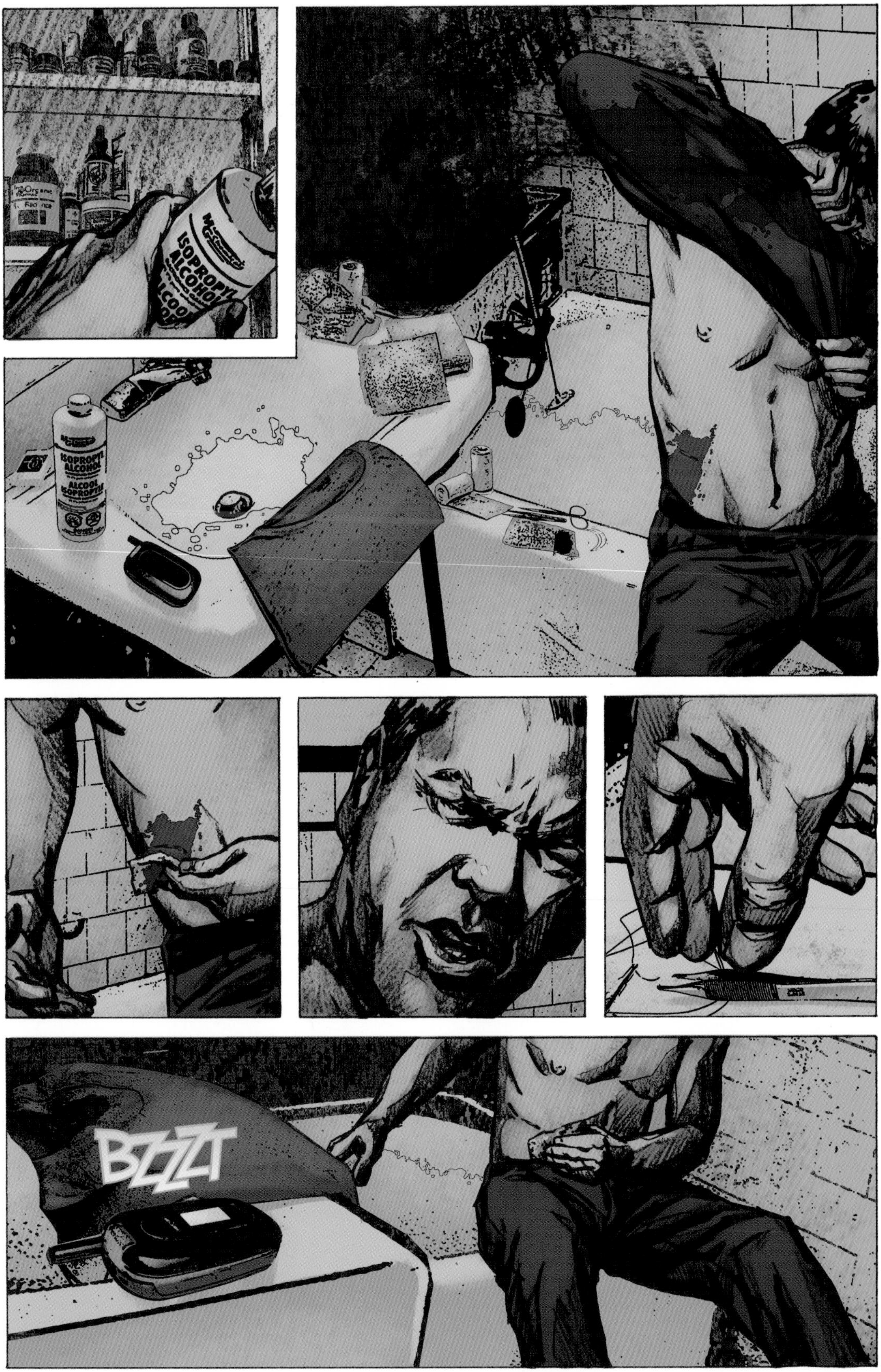
ISOPROPYL ALCOHOL
BZZZT

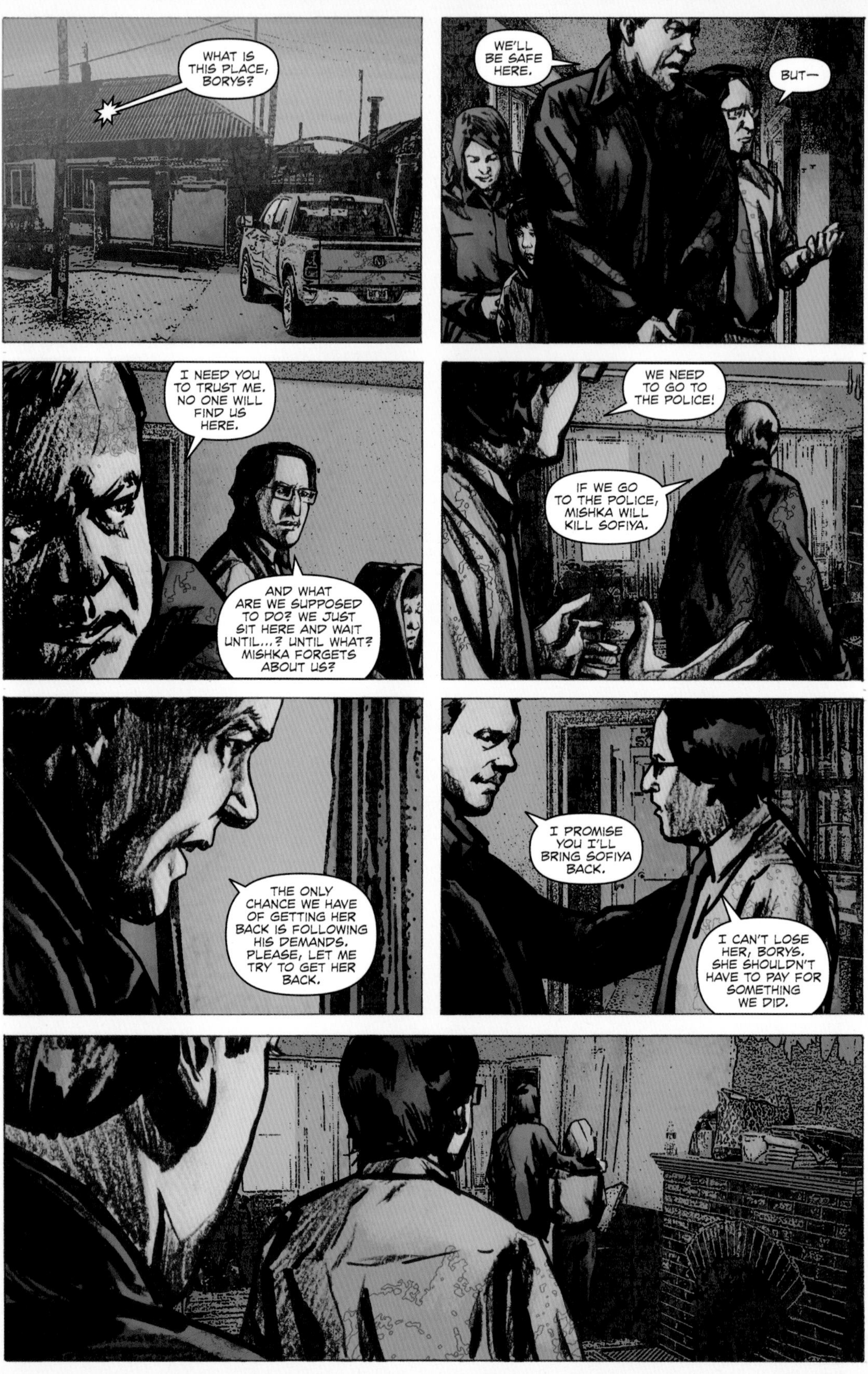
WHAT IS THIS PLACE, BORYS?
WE'LL BE SAFE HERE.
BUT—
I NEED YOU TO TRUST ME. NO ONE WILL FIND US HERE.
AND WHAT ARE WE SUPPOSED TO DO? WE JUST SIT HERE AND WAIT UNTIL...? UNTIL WHAT? MISHKA FORGETS ABOUT US?
WE NEED TO GO TO THE POLICE!
IF WE GO TO THE POLICE, MISHKA WILL KILL SOFIYA.
THE ONLY CHANCE WE HAVE OF GETTING HER BACK IS FOLLOWING HIS DEMANDS. PLEASE, LET ME TRY TO GET HER BACK.
I PROMISE YOU I'LL BRING SOFIYA BACK.
I CAN'T LOSE HER, BORYS. SHE SHOULDN'T HAVE TO PAY FOR SOMETHING WE DID.

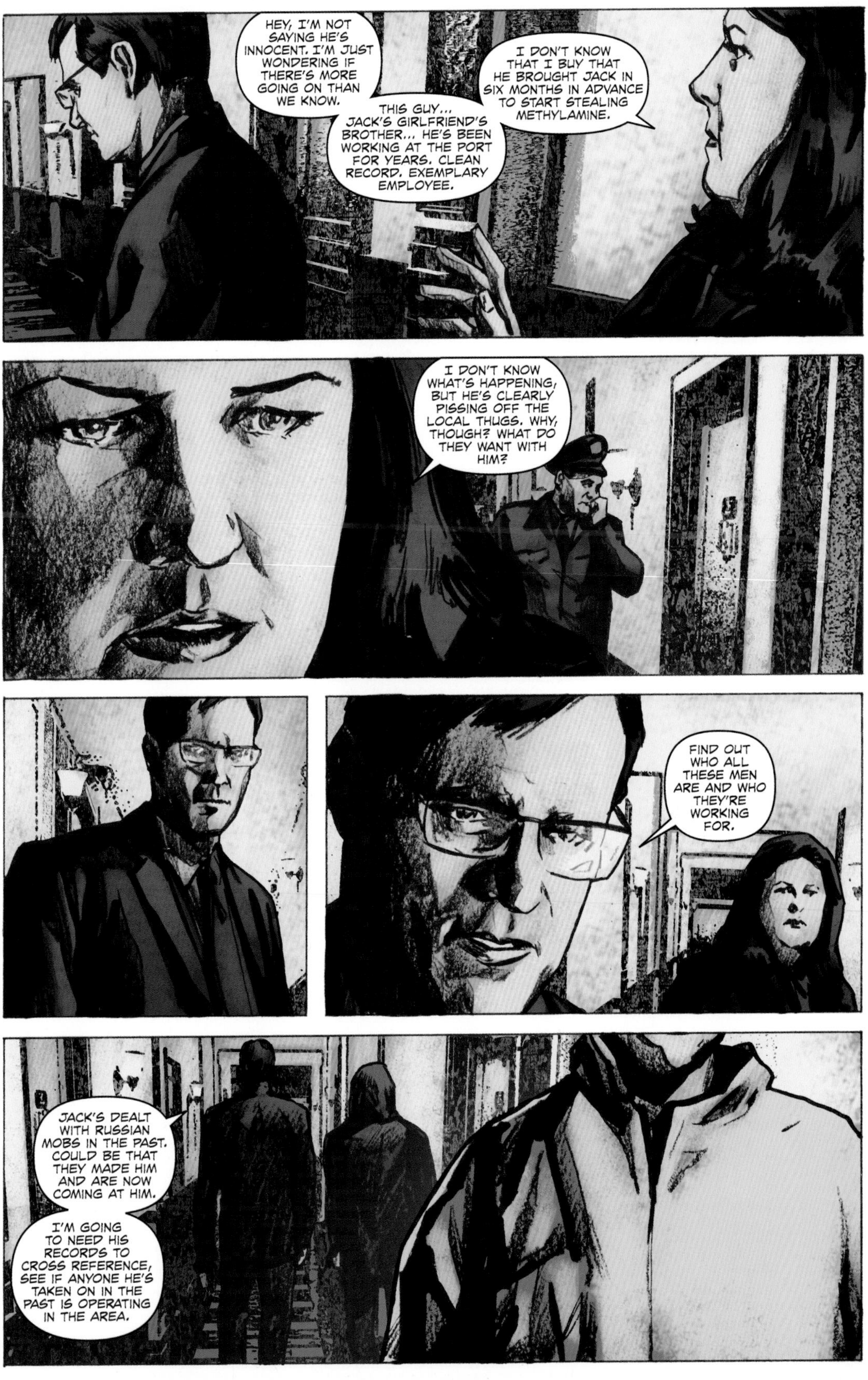
HEY, I'M NOT SAYING HE'S INNOCENT. I'M JUST WONDERING IF THERE'S MORE GOING ON THAN WE KNOW.
THIS GUY... JACK'S GIRLFRIEND'S BROTHER... HE'S BEEN WORKING AT THE PORT FOR YEARS. CLEAN RECORD. EXEMPLARY EMPLOYEE.
I DON'T KNOW THAT I BUY THAT HE BROUGHT JACK IN SIX MONTHS IN ADVANCE TO START STEALING METHYLAMINE.
I DON'T KNOW WHAT'S HAPPENING, BUT HE'S CLEARLY PISSING OFF THE LOCAL THUGS. WHY, THOUGH? WHAT DO THEY WANT WITH HIM?
FIND OUT WHO ALL THESE MEN ARE AND WHO THEY'RE WORKING FOR.
JACK'S DEALT WITH RUSSIAN MOBS IN THE PAST. COULD BE THAT THEY MADE HIM AND ARE NOW COMING AT HIM.
I'M GOING TO NEED HIS RECORDS TO CROSS REFERENCE, SEE IF ANYONE HE'S TAKEN ON IN THE PAST IS OPERATING IN THE AREA.

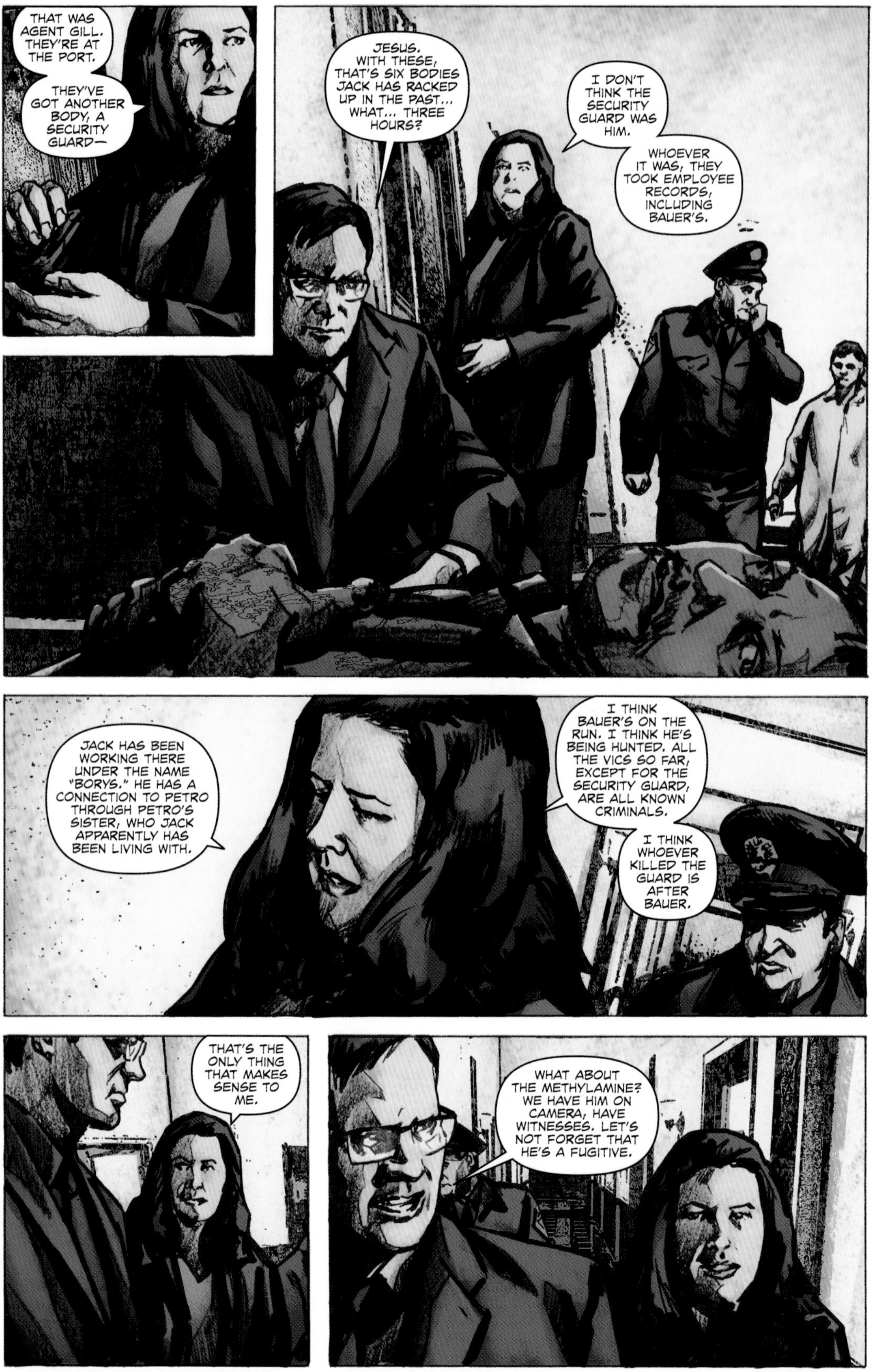
THAT WAS AGENT GILL. THEY'RE AT THE PORT.
THEY'VE GOT ANOTHER BODY, A SECURITY GUARD—
JESUS. WITH THESE, THAT'S SIX BODIES JACK HAS RACKED UP IN THE PAST... WHAT... THREE HOURS?
I DON'T THINK THE SECURITY GUARD WAS HIM.
WHOEVER IT WAS, THEY TOOK EMPLOYEE RECORDS, INCLUDING BAUER'S.
JACK HAS BEEN WORKING THERE UNDER THE NAME "BORYS." HE HAS A CONNECTION TO PETRO THROUGH PETRO'S SISTER, WHO JACK APPARENTLY HAS BEEN LIVING WITH.
I THINK BAUER'S ON THE RUN. I THINK HE'S BEING HUNTED. ALL THE VICS SO FAR, EXCEPT FOR THE SECURITY GUARD, ARE ALL KNOWN CRIMINALS.
I THINK WHOEVER KILLED THE GUARD IS AFTER BAUER.
THAT'S THE ONLY THING THAT MAKES SENSE TO ME.
WHAT ABOUT THE METHYLAMINE? WE HAVE HIM ON CAMERA, HAVE WITNESSES. LET'S NOT FORGET THAT HE'S A FUGITIVE.

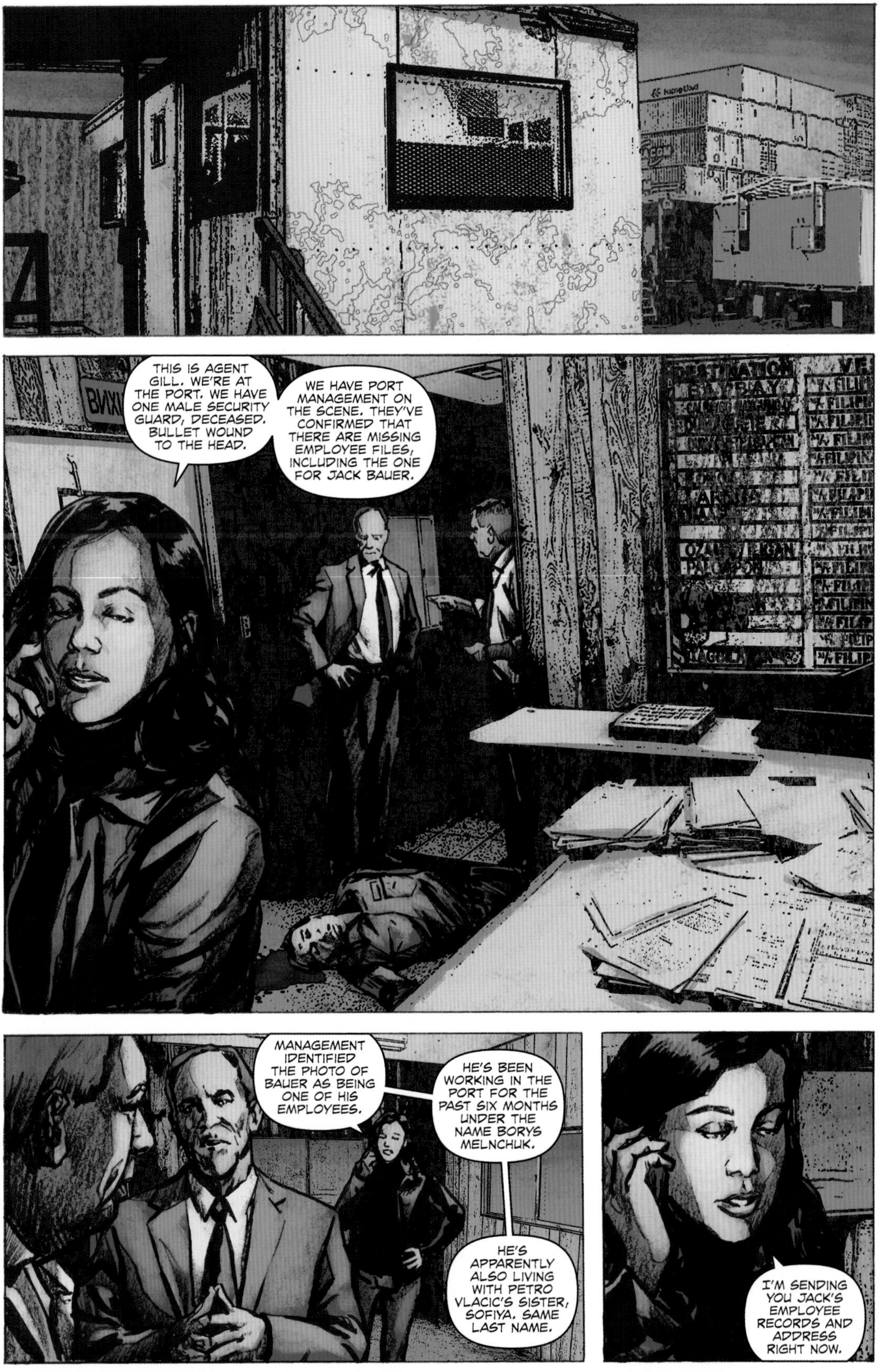
THIS IS AGENT GILL. WE'RE AT THE PORT. WE HAVE ONE MALE SECURITY GUARD, DECEASED. BULLET WOUND TO THE HEAD.
WE HAVE PORT MANAGEMENT ON THE SCENE. THEY'VE CONFIRMED THAT THERE ARE MISSING EMPLOYEE FILES, INCLUDING THE ONE FOR JACK BAUER.
MANAGEMENT IDENTIFIED THE PHOTO OF BAUER AS BEING ONE OF HIS EMPLOYEES.
HE'S BEEN WORKING IN THE PORT FOR THE PAST SIX MONTHS UNDER THE NAME BORYS MELNCHUK.
HE'S APPARENTLY ALSO LIVING WITH PETRO VLACIC'S SISTER, SOFIYA. SAME LAST NAME.
I'M SENDING YOU JACK'S EMPLOYEE RECORDS AND ADDRESS RIGHT NOW.

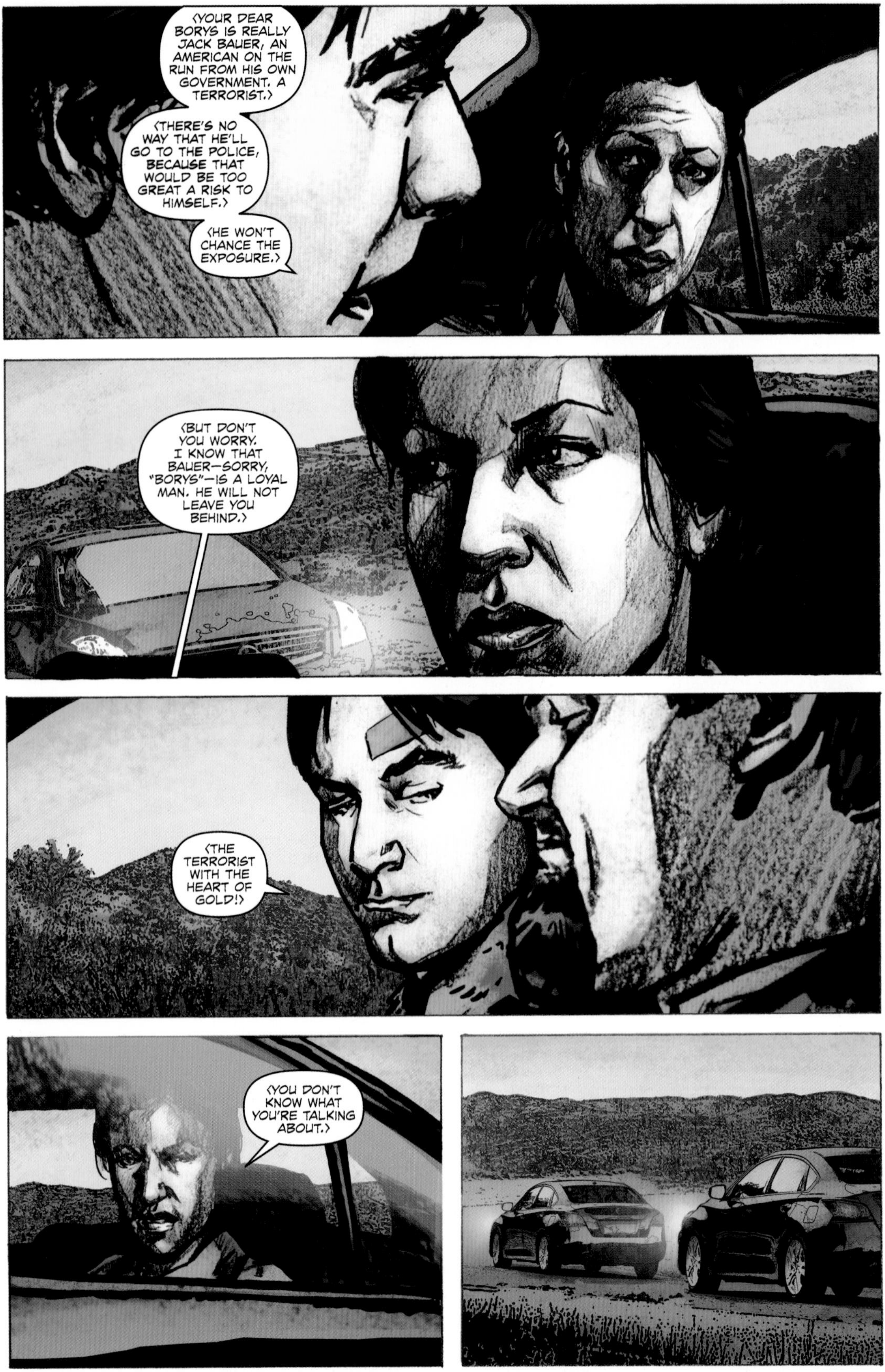

‹YOUR DEAR BORYS IS REALLY JACK BAUER, AN AMERICAN ON THE RUN FROM HIS OWN GOVERNMENT. A TERRORIST.›
‹THERE'S NO WAY THAT HE'LL GO TO THE POLICE, BECAUSE THAT WOULD BE TOO GREAT A RISK TO HIMSELF.›
‹HE WON'T CHANCE THE EXPOSURE.›
‹BUT DON'T YOU WORRY. I KNOW THAT BAUER—SORRY, "BORYS"—IS A LOYAL MAN. HE WILL NOT LEAVE YOU BEHIND.›
‹THE TERRORIST WITH THE HEART OF GOLD!›
‹YOU DON'T KNOW WHAT YOU'RE TALKING ABOUT.›

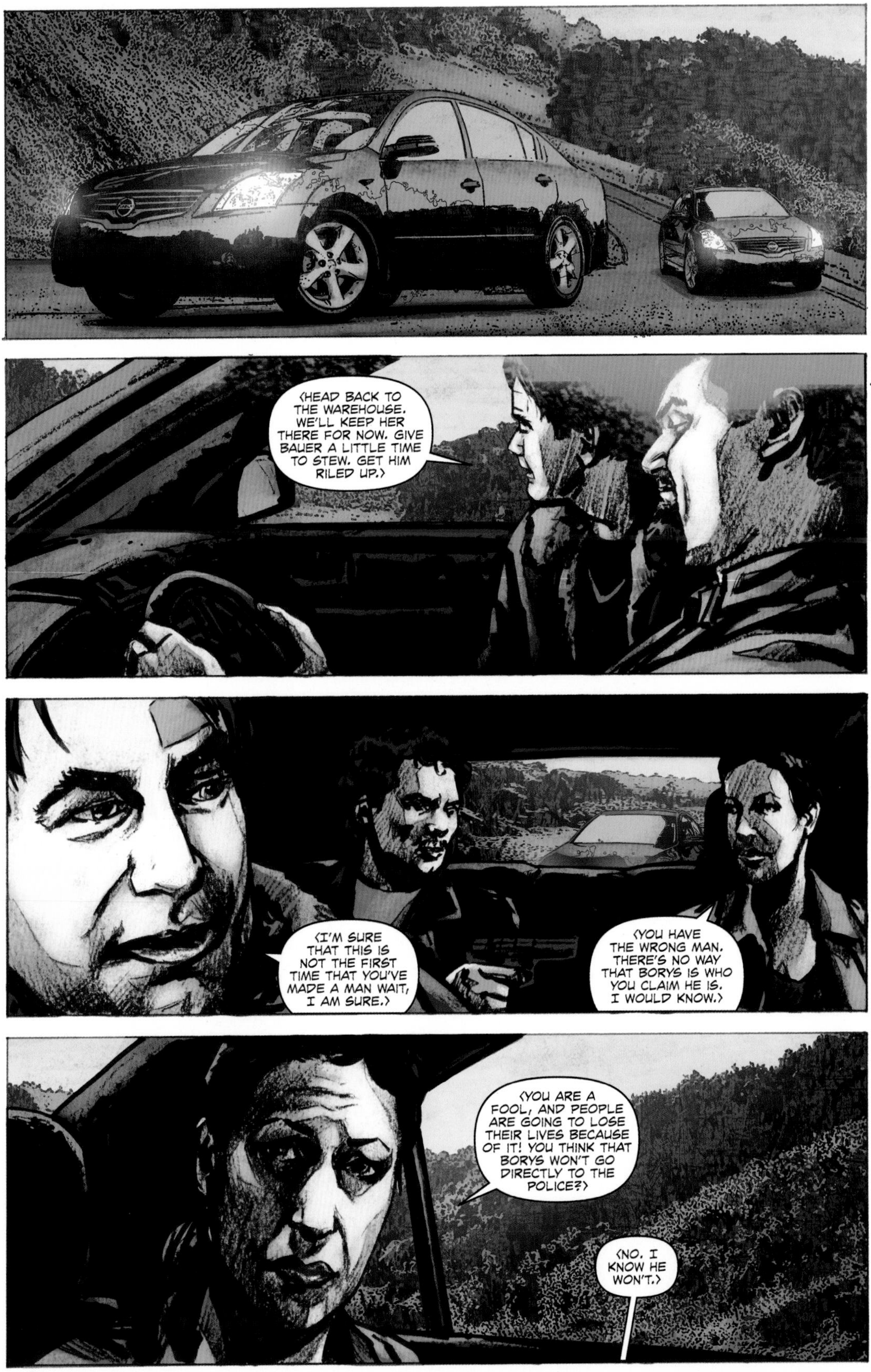
<HEAD BACK TO THE WAREHOUSE. WE'LL KEEP HER THERE FOR NOW. GIVE BAUER A LITTLE TIME TO STEW. GET HIM RILED UP.>
<I'M SURE THAT THIS IS NOT THE FIRST TIME THAT YOU'VE MADE A MAN WAIT, I AM SURE.>
<YOU HAVE THE WRONG MAN. THERE'S NO WAY THAT BORYS IS WHO YOU CLAIM HE IS. I WOULD KNOW.>
<YOU ARE A FOOL, AND PEOPLE ARE GOING TO LOSE THEIR LIVES BECAUSE OF IT! YOU THINK THAT BORYS WON'T GO DIRECTLY TO THE POLICE?>
<NO. I KNOW HE WON'T.>

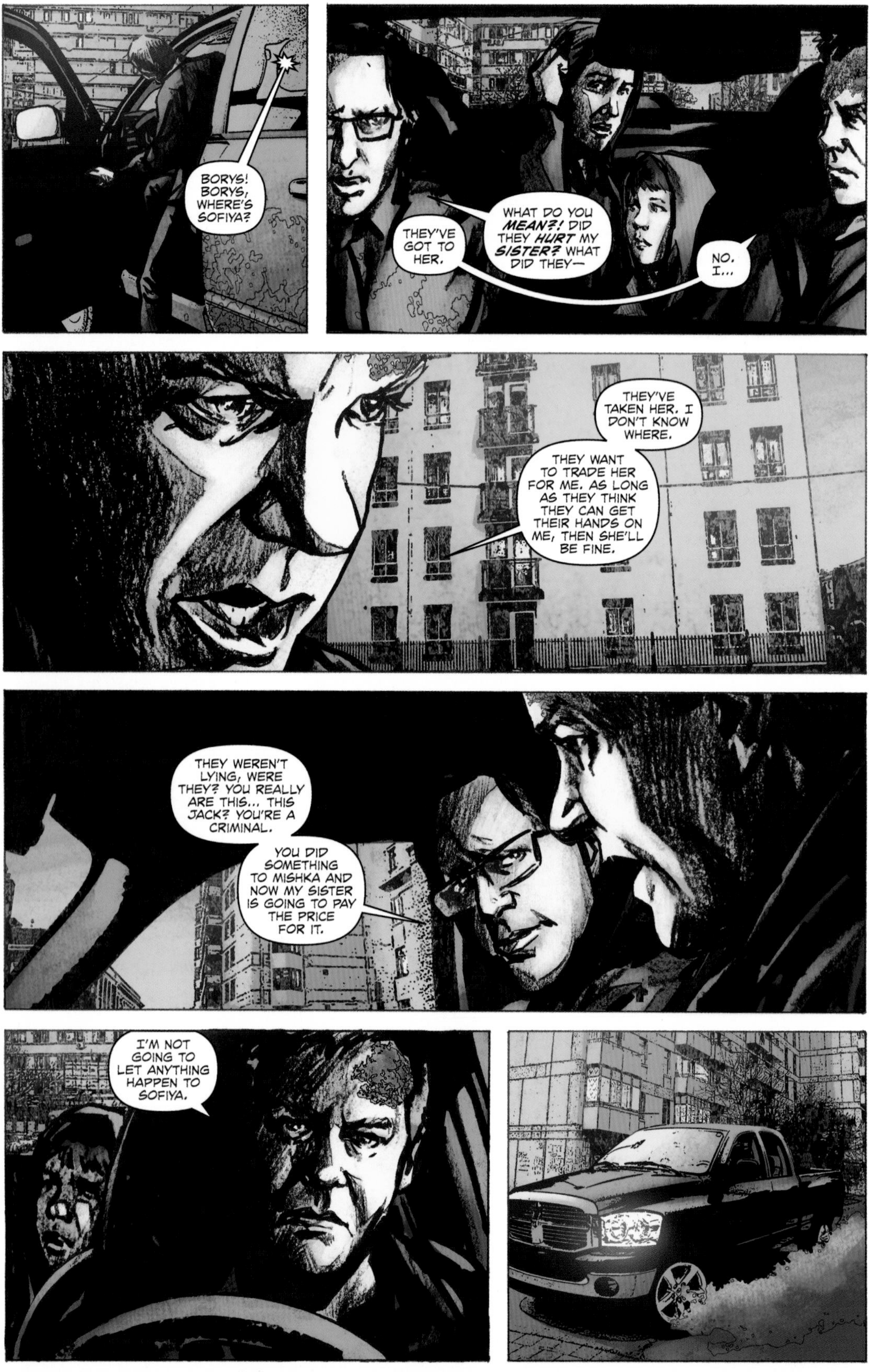
BORYS! BORYS, WHERE'S SOFIYA?
THEY'VE GOT TO HER.
WHAT DO YOU ***MEAN?!*** DID THEY ***HURT*** MY ***SISTER?*** WHAT DID THEY—
NO. I...
THEY'VE TAKEN HER. I DON'T KNOW WHERE.
THEY WANT TO TRADE HER FOR ME. AS LONG AS THEY THINK THEY CAN GET THEIR HANDS ON ME, THEN SHE'LL BE FINE.
THEY WEREN'T LYING, WERE THEY? YOU REALLY ARE THIS... THIS JACK? YOU'RE A CRIMINAL.
YOU DID SOMETHING TO MISHKA AND NOW MY SISTER IS GOING TO PAY THE PRICE FOR IT.
I'M NOT GOING TO LET ANYTHING HAPPEN TO SOFIYA.

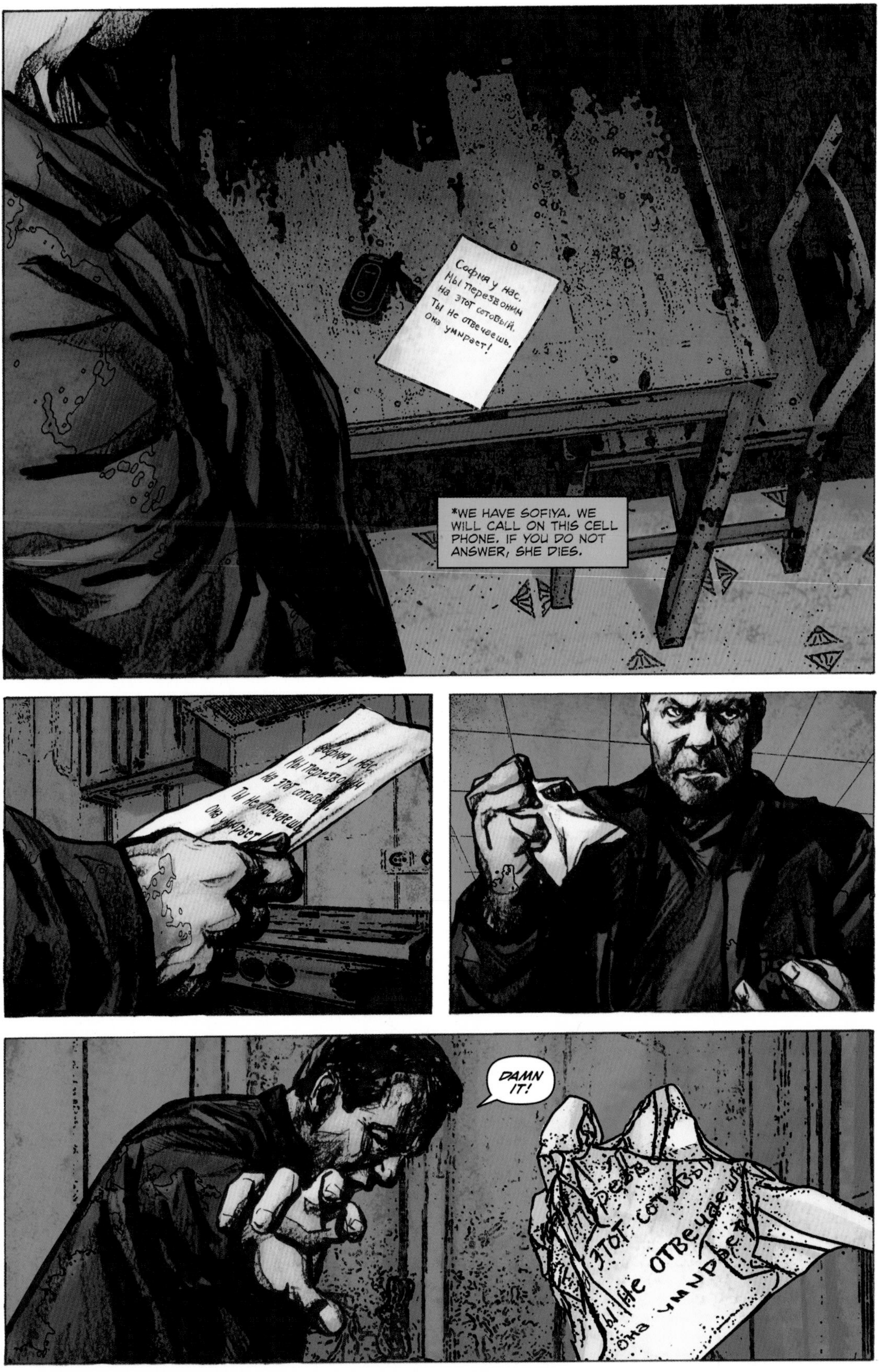
Софня у нас.
Мы перезвоним
на этот сотовый.
Ты Не отвечаешь.
Она умнрает!
*WE HAVE SOFIYA. WE WILL CALL ON THIS CELL PHONE. IF YOU DO NOT ANSWER, SHE DIES.
DAMN IT!

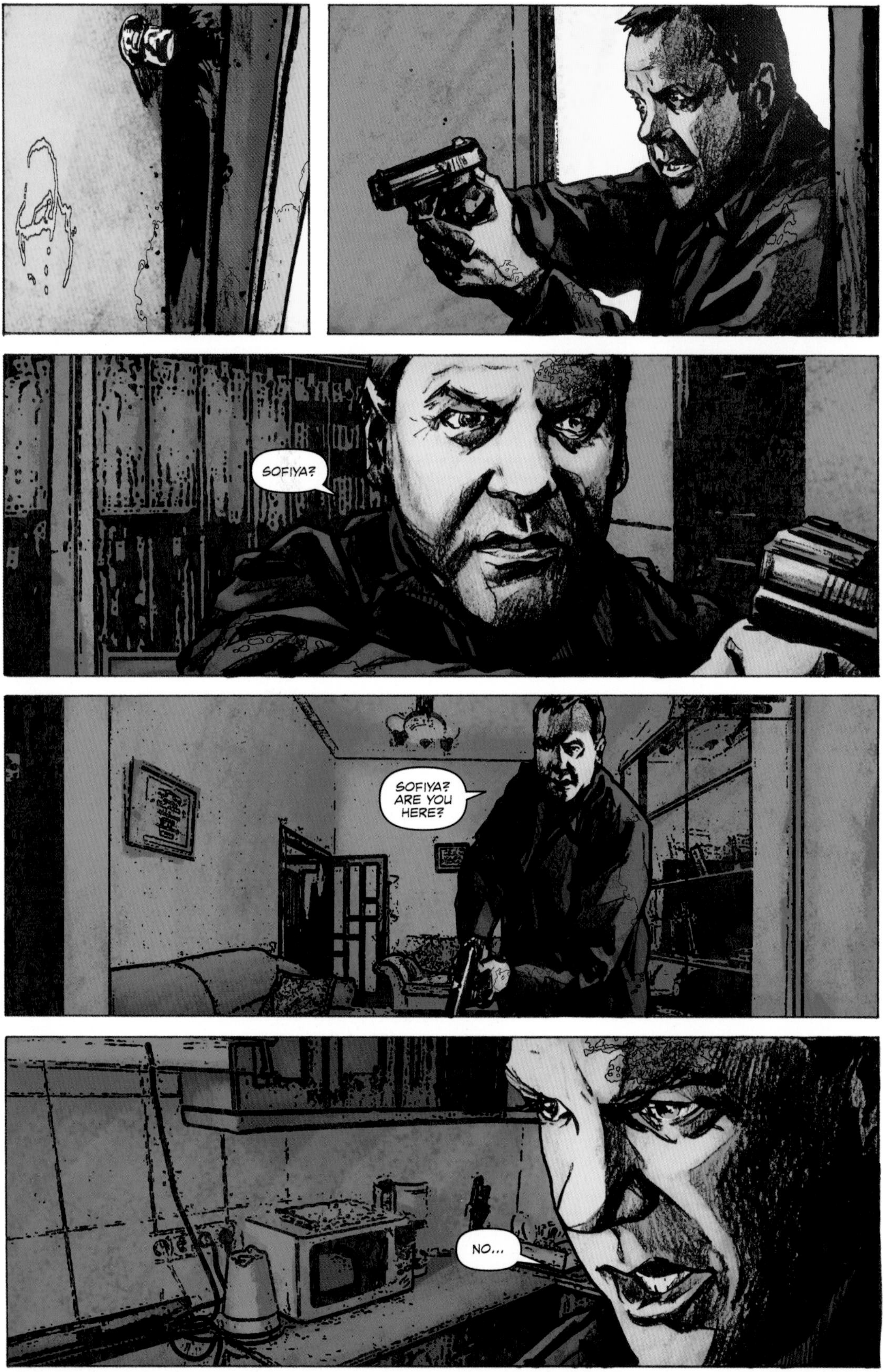
SOFIYA?
SOFIYA? ARE YOU HERE?
NO...

3 ART BY DAVIDE FURNÓ

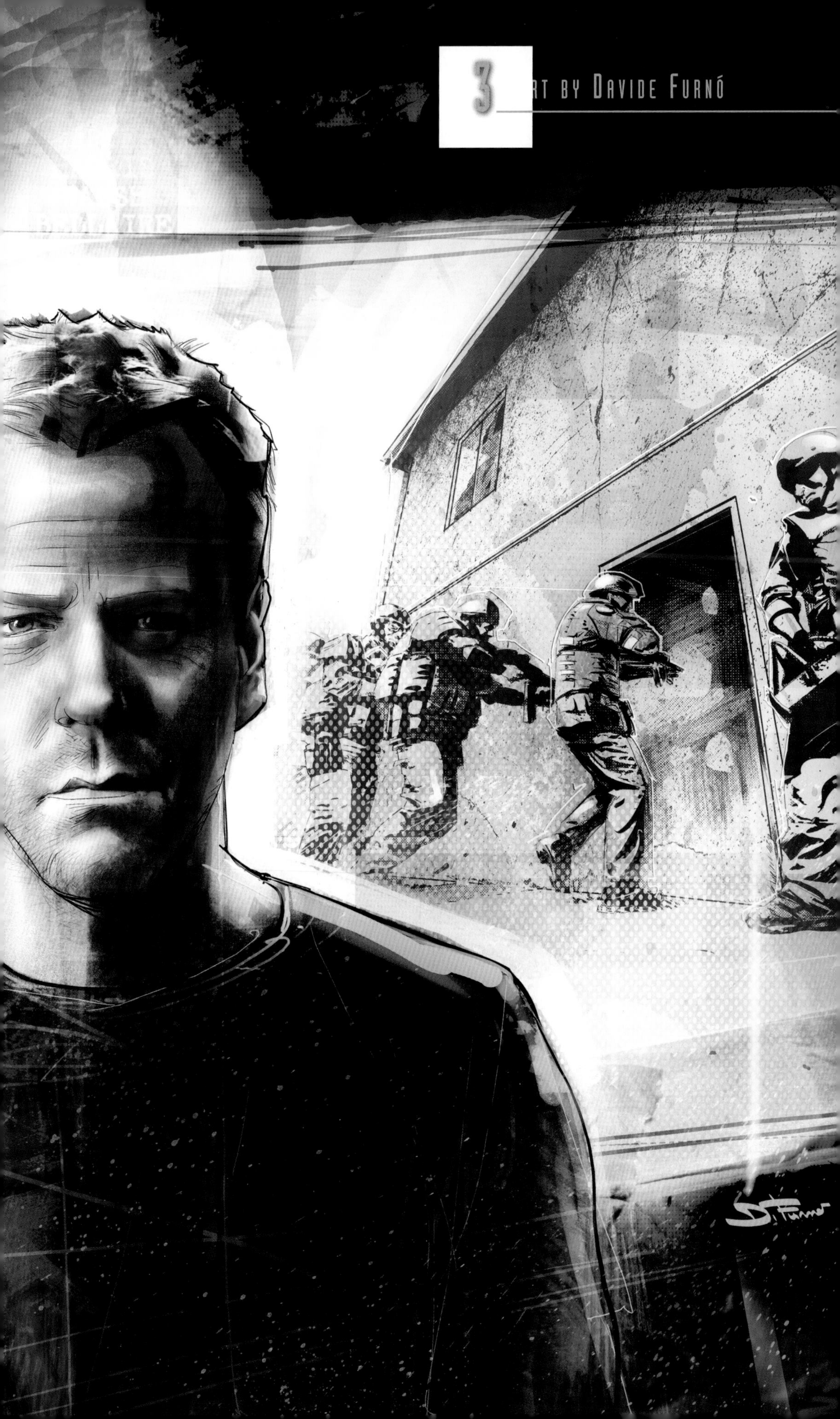

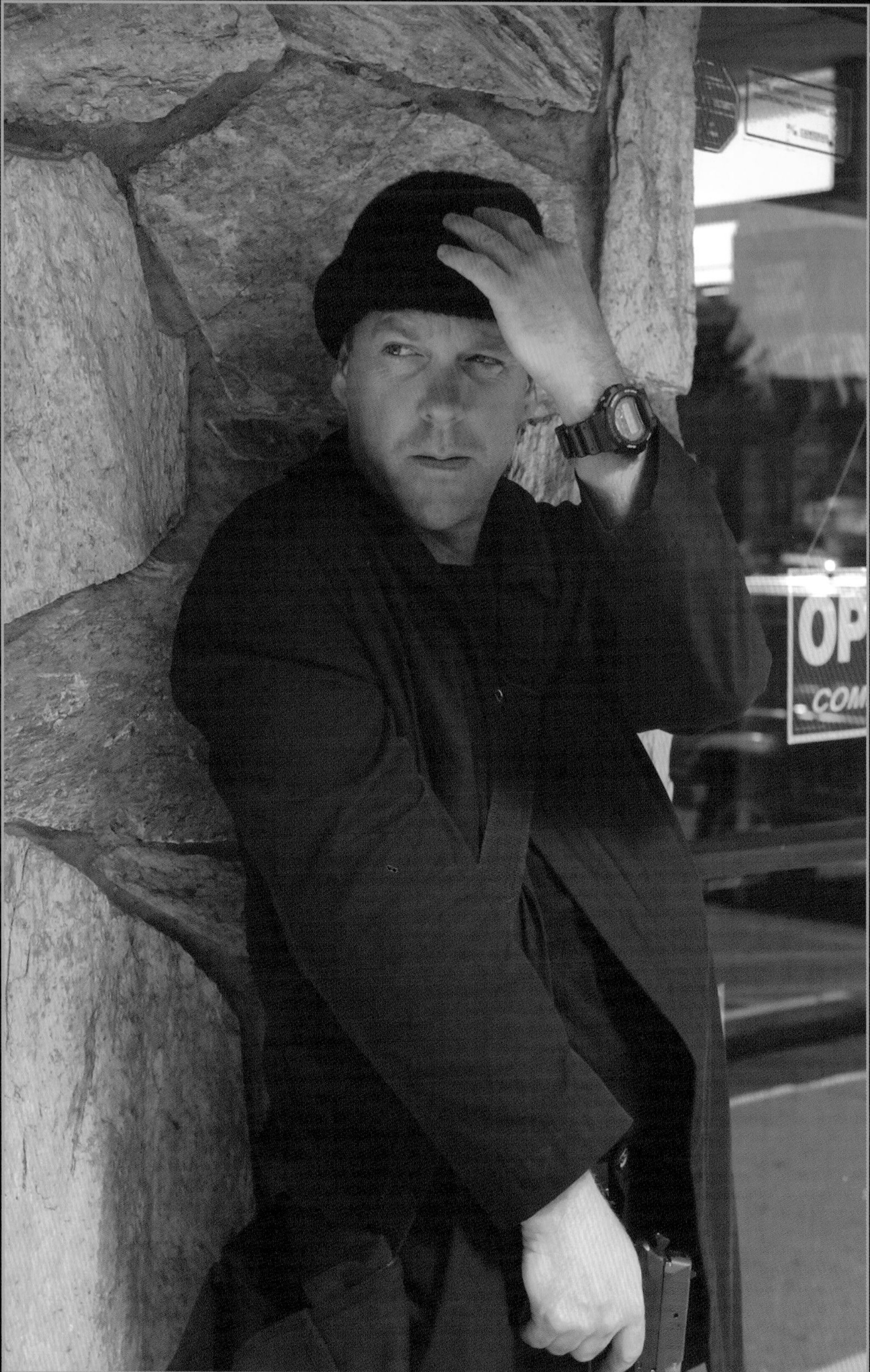

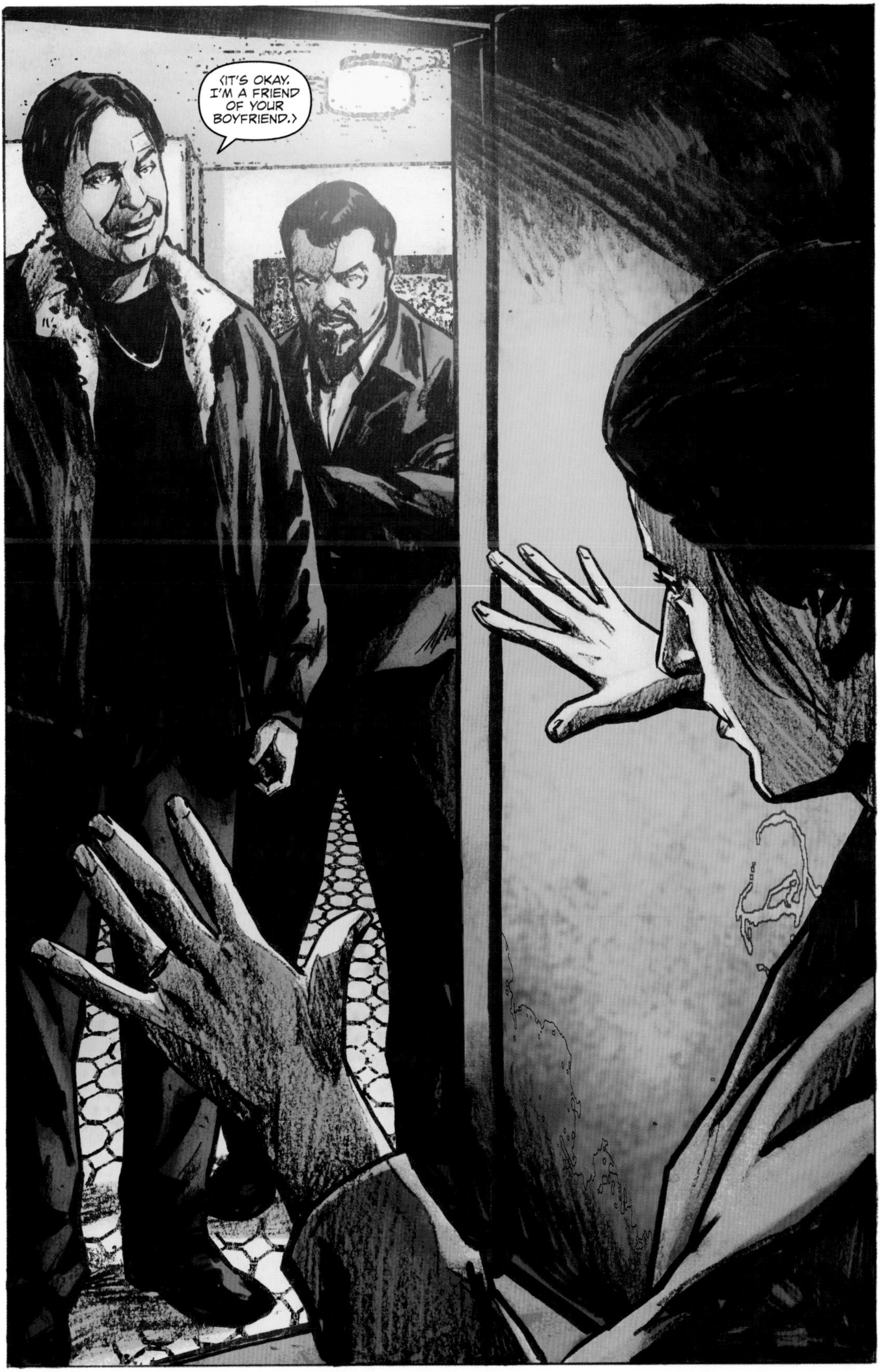
<IT'S OKAY. I'M A FRIEND OF YOUR BOYFRIEND.>

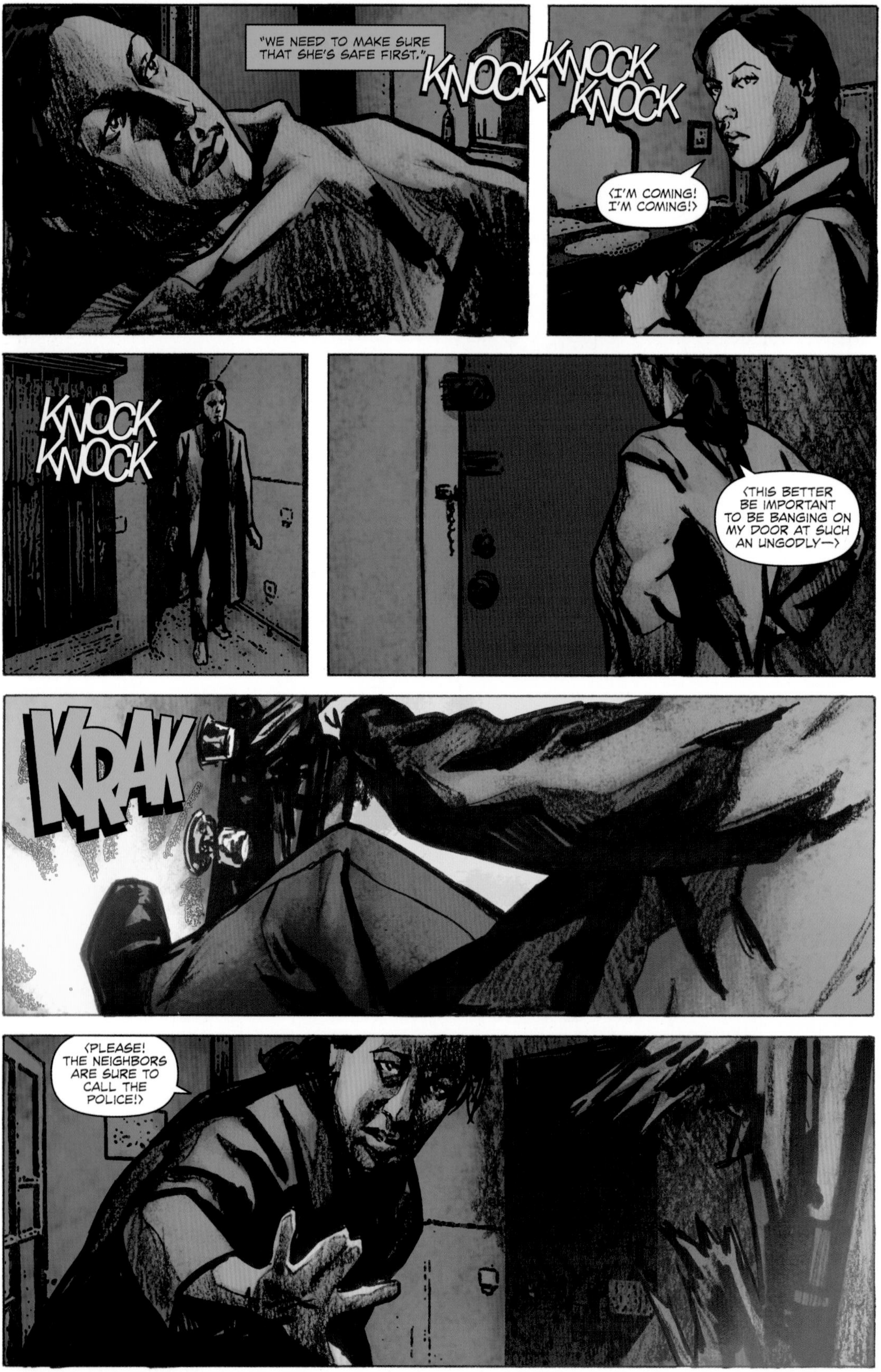
"WE NEED TO MAKE SURE THAT SHE'S SAFE FIRST."
KNOCK KNOCK KNOCK
‹I'M COMING! I'M COMING!›
KNOCK KNOCK
‹THIS BETTER BE IMPORTANT TO BE BANGING ON MY DOOR AT SUCH AN UNGODLY—›
KRAK
‹PLEASE! THE NEIGHBORS ARE SURE TO CALL THE POLICE!›

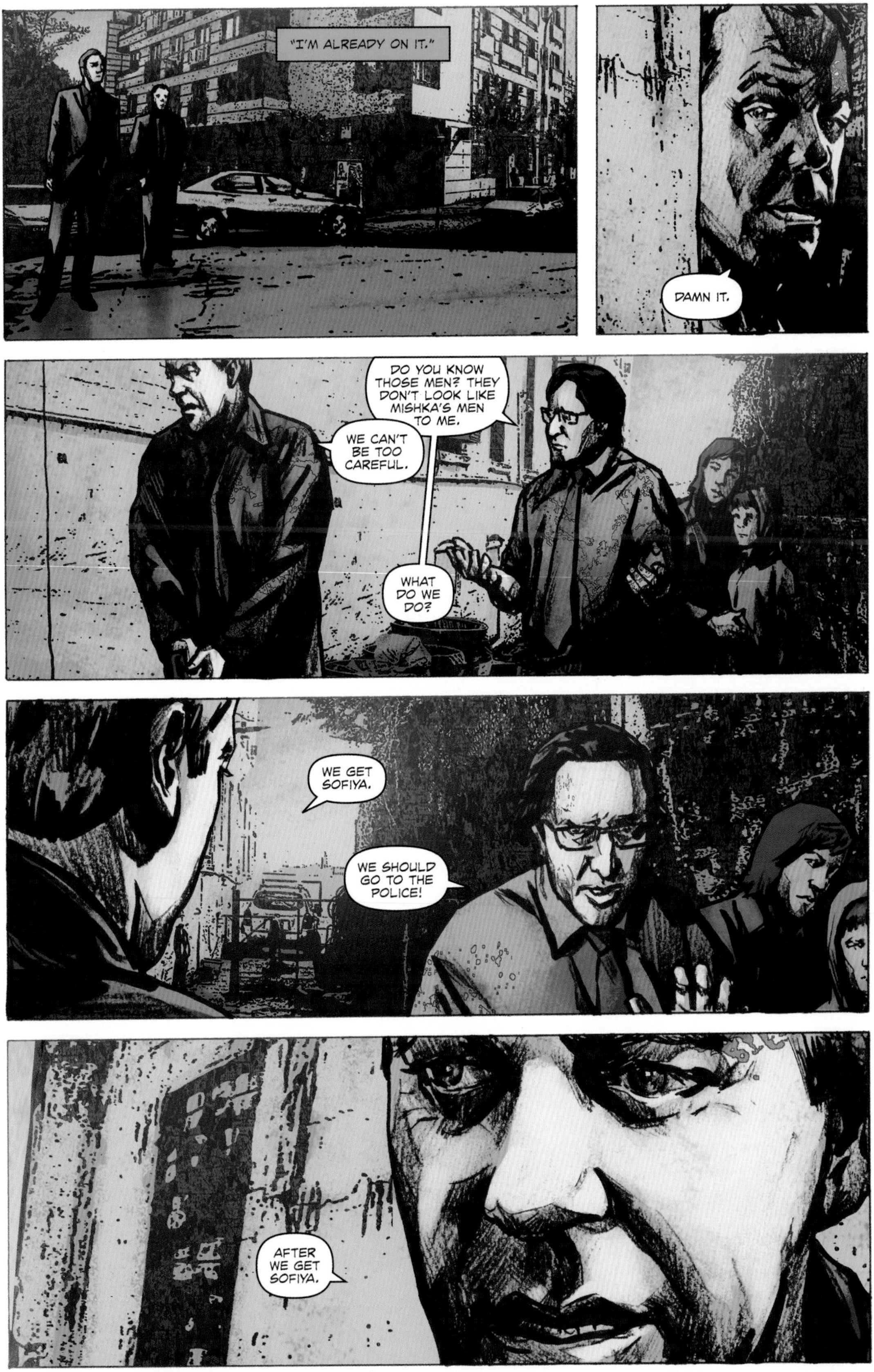
"I'M ALREADY ON IT."
DAMN IT.
DO YOU KNOW THOSE MEN? THEY DON'T LOOK LIKE MISHKA'S MEN TO ME.
WE CAN'T BE TOO CAREFUL.
WHAT DO WE DO?
WE GET SOFIYA.
WE SHOULD GO TO THE POLICE!
AFTER WE GET SOFIYA.

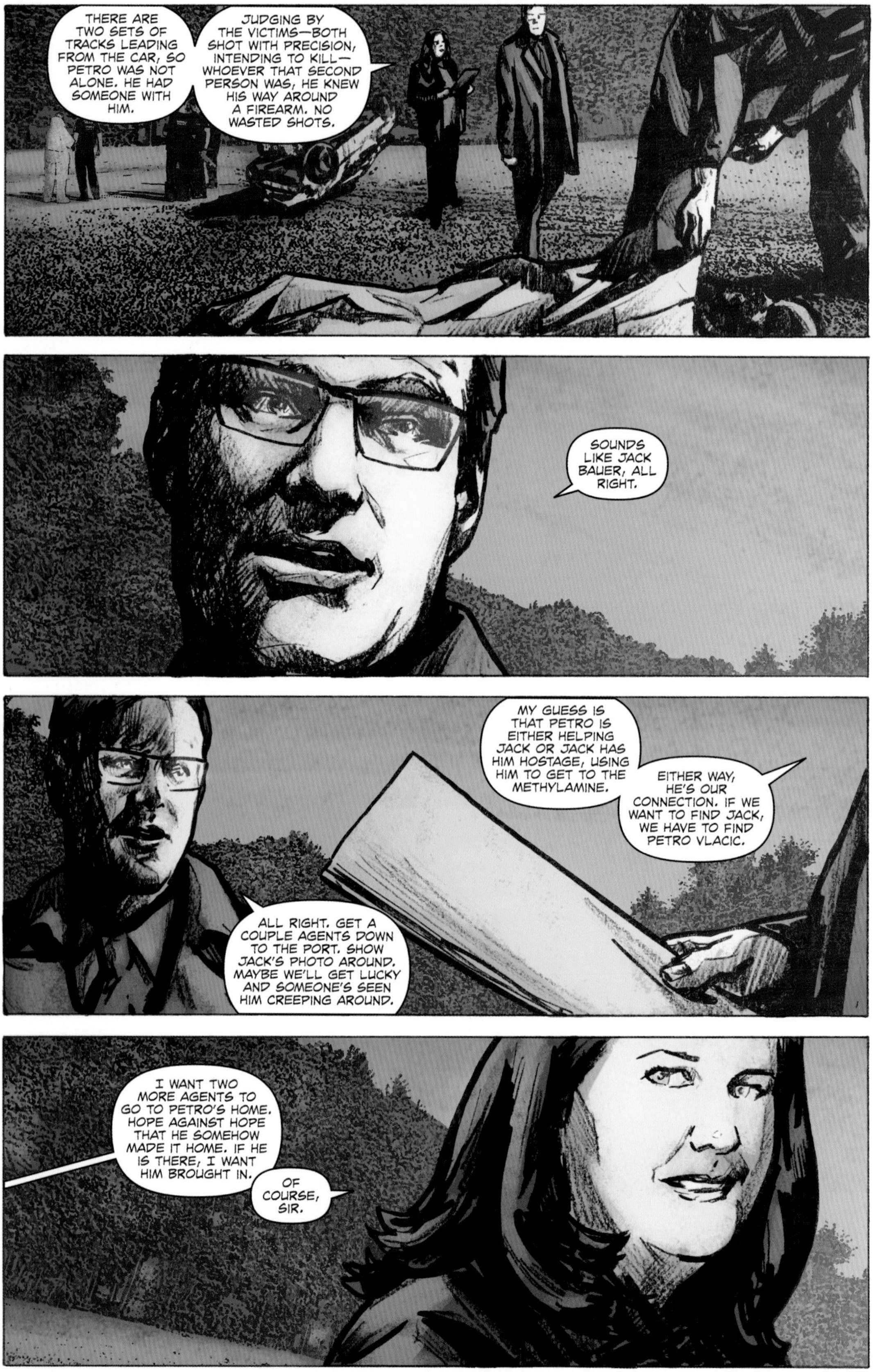
THERE ARE TWO SETS OF TRACKS LEADING FROM THE CAR, SO PETRO WAS NOT ALONE. HE HAD SOMEONE WITH HIM.
JUDGING BY THE VICTIMS—BOTH SHOT WITH PRECISION, INTENDING TO KILL—WHOEVER THAT SECOND PERSON WAS, HE KNEW HIS WAY AROUND A FIREARM. NO WASTED SHOTS.
SOUNDS LIKE JACK BAUER, ALL RIGHT.
MY GUESS IS THAT PETRO IS EITHER HELPING JACK OR JACK HAS HIM HOSTAGE, USING HIM TO GET TO THE METHYLAMINE.
EITHER WAY, HE'S OUR CONNECTION. IF WE WANT TO FIND JACK, WE HAVE TO FIND PETRO VLACIC.
ALL RIGHT. GET A COUPLE AGENTS DOWN TO THE PORT. SHOW JACK'S PHOTO AROUND. MAYBE WE'LL GET LUCKY AND SOMEONE'S SEEN HIM CREEPING AROUND.
I WANT TWO MORE AGENTS TO GO TO PETRO'S HOME. HOPE AGAINST HOPE THAT HE SOMEHOW MADE IT HOME. IF HE IS THERE, I WANT HIM BROUGHT IN.
OF COURSE, SIR.

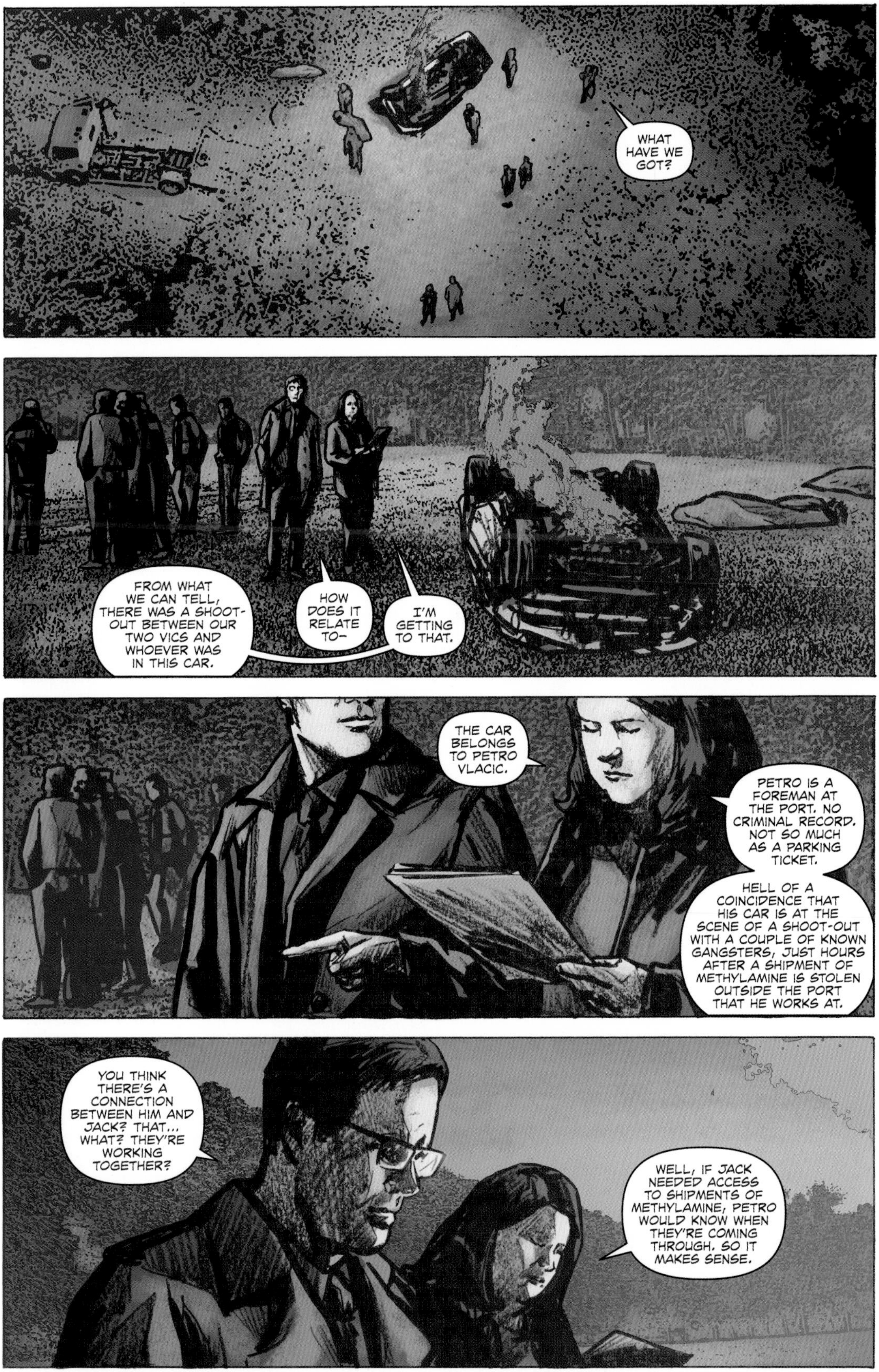
WHAT HAVE WE GOT?
FROM WHAT WE CAN TELL, THERE WAS A SHOOT-OUT BETWEEN OUR TWO VICS AND WHOEVER WAS IN THIS CAR.
HOW DOES IT RELATE TO—
I'M GETTING TO THAT.
THE CAR BELONGS TO PETRO VLACIC.
PETRO IS A FOREMAN AT THE PORT. NO CRIMINAL RECORD. NOT SO MUCH AS A PARKING TICKET.
HELL OF A COINCIDENCE THAT HIS CAR IS AT THE SCENE OF A SHOOT-OUT WITH A COUPLE OF KNOWN GANGSTERS, JUST HOURS AFTER A SHIPMENT OF METHYLAMINE IS STOLEN OUTSIDE THE PORT THAT HE WORKS AT.
YOU THINK THERE'S A CONNECTION BETWEEN HIM AND JACK? THAT... WHAT? THEY'RE WORKING TOGETHER?
WELL, IF JACK NEEDED ACCESS TO SHIPMENTS OF METHYLAMINE, PETRO WOULD KNOW WHEN THEY'RE COMING THROUGH. SO IT MAKES SENSE.

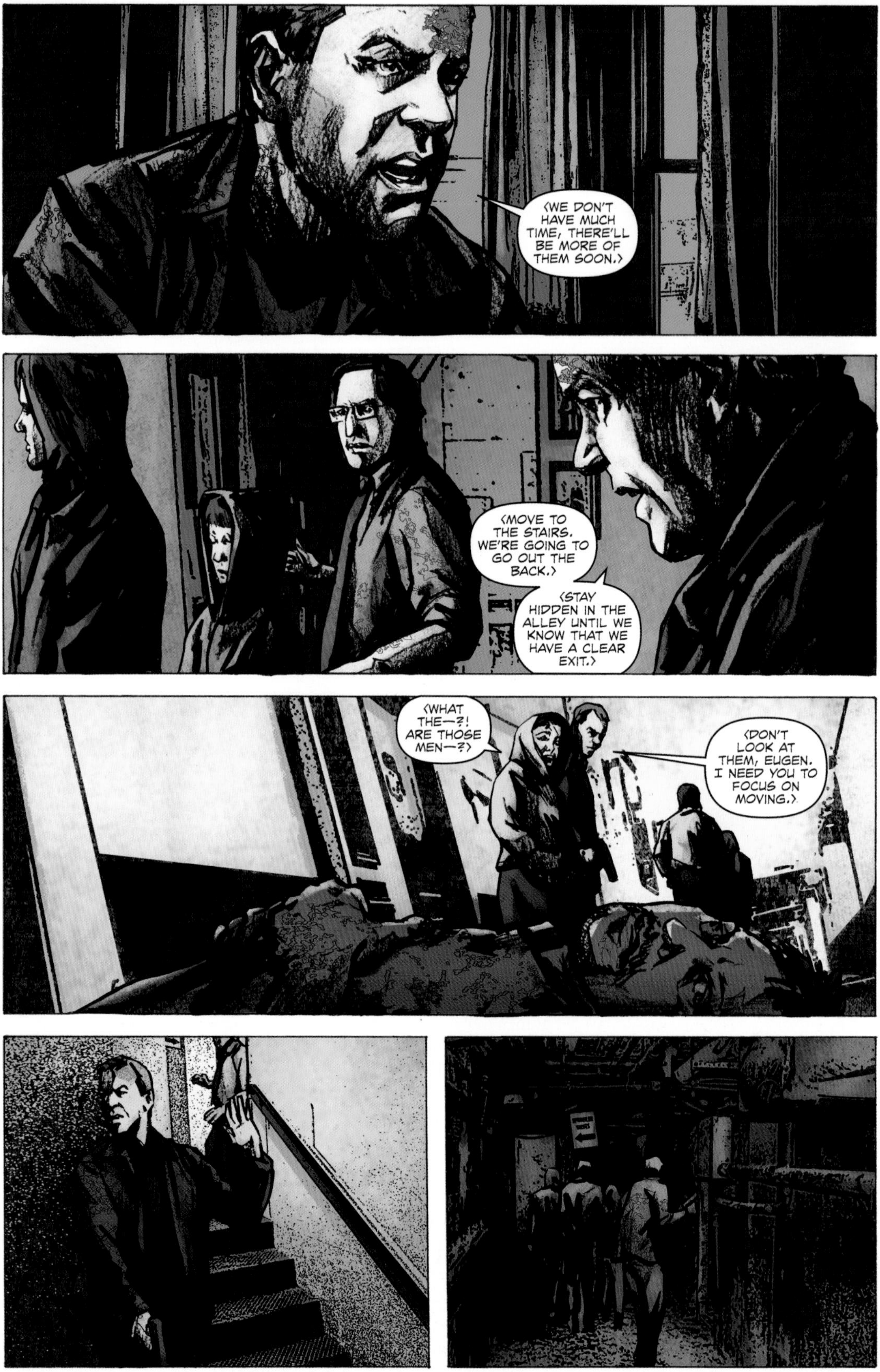
‹WE DON'T HAVE MUCH TIME, THERE'LL BE MORE OF THEM SOON.›
‹MOVE TO THE STAIRS. WE'RE GOING TO GO OUT THE BACK.›
‹STAY HIDDEN IN THE ALLEY UNTIL WE KNOW THAT WE HAVE A CLEAR EXIT.›
‹WHAT THE—?! ARE THOSE MEN—?›
‹DON'T LOOK AT THEM, EUGEN. I NEED YOU TO FOCUS ON MOVING.›

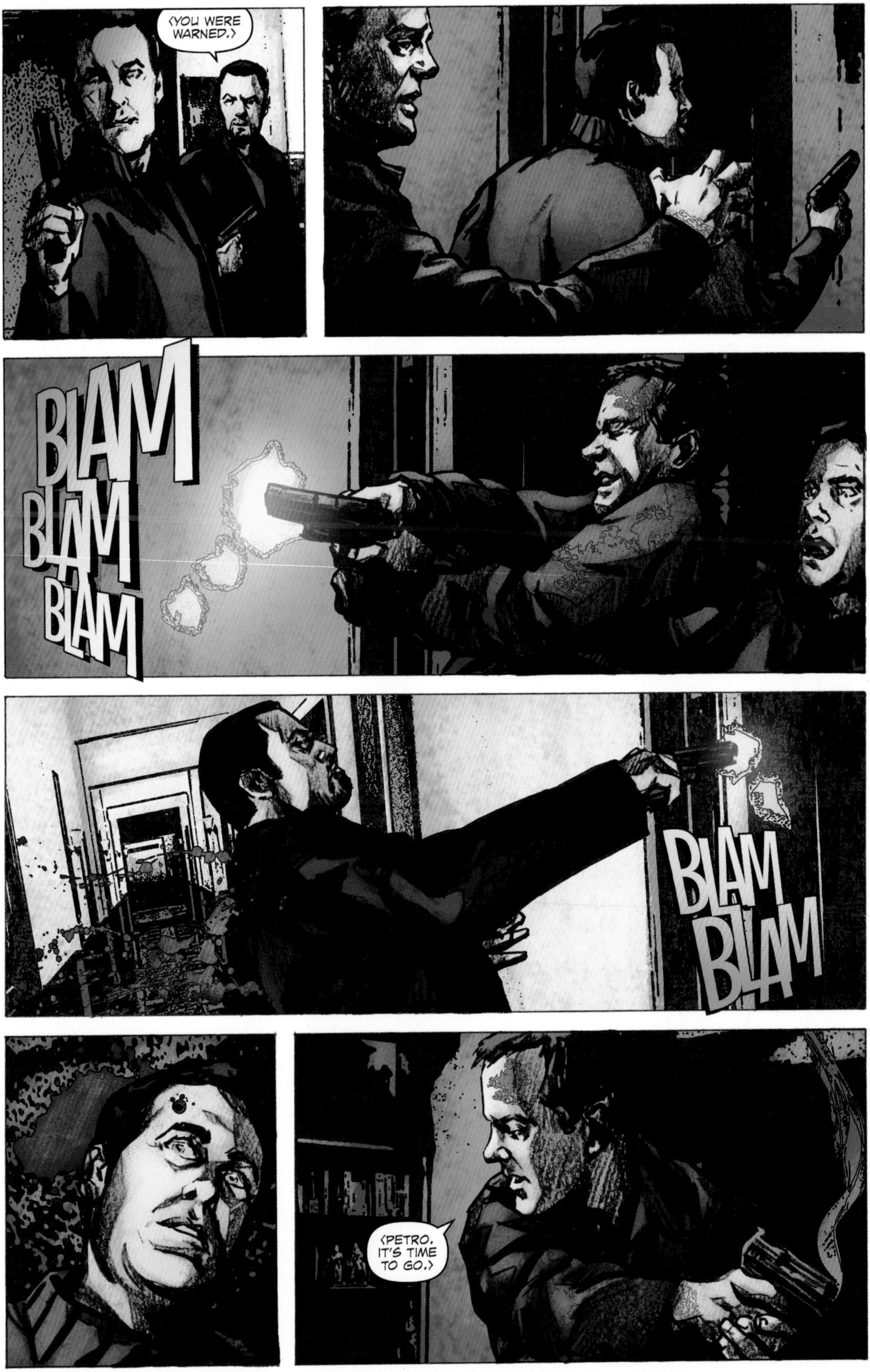
‹YOU WERE WARNED.›
BLAM
BLAM
BLAM
BLAM
BLAM
‹PETRO. IT'S TIME TO GO.›

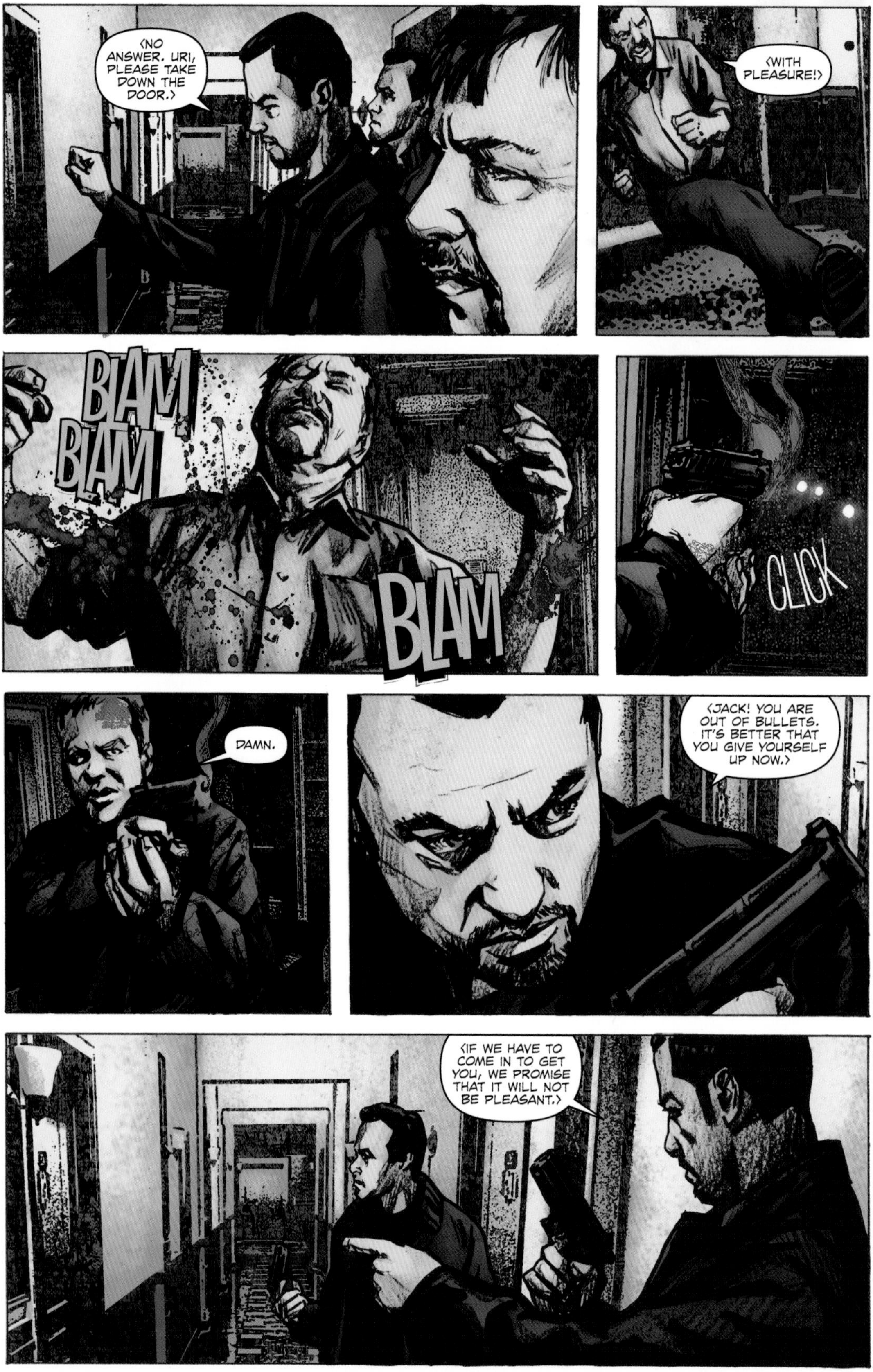

‹NO ANSWER. URI, PLEASE TAKE DOWN THE DOOR.›
‹WITH PLEASURE!›
BLAM
BLAM
BLAM
CLICK
DAMN.
‹JACK! YOU ARE OUT OF BULLETS. IT'S BETTER THAT YOU GIVE YOURSELF UP NOW.›
‹IF WE HAVE TO COME IN TO GET YOU, WE PROMISE THAT IT WILL NOT BE PLEASANT.›

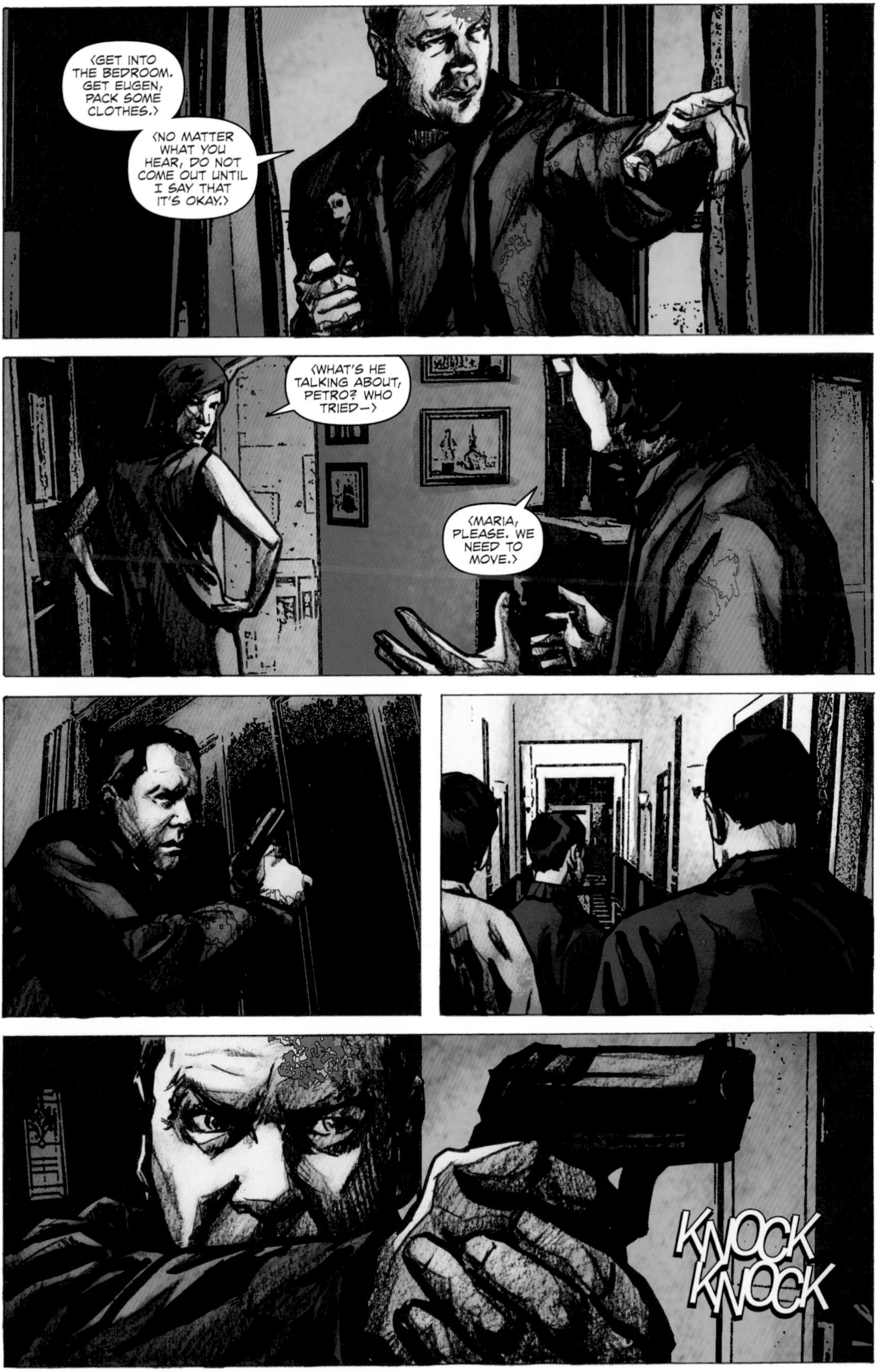
⟨GET INTO THE BEDROOM. GET EUGEN, PACK SOME CLOTHES.⟩
⟨NO MATTER WHAT YOU HEAR, DO NOT COME OUT UNTIL I SAY THAT IT'S OKAY.⟩
⟨WHAT'S HE TALKING ABOUT, PETRO? WHO TRIED—⟩
⟨MARIA, PLEASE. WE NEED TO MOVE.⟩
KNOCK KNOCK

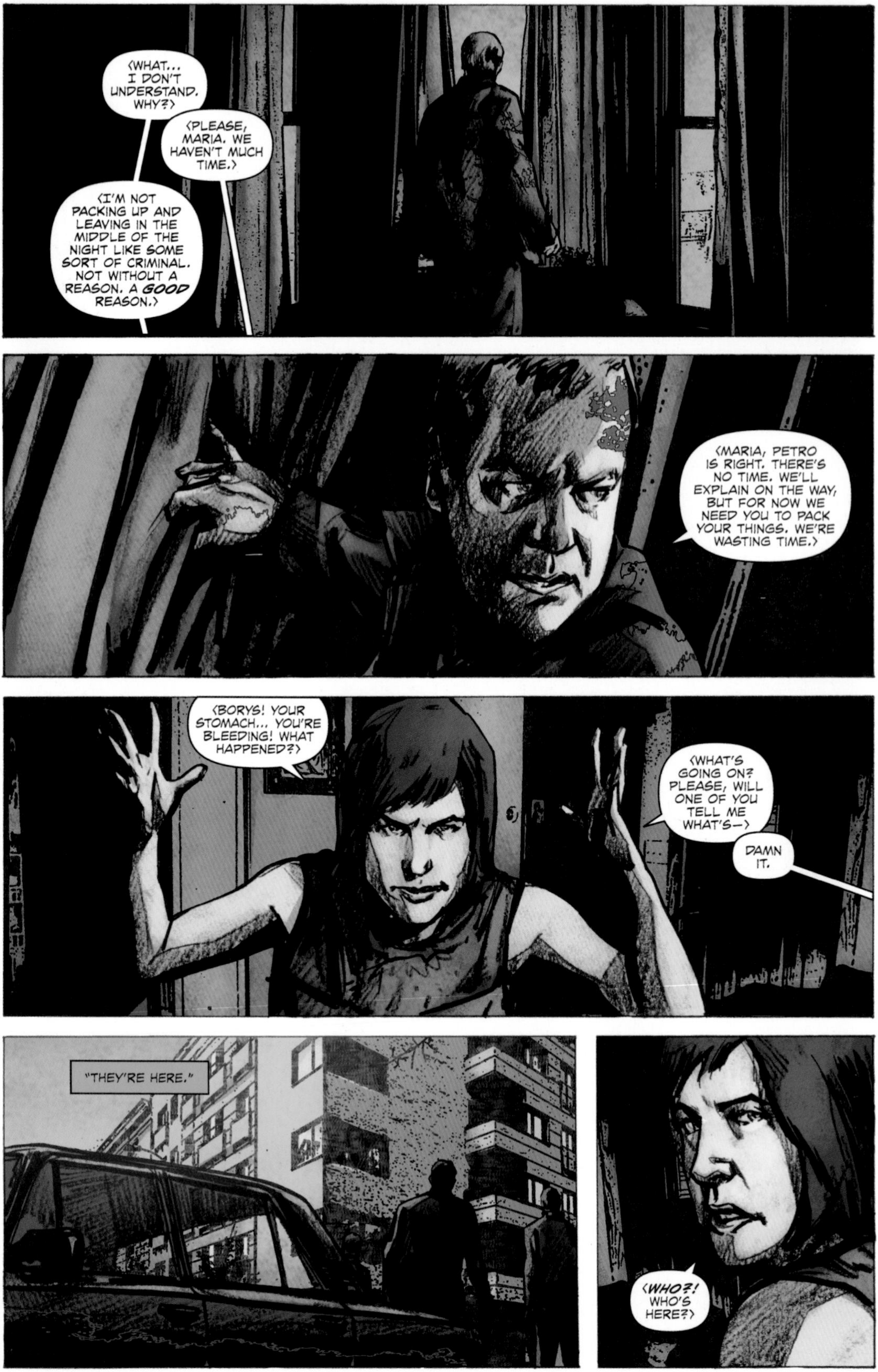

⟨WHAT... I DON'T UNDERSTAND. WHY?⟩
⟨PLEASE, MARIA. WE HAVEN'T MUCH TIME.⟩
⟨I'M NOT PACKING UP AND LEAVING IN THE MIDDLE OF THE NIGHT LIKE SOME SORT OF CRIMINAL. NOT WITHOUT A REASON. A ***GOOD*** REASON.⟩
⟨MARIA, PETRO IS RIGHT. THERE'S NO TIME. WE'LL EXPLAIN ON THE WAY, BUT FOR NOW WE NEED YOU TO PACK YOUR THINGS. WE'RE WASTING TIME.⟩
⟨BORYS! YOUR STOMACH... YOU'RE BLEEDING! WHAT HAPPENED?⟩
⟨WHAT'S GOING ON? PLEASE, WILL ONE OF YOU TELL ME WHAT'S—⟩
DAMN IT.
"THEY'RE HERE."
⟨***WHO?!*** WHO'S HERE?⟩

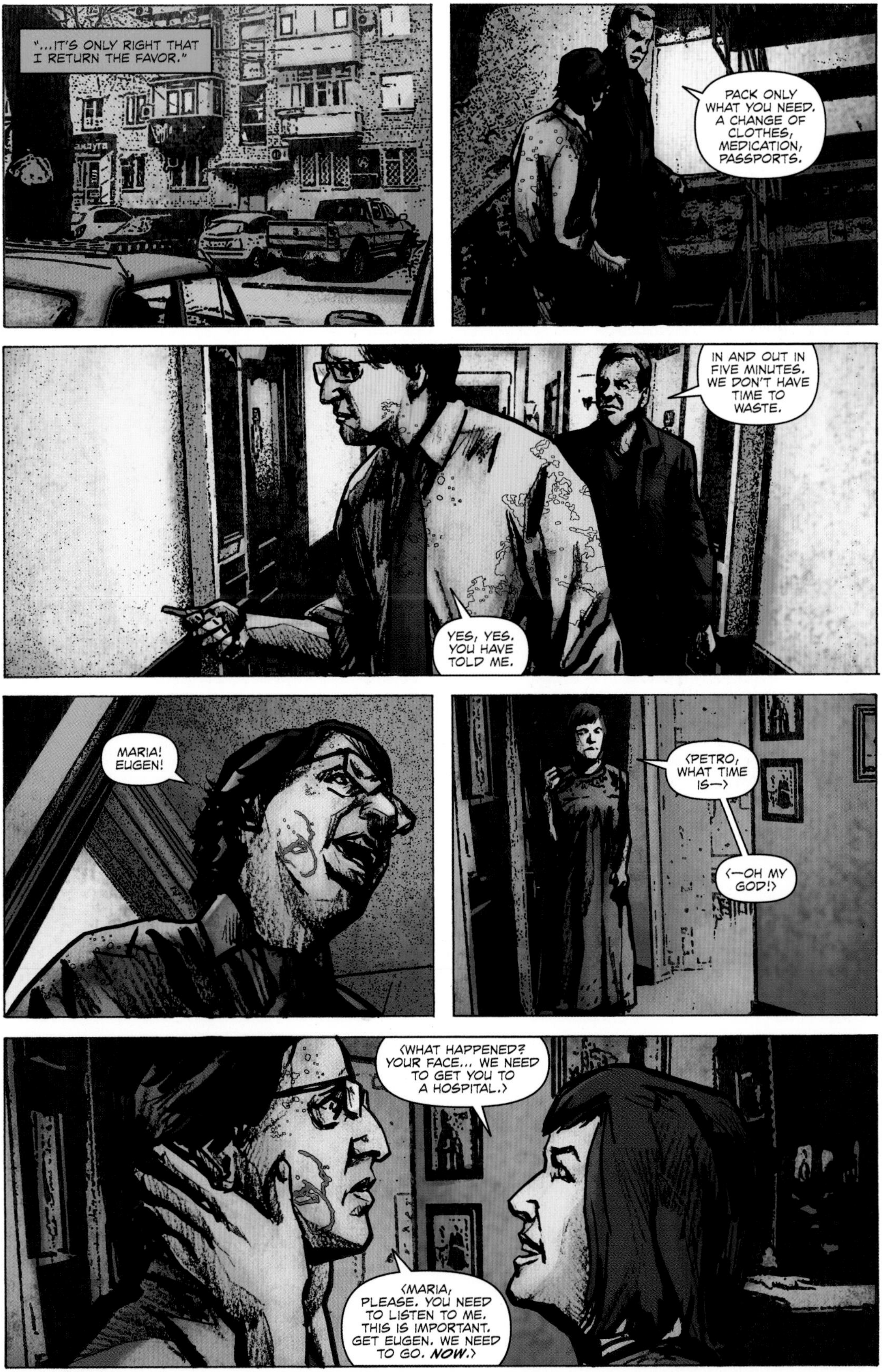
"...IT'S ONLY RIGHT THAT I RETURN THE FAVOR."
PACK ONLY WHAT YOU NEED. A CHANGE OF CLOTHES, MEDICATION, PASSPORTS.
IN AND OUT IN FIVE MINUTES. WE DON'T HAVE TIME TO WASTE.
YES, YES. YOU HAVE TOLD ME.
MARIA! EUGEN!
<PETRO, WHAT TIME IS—>
<—OH MY GOD!>
<WHAT HAPPENED? YOUR FACE... WE NEED TO GET YOU TO A HOSPITAL.>
<MARIA, PLEASE. YOU NEED TO LISTEN TO ME. THIS IS IMPORTANT. GET EUGEN. WE NEED TO GO. ***NOW***.>

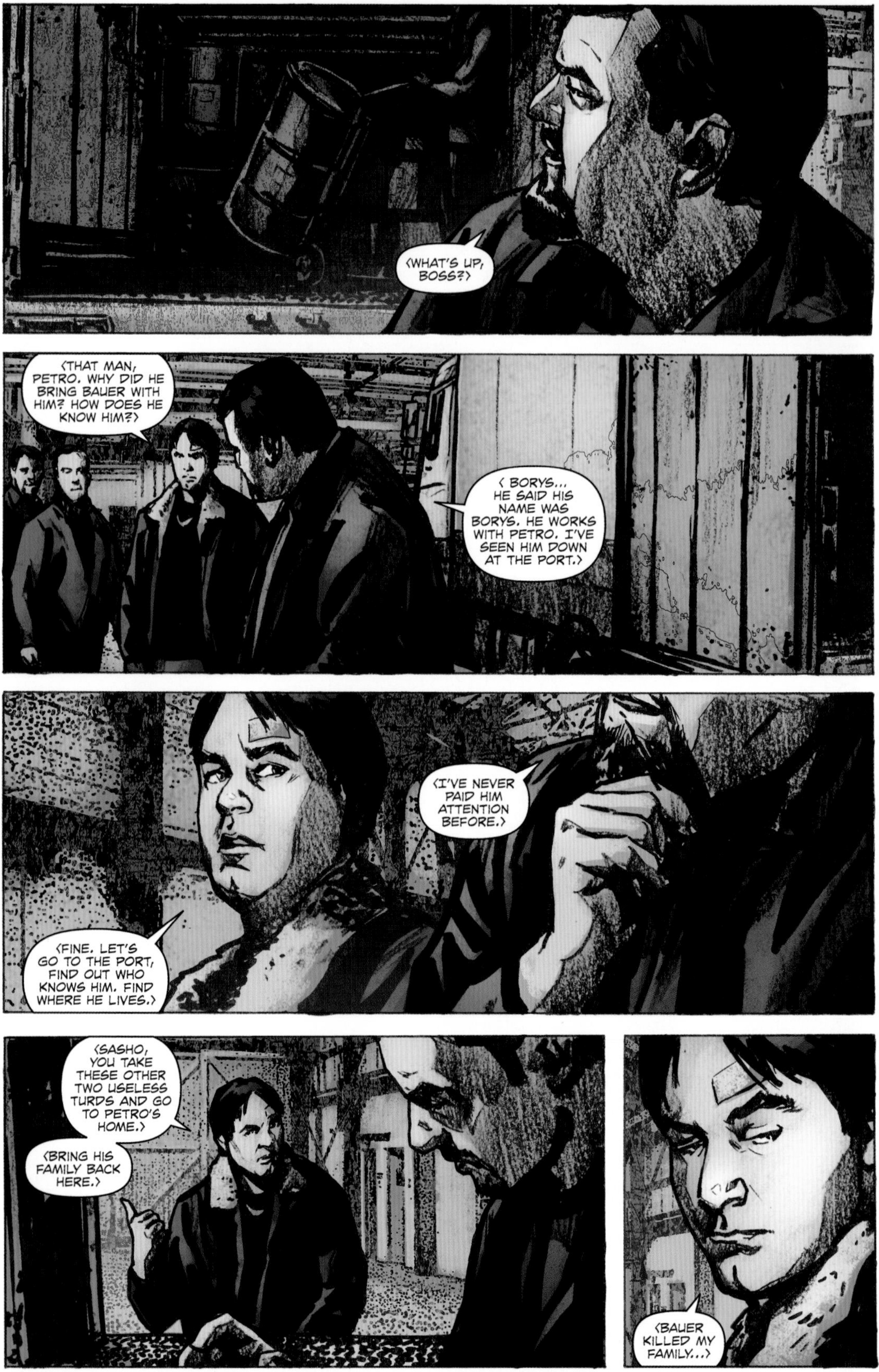
‹WHAT'S UP, BOSS?›
‹THAT MAN, PETRO. WHY DID HE BRING BAUER WITH HIM? HOW DOES HE KNOW HIM?›
‹ BORYS... HE SAID HIS NAME WAS BORYS. HE WORKS WITH PETRO. I'VE SEEN HIM DOWN AT THE PORT.›
‹I'VE NEVER PAID HIM ATTENTION BEFORE.›
‹FINE. LET'S GO TO THE PORT, FIND OUT WHO KNOWS HIM. FIND WHERE HE LIVES.›
‹SASHO, YOU TAKE THESE OTHER TWO USELESS TURDS AND GO TO PETRO'S HOME.›
‹BRING HIS FAMILY BACK HERE.›
‹BAUER KILLED MY FAMILY...›

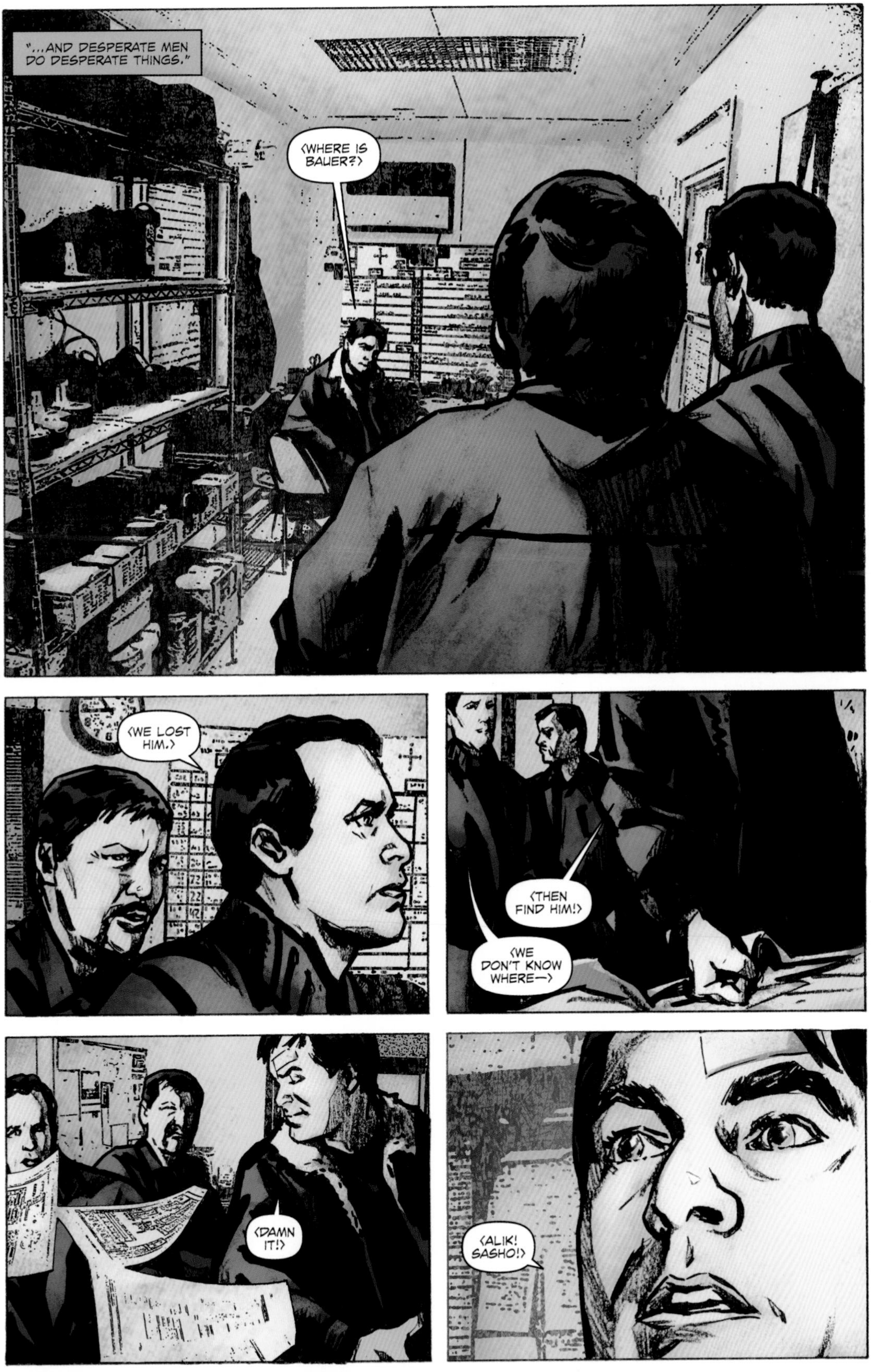
"...AND DESPERATE MEN DO DESPERATE THINGS."
‹WHERE IS BAUER?›
‹WE LOST HIM.›
‹THEN FIND HIM!›
‹WE DON'T KNOW WHERE—›
‹DAMN IT!›
‹ALIK! SASHO!›

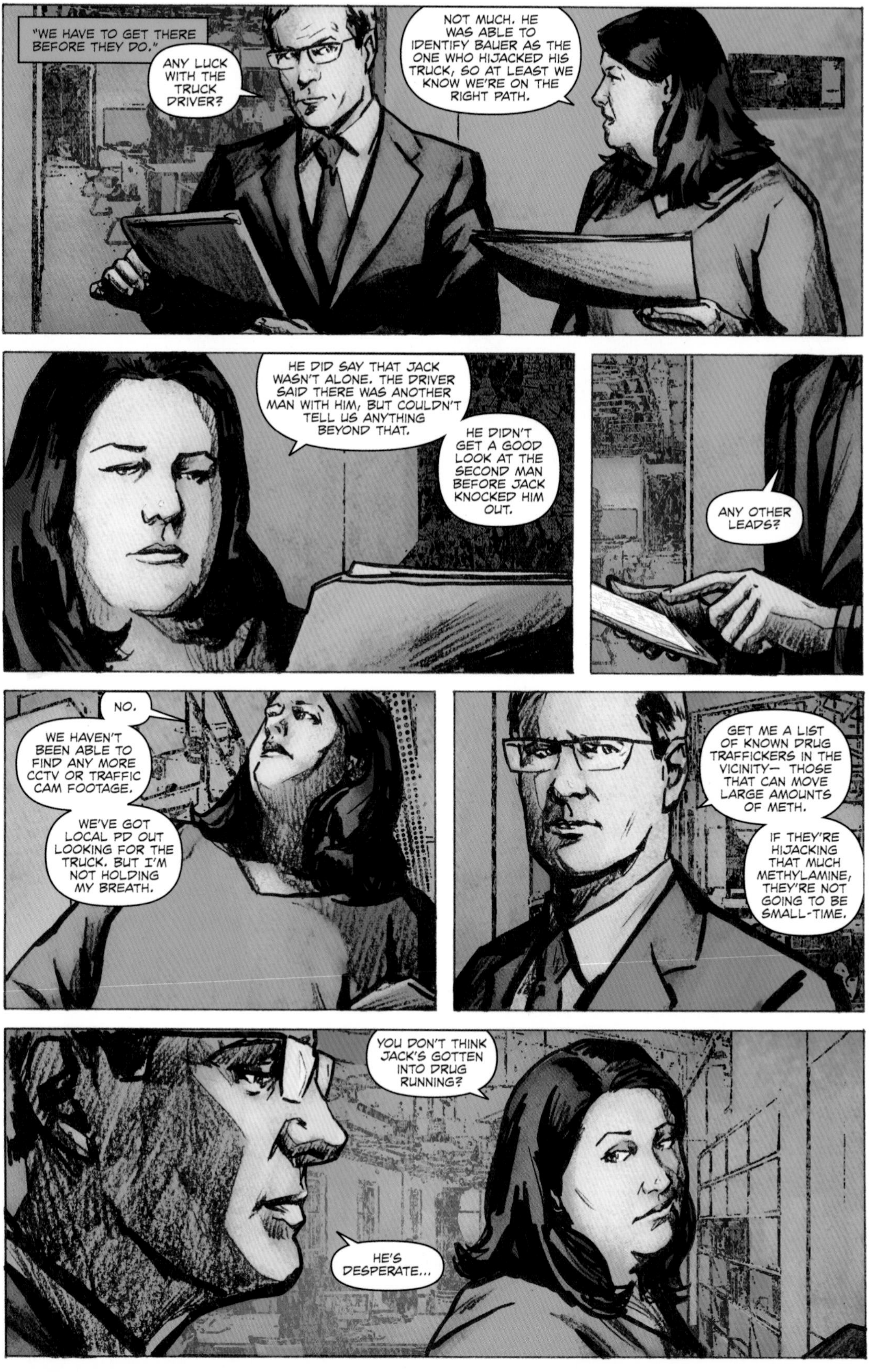
"WE HAVE TO GET THERE BEFORE THEY DO."
ANY LUCK WITH THE TRUCK DRIVER?
NOT MUCH. HE WAS ABLE TO IDENTIFY BAUER AS THE ONE WHO HIJACKED HIS TRUCK, SO AT LEAST WE KNOW WE'RE ON THE RIGHT PATH.
HE DID SAY THAT JACK WASN'T ALONE. THE DRIVER SAID THERE WAS ANOTHER MAN WITH HIM, BUT COULDN'T TELL US ANYTHING BEYOND THAT.
HE DIDN'T GET A GOOD LOOK AT THE SECOND MAN BEFORE JACK KNOCKED HIM OUT.
ANY OTHER LEADS?
NO.
WE HAVEN'T BEEN ABLE TO FIND ANY MORE CCTV OR TRAFFIC CAM FOOTAGE.
WE'VE GOT LOCAL PD OUT LOOKING FOR THE TRUCK. BUT I'M NOT HOLDING MY BREATH.
GET ME A LIST OF KNOWN DRUG TRAFFICKERS IN THE VICINITY— THOSE THAT CAN MOVE LARGE AMOUNTS OF METH.
IF THEY'RE HIJACKING THAT MUCH METHYLAMINE, THEY'RE NOT GOING TO BE SMALL-TIME.
YOU DON'T THINK JACK'S GOTTEN INTO DRUG RUNNING?
HE'S DESPERATE...

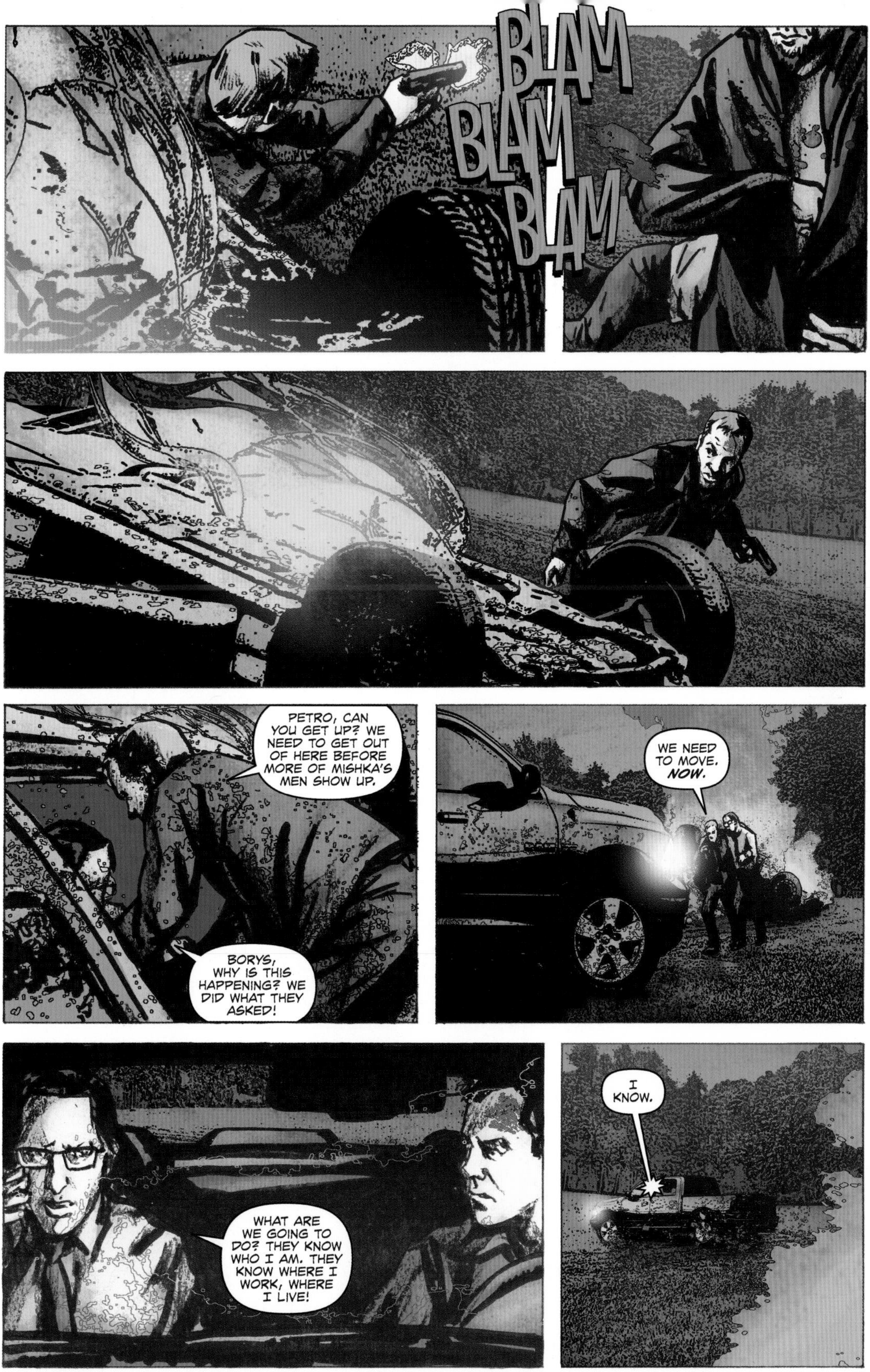
BLAM
BLAM
BLAM
PETRO, CAN YOU GET UP? WE NEED TO GET OUT OF HERE BEFORE MORE OF MISHKA'S MEN SHOW UP.
BORYS, WHY IS THIS HAPPENING? WE DID WHAT THEY ASKED!
WE NEED TO MOVE. ***NOW.***
WHAT ARE WE GOING TO DO? THEY KNOW WHO I AM. THEY KNOW WHERE I WORK, WHERE I LIVE!
I KNOW.

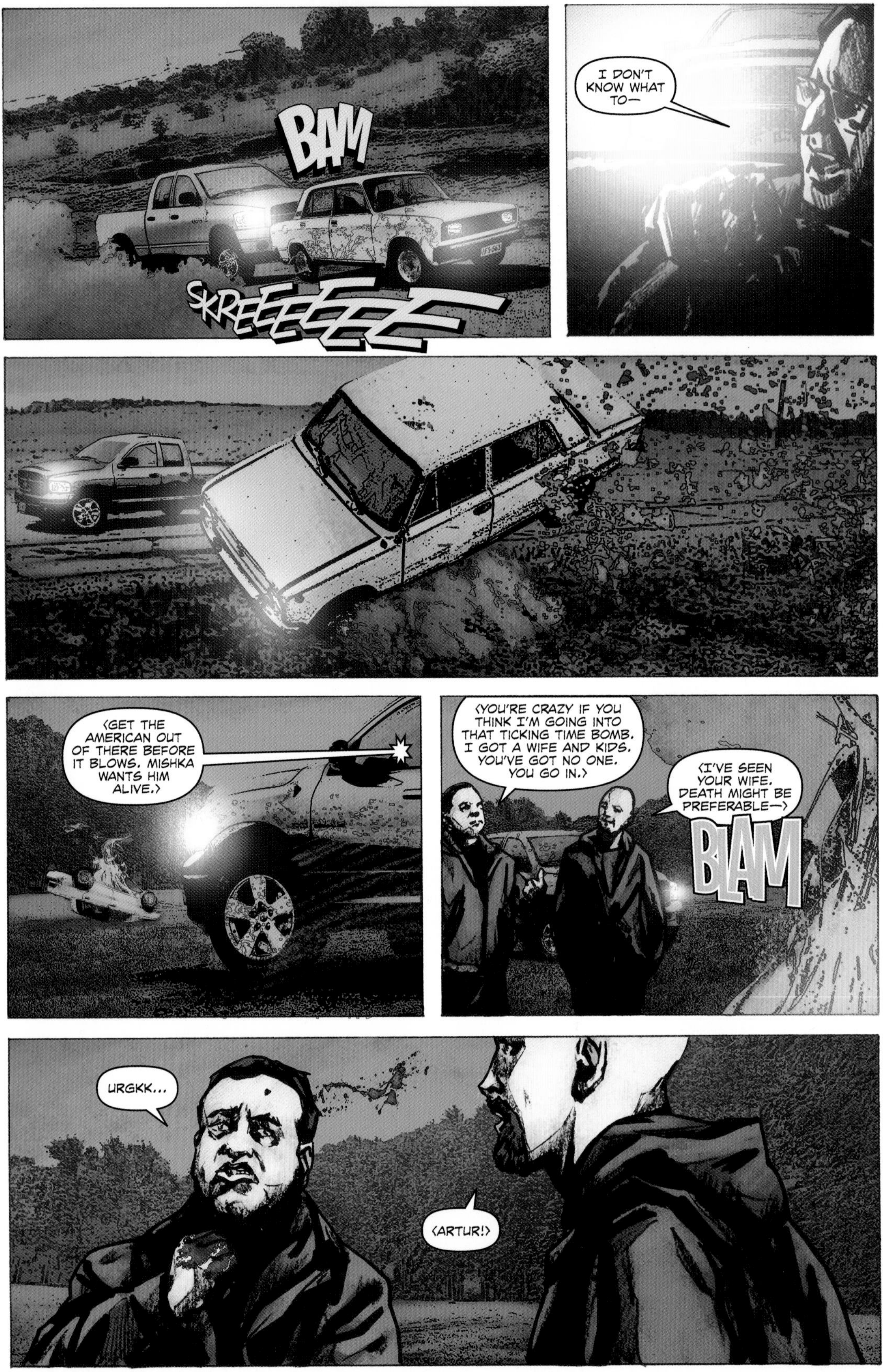
BAM
SKREEEEEEE
I DON'T KNOW WHAT TO—
‹GET THE AMERICAN OUT OF THERE BEFORE IT BLOWS. MISHKA WANTS HIM ALIVE.›
‹YOU'RE CRAZY IF YOU THINK I'M GOING INTO THAT TICKING TIME BOMB. I GOT A WIFE AND KIDS. YOU'VE GOT NO ONE. YOU GO IN.›
‹I'VE SEEN YOUR WIFE. DEATH MIGHT BE PREFERABLE—›
BLAM
URGKK...
‹ARTUR!›

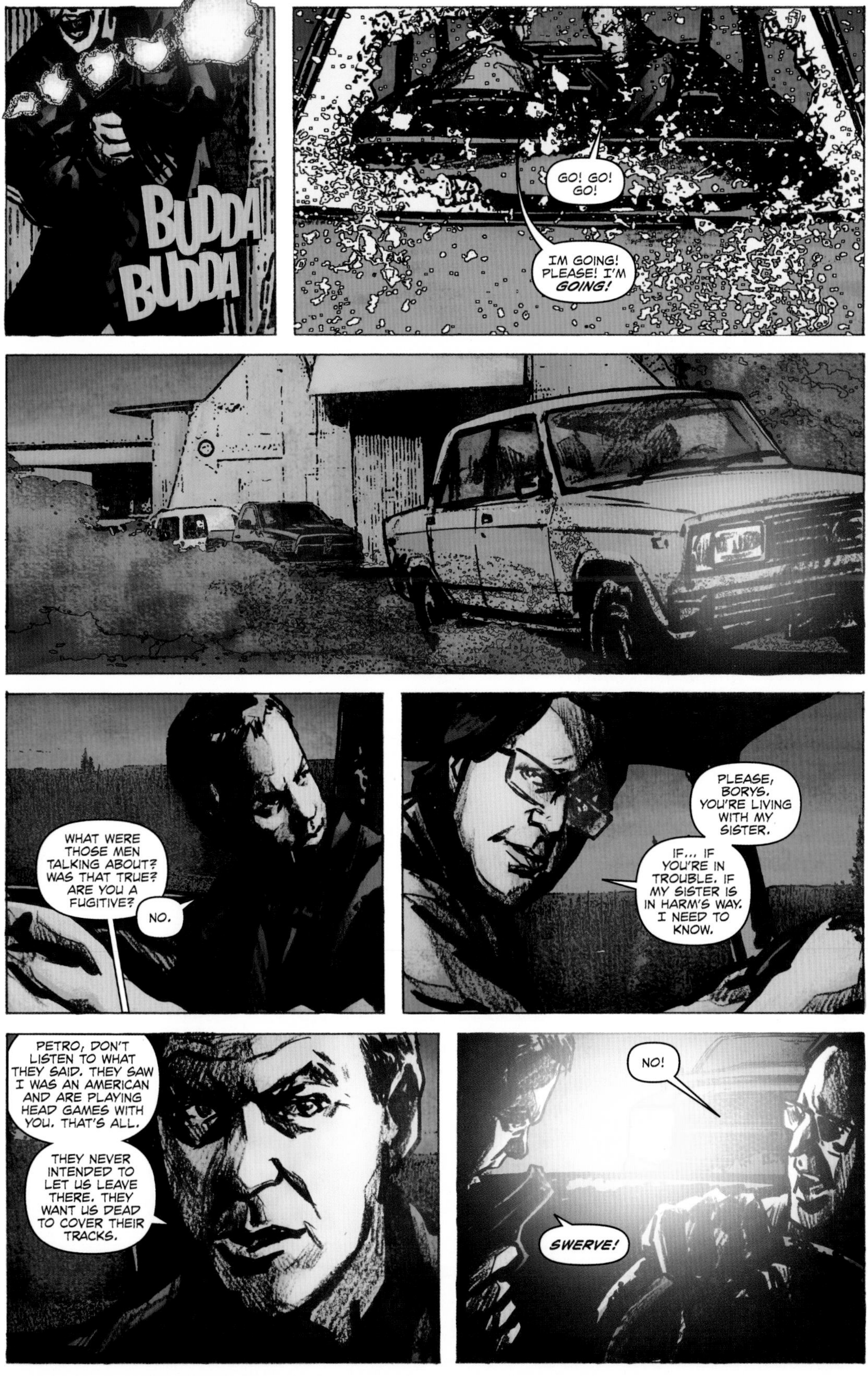
BUDDA BUDDA
GO! GO! GO!
IM GOING! PLEASE! I'M *GOING!*
WHAT WERE THOSE MEN TALKING ABOUT? WAS THAT TRUE? ARE YOU A FUGITIVE?
NO.
PLEASE, BORYS. YOU'RE LIVING WITH MY SISTER.
IF... IF YOU'RE IN TROUBLE. IF MY SISTER IS IN HARM'S WAY. I NEED TO KNOW.
PETRO, DON'T LISTEN TO WHAT THEY SAID. THEY SAW I WAS AN AMERICAN AND ARE PLAYING HEAD GAMES WITH YOU. THAT'S ALL.
THEY NEVER INTENDED TO LET US LEAVE THERE. THEY WANT US DEAD TO COVER THEIR TRACKS.
NO!
SWERVE!

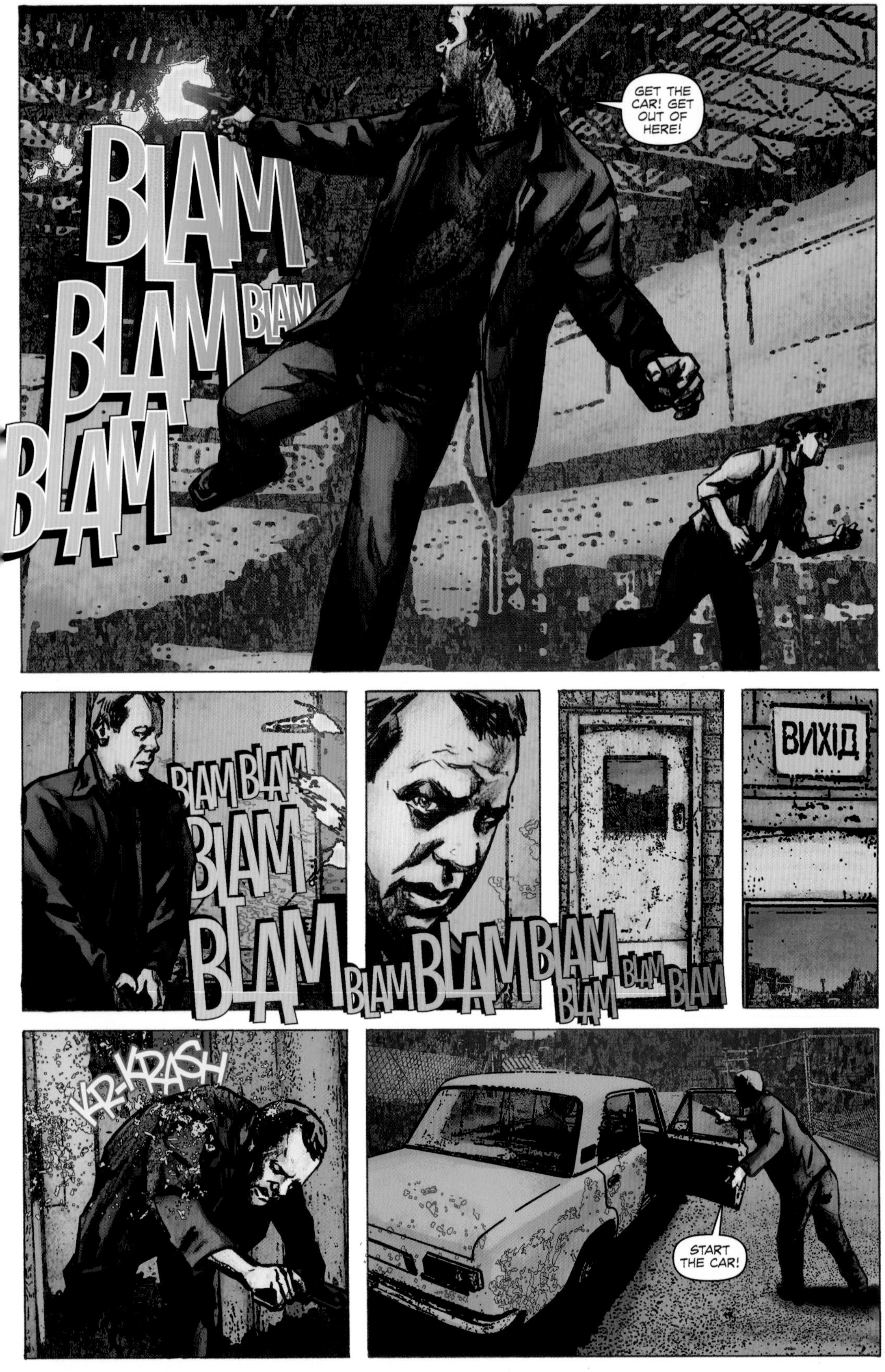
GET THE CAR! GET OUT OF HERE!
BLAM BLAM BLAM BLAM
BLAM BLAM BLAM BLAM BLAM BLAM BLAM BLAM BLAM BLAM BLAM
ВИХІД
KR-KRASH
START THE CAR!

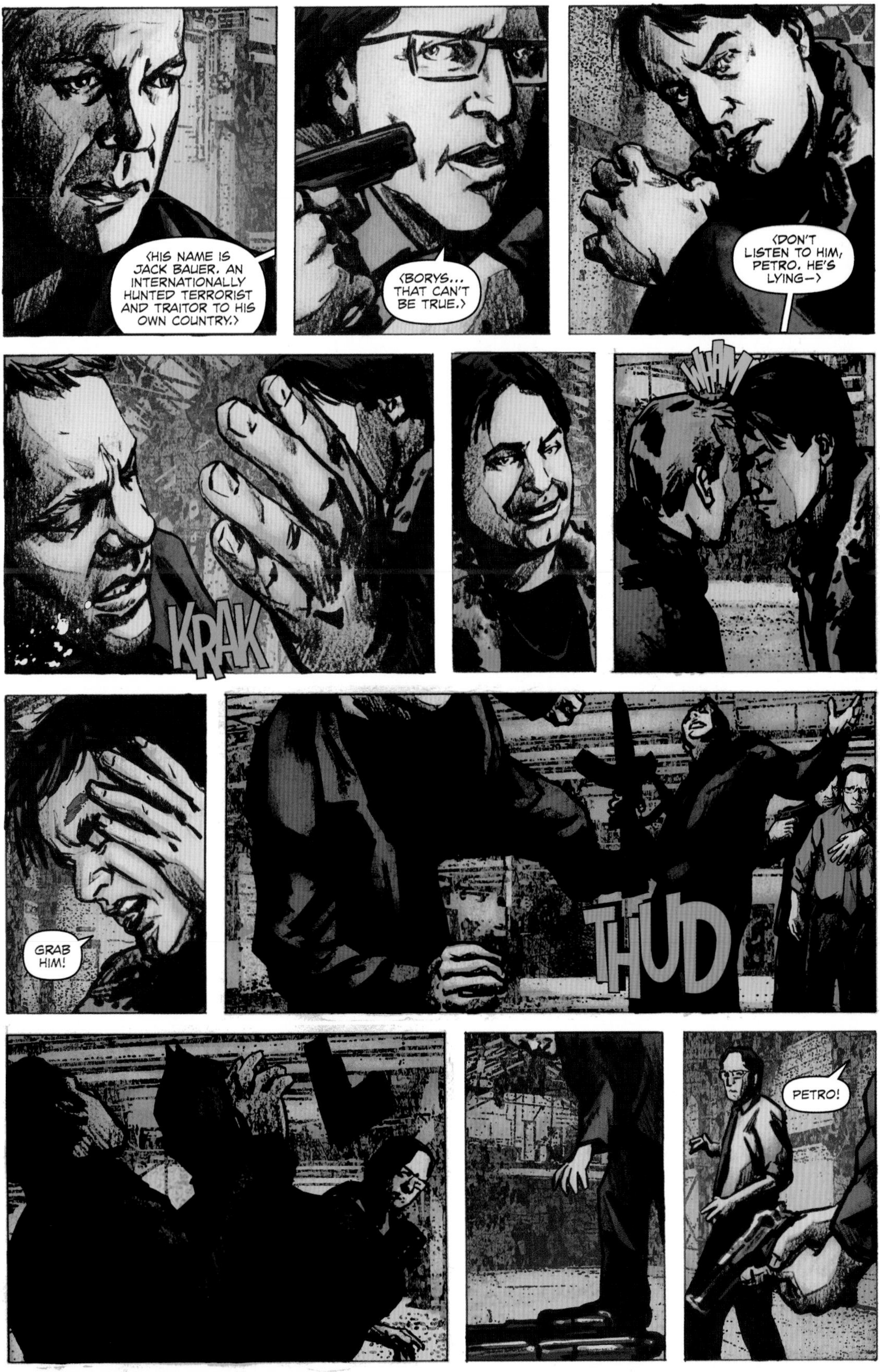

‹HIS NAME IS JACK BAUER. AN INTERNATIONALLY HUNTED TERRORIST AND TRAITOR TO HIS OWN COUNTRY.›
‹BORYS... THAT CAN'T BE TRUE.›
‹DON'T LISTEN TO HIM, PETRO. HE'S LYING—›
KRAK
WHAM
GRAB HIM!
THUD
PETRO!

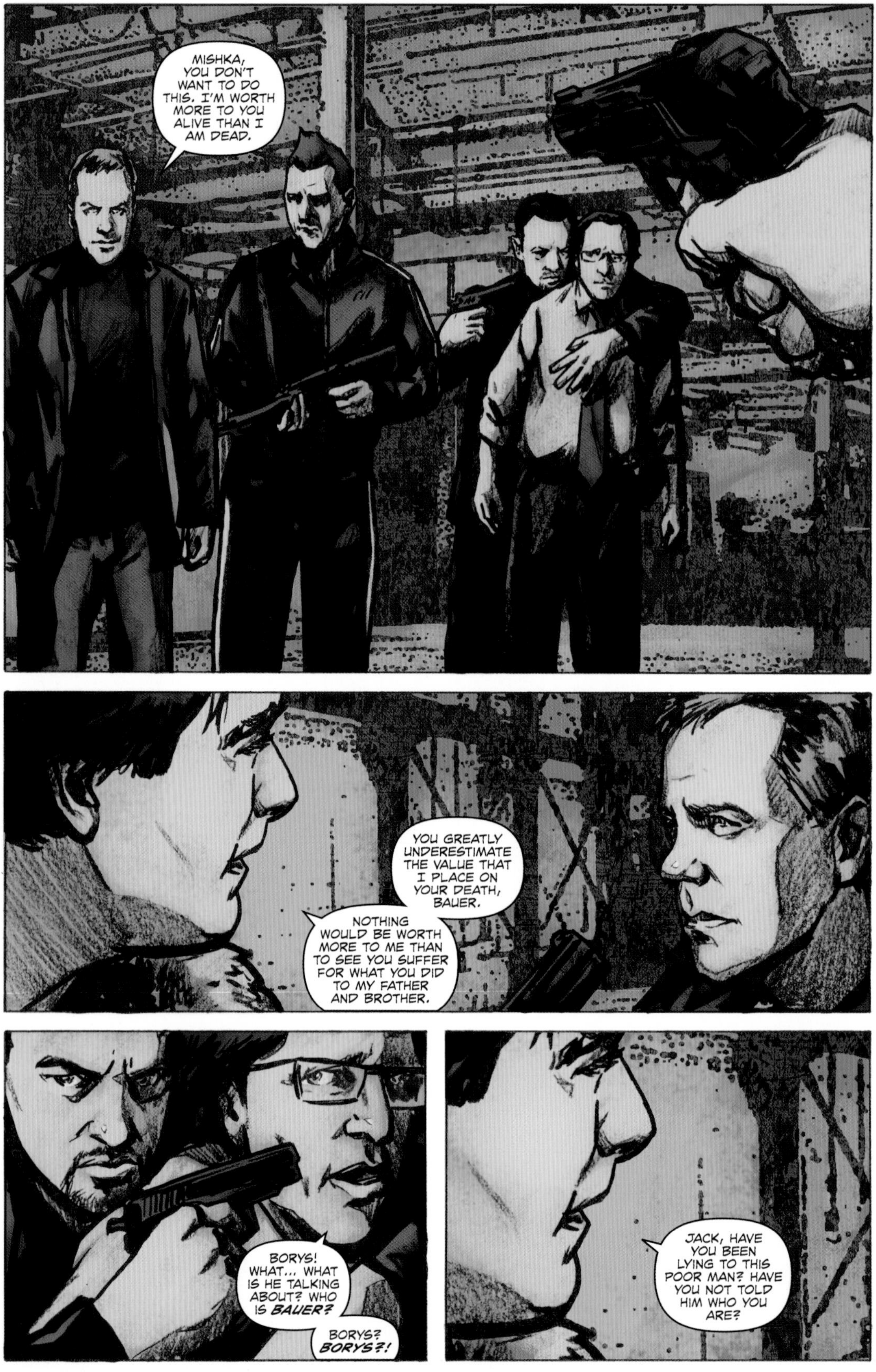
MISHKA, YOU DON'T WANT TO DO THIS. I'M WORTH MORE TO YOU ALIVE THAN I AM DEAD.
YOU GREATLY UNDERESTIMATE THE VALUE THAT I PLACE ON YOUR DEATH, BAUER.
NOTHING WOULD BE WORTH MORE TO ME THAN TO SEE YOU SUFFER FOR WHAT YOU DID TO MY FATHER AND BROTHER.
BORYS! WHAT... WHAT IS HE TALKING ABOUT? WHO IS *BAUER?*
BORYS? ***BORYS?!***
JACK, HAVE YOU BEEN LYING TO THIS POOR MAN? HAVE YOU NOT TOLD HIM WHO YOU ARE?

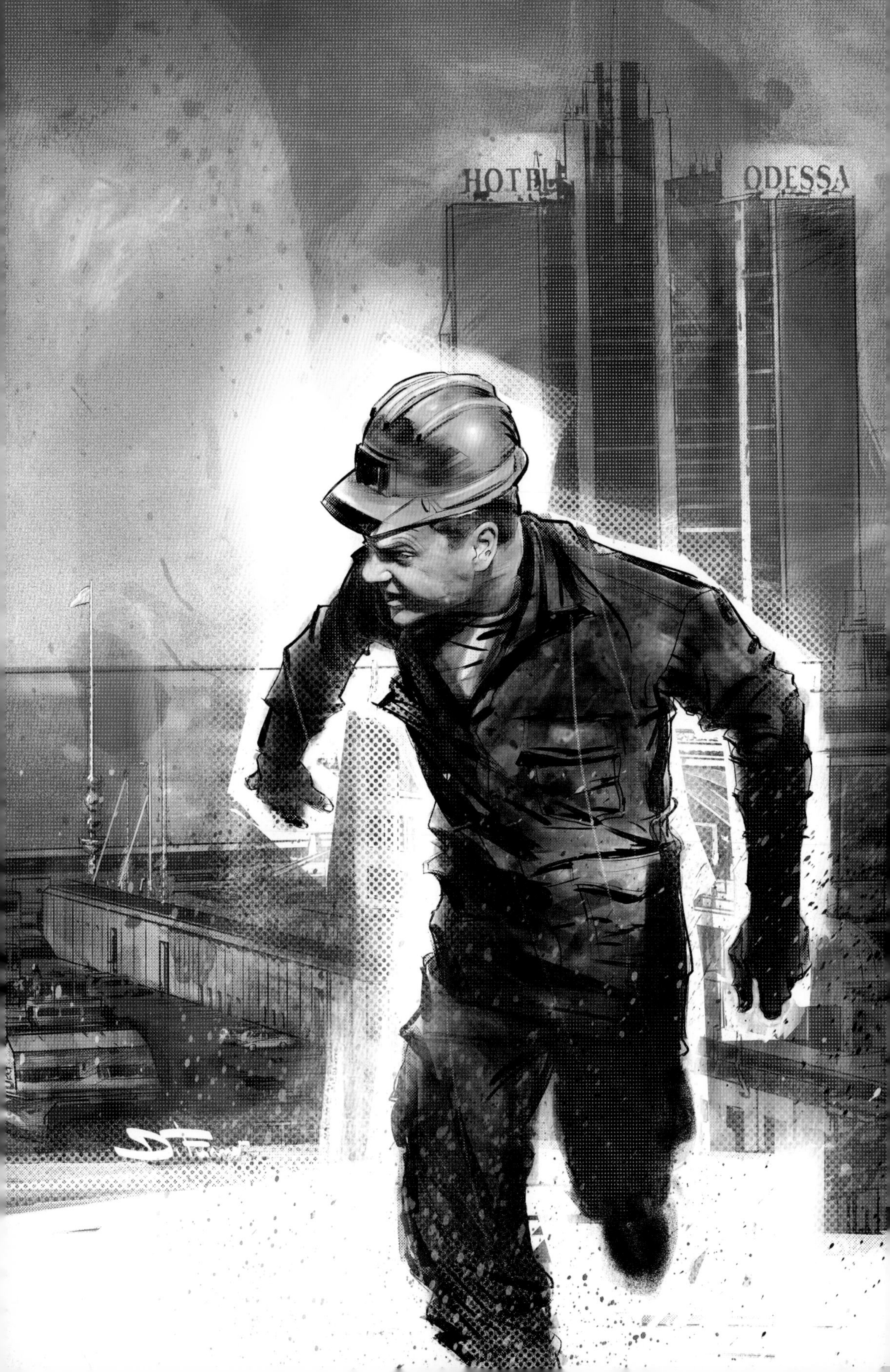
HOTEL
ODESSA

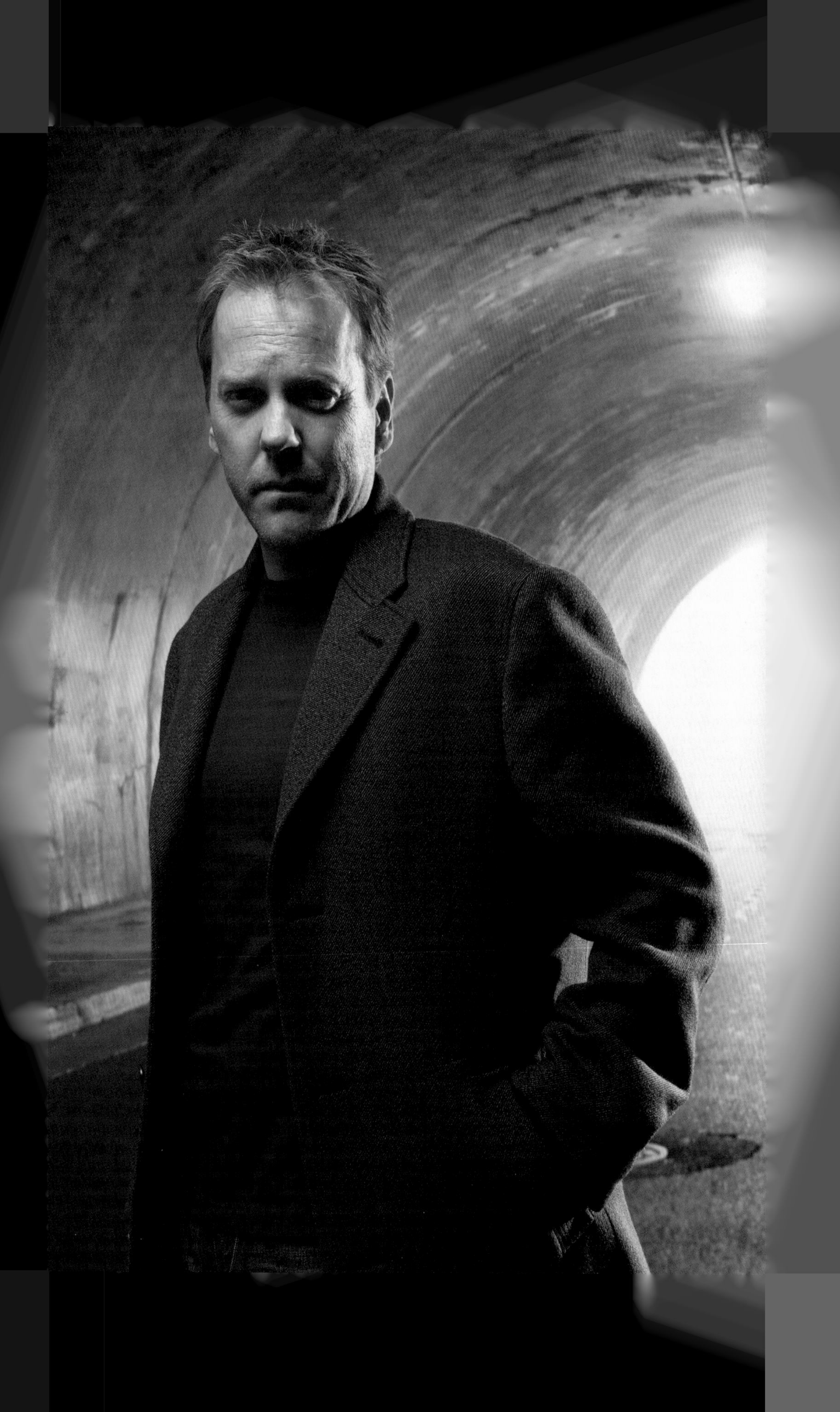

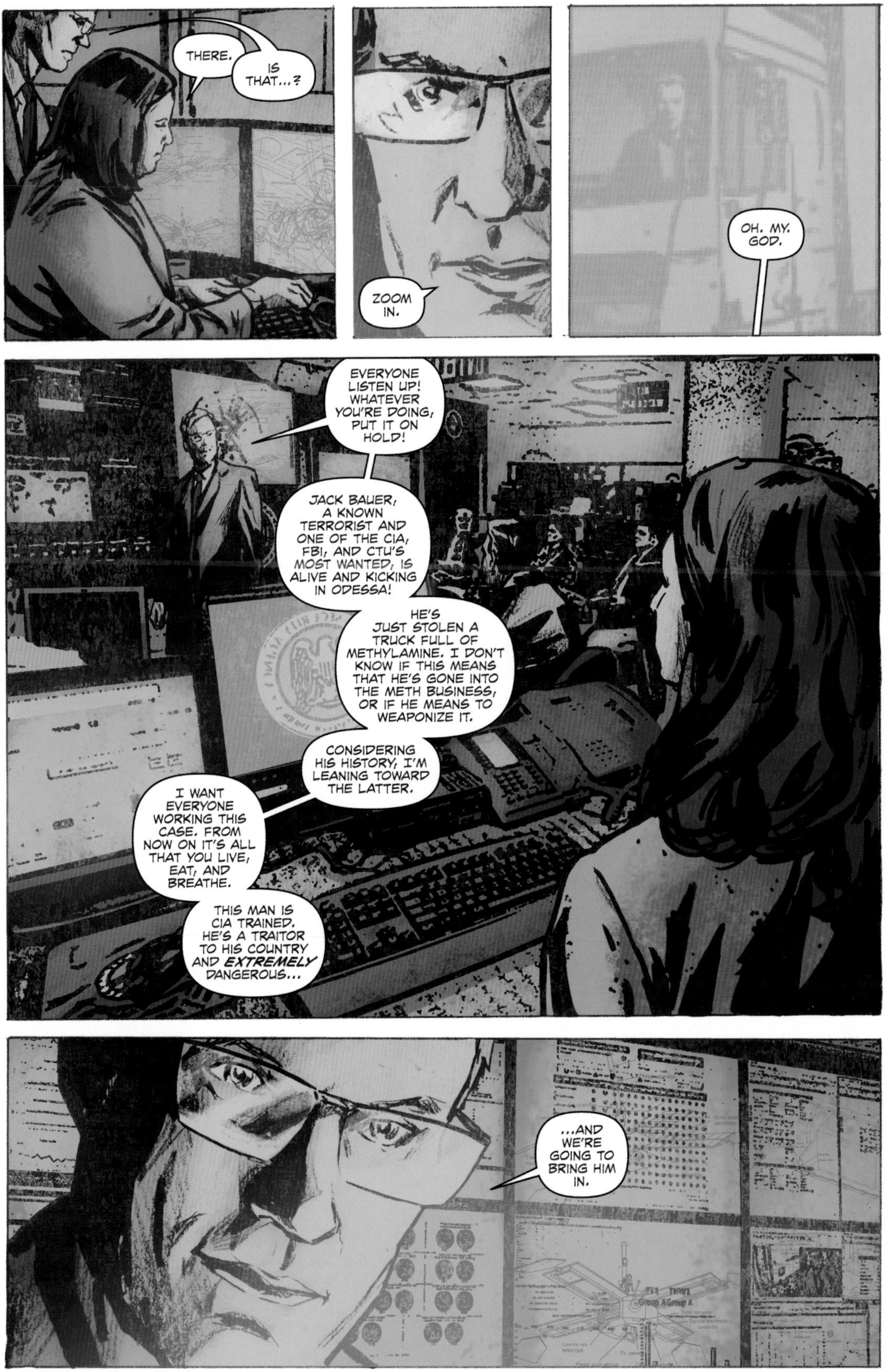
THERE.
IS THAT...?
ZOOM IN.
OH. MY. GOD.
EVERYONE LISTEN UP! WHATEVER YOU'RE DOING, PUT IT ON HOLD!
JACK BAUER, A KNOWN TERRORIST AND ONE OF THE CIA, FBI, AND CTU'S MOST WANTED, IS ALIVE AND KICKING IN ODESSA!
HE'S JUST STOLEN A TRUCK FULL OF METHYLAMINE. I DON'T KNOW IF THIS MEANS THAT HE'S GONE INTO THE METH BUSINESS, OR IF HE MEANS TO WEAPONIZE IT.
CONSIDERING HIS HISTORY, I'M LEANING TOWARD THE LATTER.
I WANT EVERYONE WORKING THIS CASE. FROM NOW ON IT'S ALL THAT YOU LIVE, EAT, AND BREATHE.
THIS MAN IS CIA TRAINED. HE'S A TRAITOR TO HIS COUNTRY AND *EXTREMELY* DANGEROUS...
...AND WE'RE GOING TO BRING HIM IN.

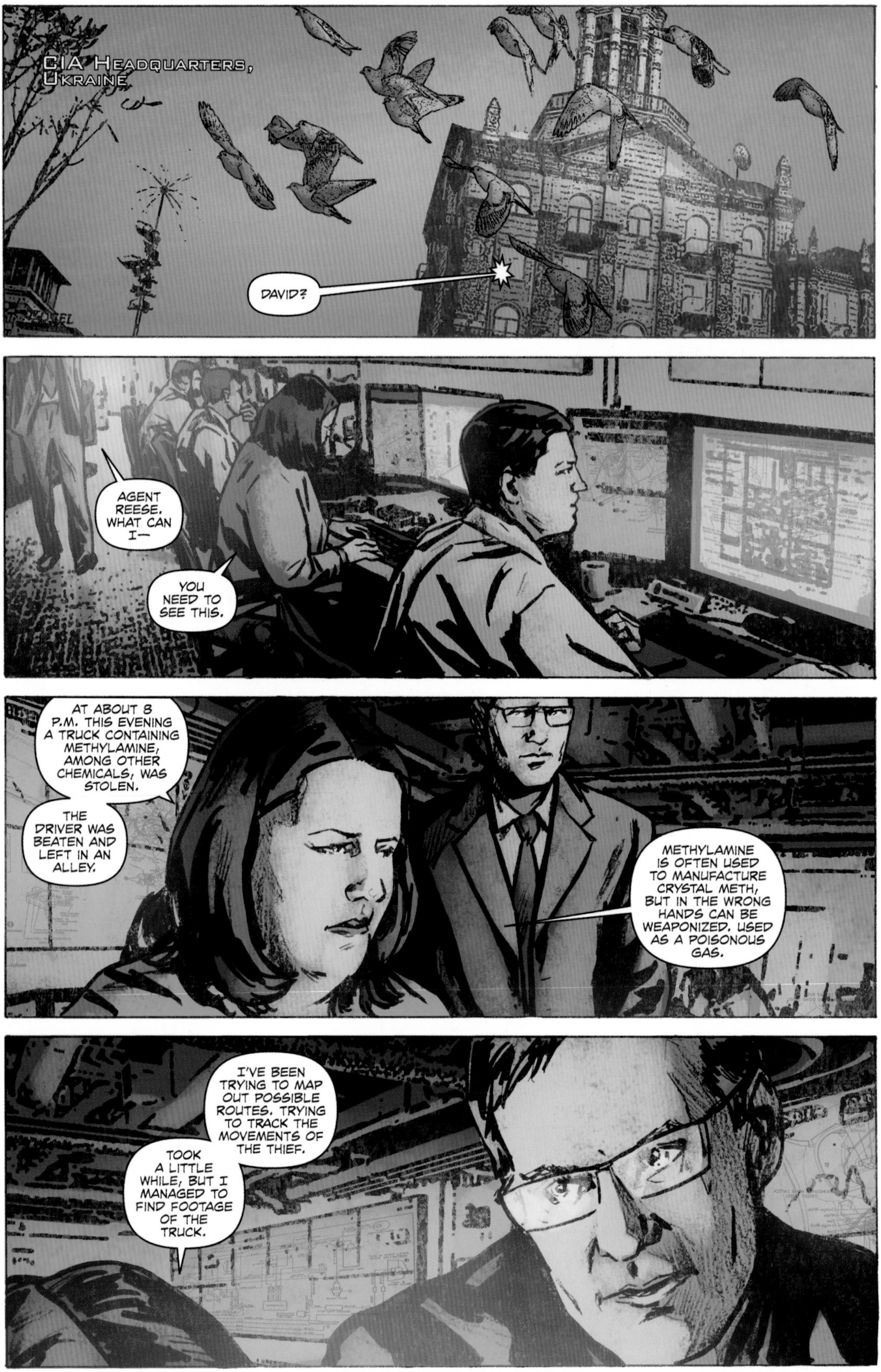
CIA Headquarters,
Ukraine
DAVID?
AGENT REESE. WHAT CAN I—
YOU NEED TO SEE THIS.
AT ABOUT 8 P.M. THIS EVENING A TRUCK CONTAINING METHYLAMINE, AMONG OTHER CHEMICALS, WAS STOLEN.
THE DRIVER WAS BEATEN AND LEFT IN AN ALLEY.
METHYLAMINE IS OFTEN USED TO MANUFACTURE CRYSTAL METH, BUT IN THE WRONG HANDS CAN BE WEAPONIZED. USED AS A POISONOUS GAS.
I'VE BEEN TRYING TO MAP OUT POSSIBLE ROUTES. TRYING TO TRACK THE MOVEMENTS OF THE THIEF.
TOOK A LITTLE WHILE, BUT I MANAGED TO FIND FOOTAGE OF THE TRUCK.

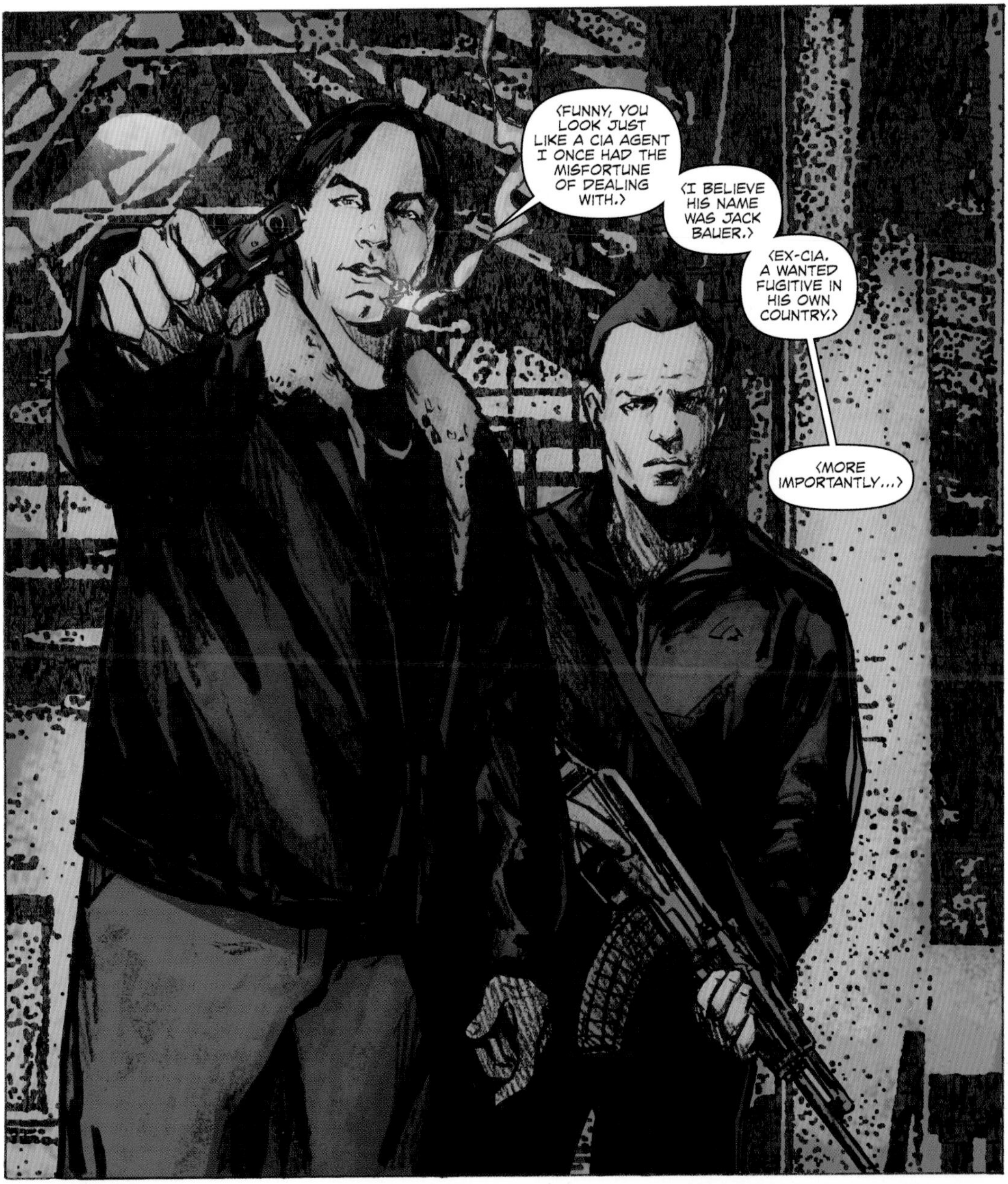
‹FUNNY, YOU LOOK JUST LIKE A CIA AGENT I ONCE HAD THE MISFORTUNE OF DEALING WITH.›
‹I BELIEVE HIS NAME WAS JACK BAUER.›
‹EX-CIA. A WANTED FUGITIVE IN HIS OWN COUNTRY.›
‹MORE IMPORTANTLY...›

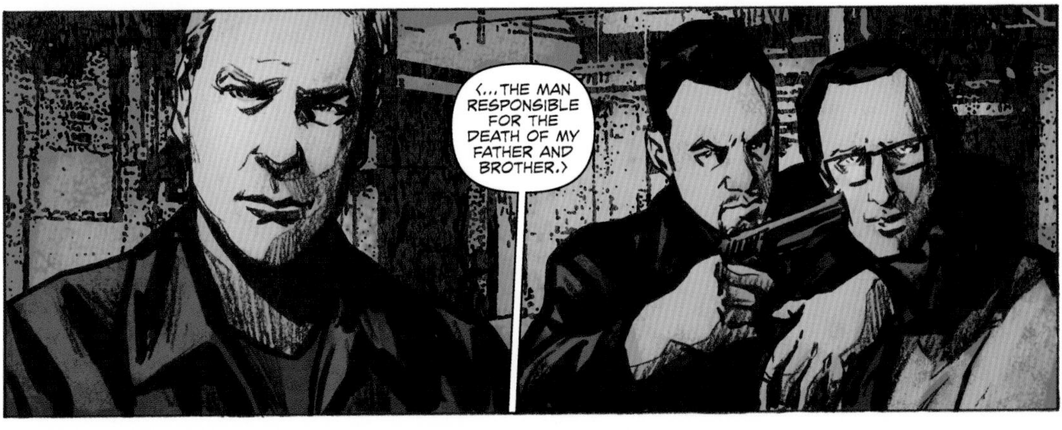
‹...THE MAN RESPONSIBLE FOR THE DEATH OF MY FATHER AND BROTHER.›

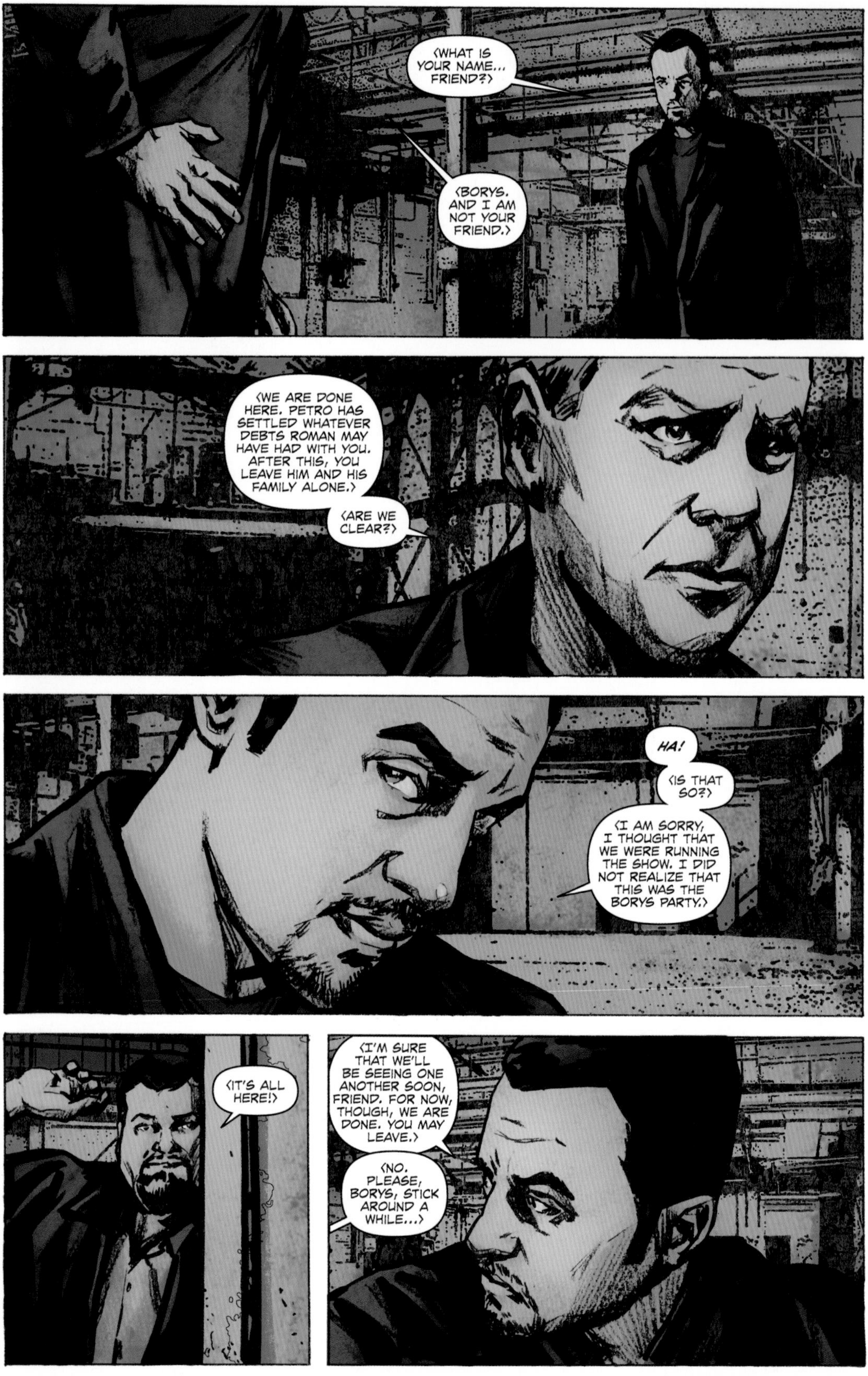
<WHAT IS YOUR NAME... FRIEND?>
<BORYS. AND I AM NOT YOUR FRIEND.>
<WE ARE DONE HERE. PETRO HAS SETTLED WHATEVER DEBTS ROMAN MAY HAVE HAD WITH YOU. AFTER THIS, YOU LEAVE HIM AND HIS FAMILY ALONE.>
<ARE WE CLEAR?>
HA!
<IS THAT SO?>
<I AM SORRY, I THOUGHT THAT WE WERE RUNNING THE SHOW. I DID NOT REALIZE THAT THIS WAS THE BORYS PARTY.>
<IT'S ALL HERE!>
<I'M SURE THAT WE'LL BE SEEING ONE ANOTHER SOON, FRIEND. FOR NOW, THOUGH, WE ARE DONE. YOU MAY LEAVE.>
<NO. PLEASE, BORYS, STICK AROUND A WHILE...>

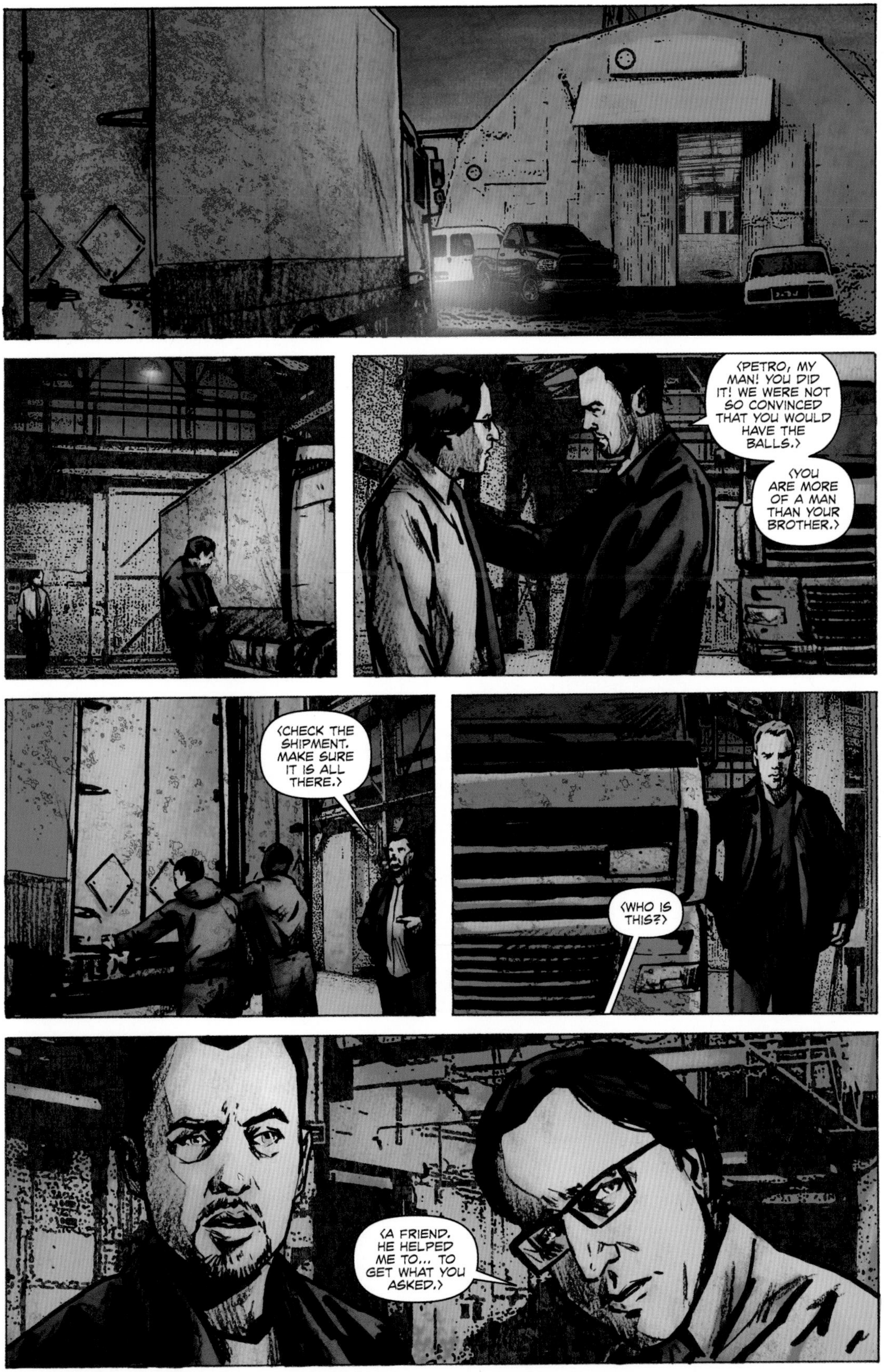

‹PETRO, MY MAN! YOU DID IT! WE WERE NOT SO CONVINCED THAT YOU WOULD HAVE THE BALLS.›
‹YOU ARE MORE OF A MAN THAN YOUR BROTHER.›
‹CHECK THE SHIPMENT. MAKE SURE IT IS ALL THERE.›
‹WHO IS THIS?›
‹A FRIEND. HE HELPED ME TO... TO GET WHAT YOU ASKED.›

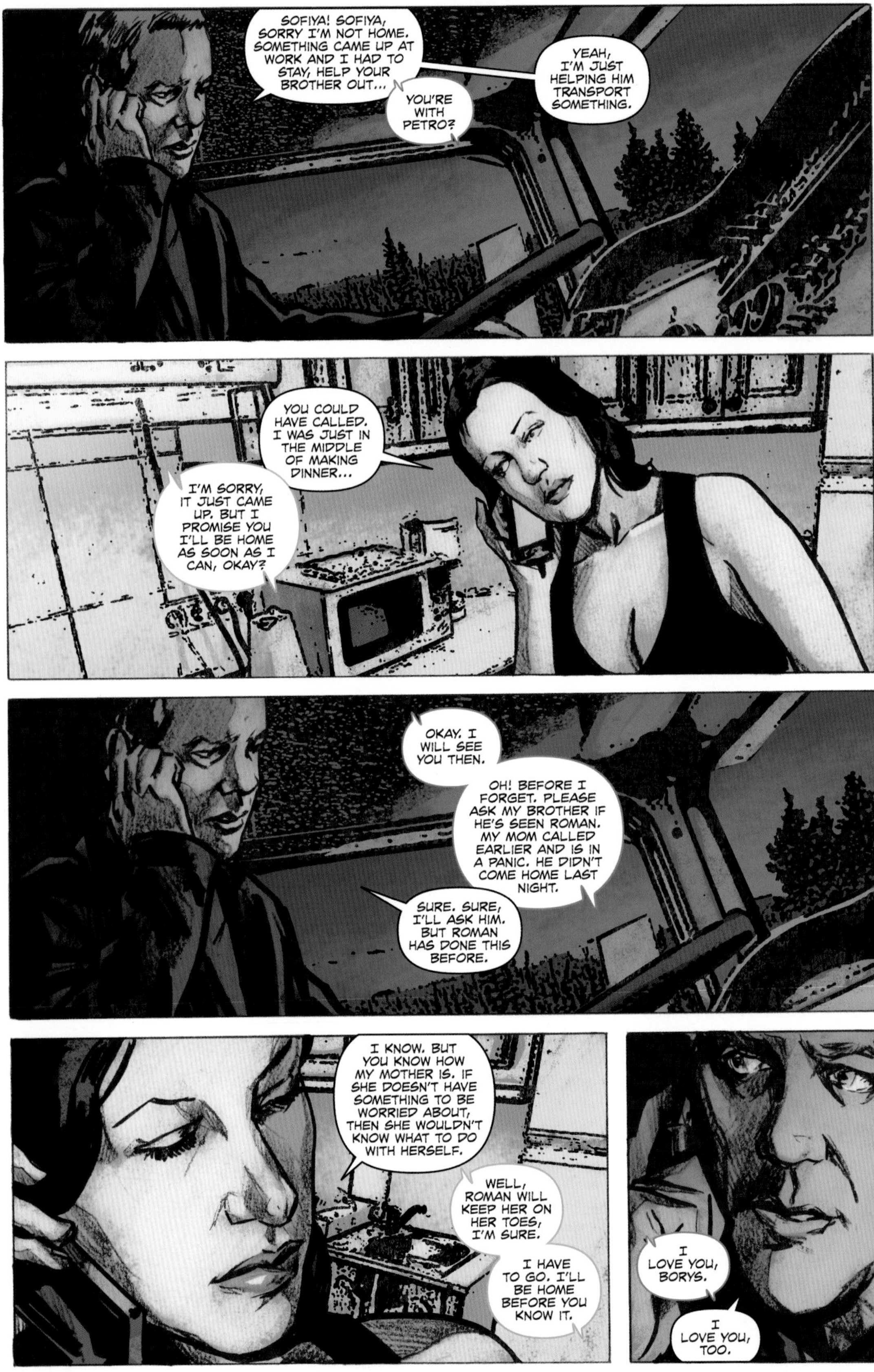
SOFIYA! SOFIYA, SORRY I'M NOT HOME. SOMETHING CAME UP AT WORK AND I HAD TO STAY, HELP YOUR BROTHER OUT...
YOU'RE WITH PETRO?
YEAH, I'M JUST HELPING HIM TRANSPORT SOMETHING.
YOU COULD HAVE CALLED. I WAS JUST IN THE MIDDLE OF MAKING DINNER...
I'M SORRY, IT JUST CAME UP. BUT I PROMISE YOU I'LL BE HOME AS SOON AS I CAN, OKAY?
OKAY. I WILL SEE YOU THEN.
OH! BEFORE I FORGET. PLEASE ASK MY BROTHER IF HE'S SEEN ROMAN. MY MOM CALLED EARLIER AND IS IN A PANIC. HE DIDN'T COME HOME LAST NIGHT.
SURE. SURE, I'LL ASK HIM. BUT ROMAN HAS DONE THIS BEFORE.
I KNOW. BUT YOU KNOW HOW MY MOTHER IS. IF SHE DOESN'T HAVE SOMETHING TO BE WORRIED ABOUT, THEN SHE WOULDN'T KNOW WHAT TO DO WITH HERSELF.
WELL, ROMAN WILL KEEP HER ON HER TOES, I'M SURE.
I HAVE TO GO. I'LL BE HOME BEFORE YOU KNOW IT.
I LOVE YOU, BORYS.
I LOVE YOU, TOO.

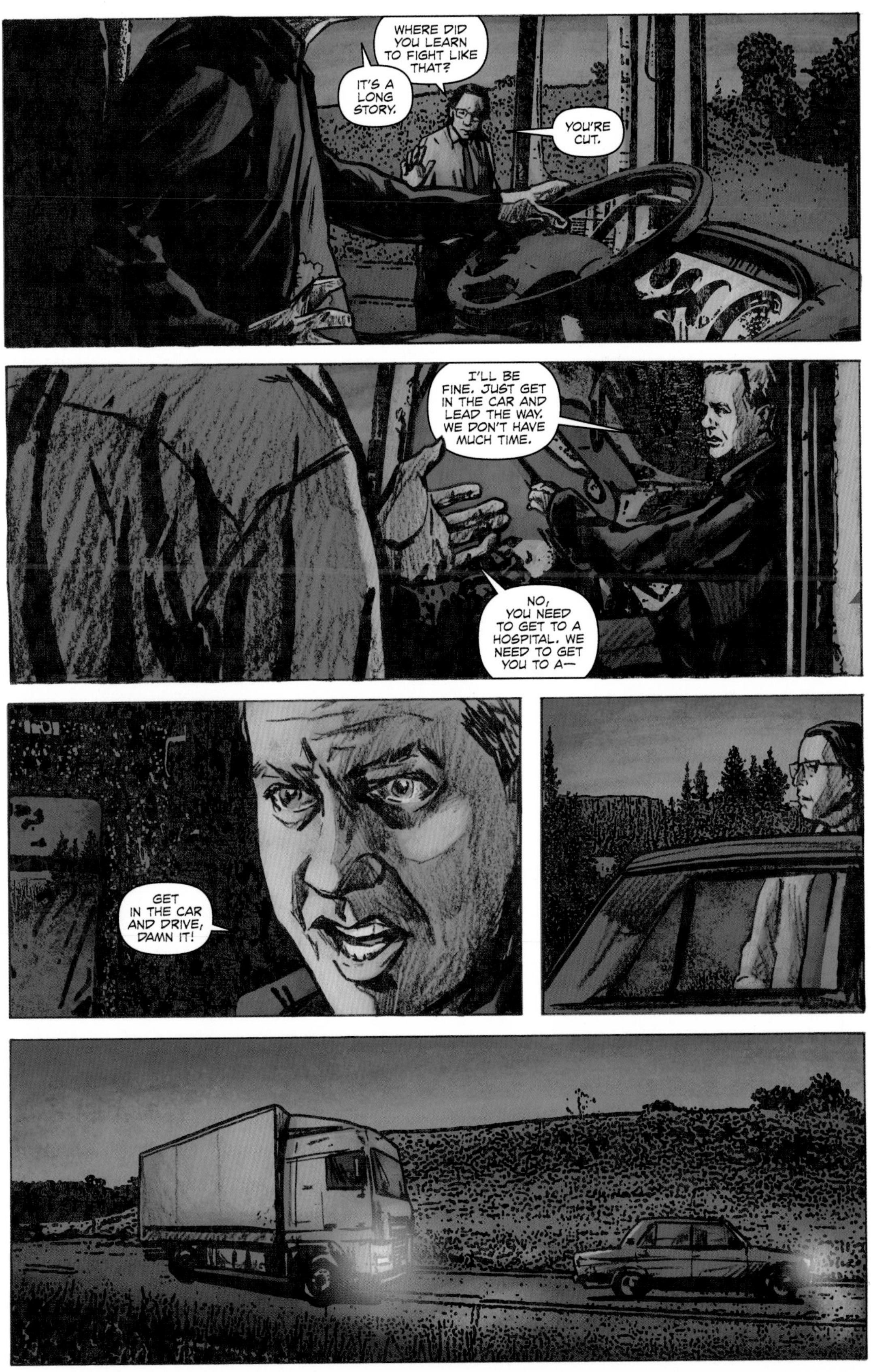
WHERE DID YOU LEARN TO FIGHT LIKE THAT?
IT'S A LONG STORY.
YOU'RE CUT.
I'LL BE FINE. JUST GET IN THE CAR AND LEAD THE WAY. WE DON'T HAVE MUCH TIME.
NO, YOU NEED TO GET TO A HOSPITAL. WE NEED TO GET YOU TO A—
GET IN THE CAR AND DRIVE, DAMN IT!

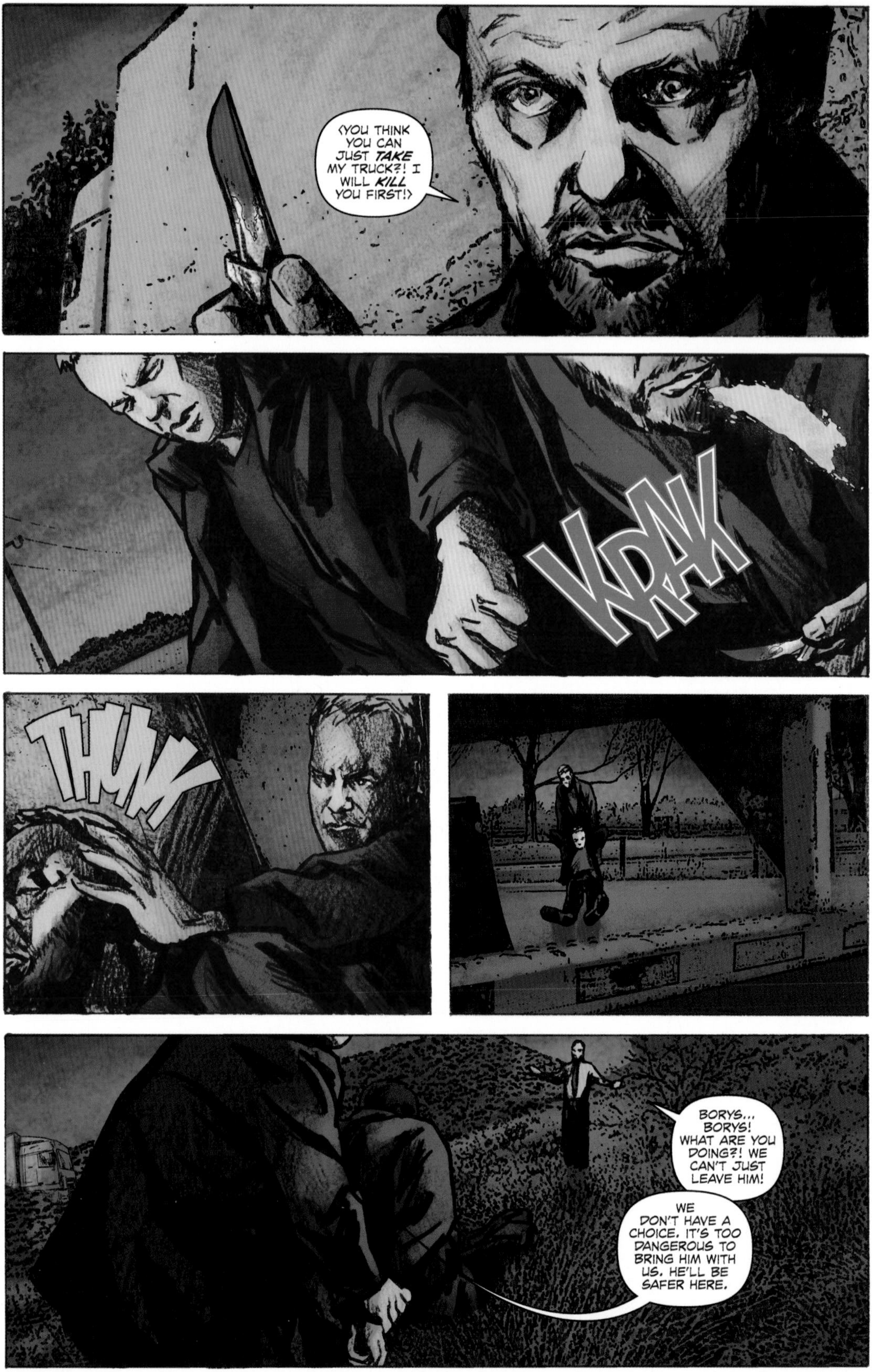

‹YOU THINK YOU CAN JUST TAKE MY TRUCK?! I WILL KILL YOU FIRST!›
KRAK
THUNK
BORYS... BORYS! WHAT ARE YOU DOING?! WE CAN'T JUST LEAVE HIM!
WE DON'T HAVE A CHOICE. IT'S TOO DANGEROUS TO BRING HIM WITH US. HE'LL BE SAFER HERE.

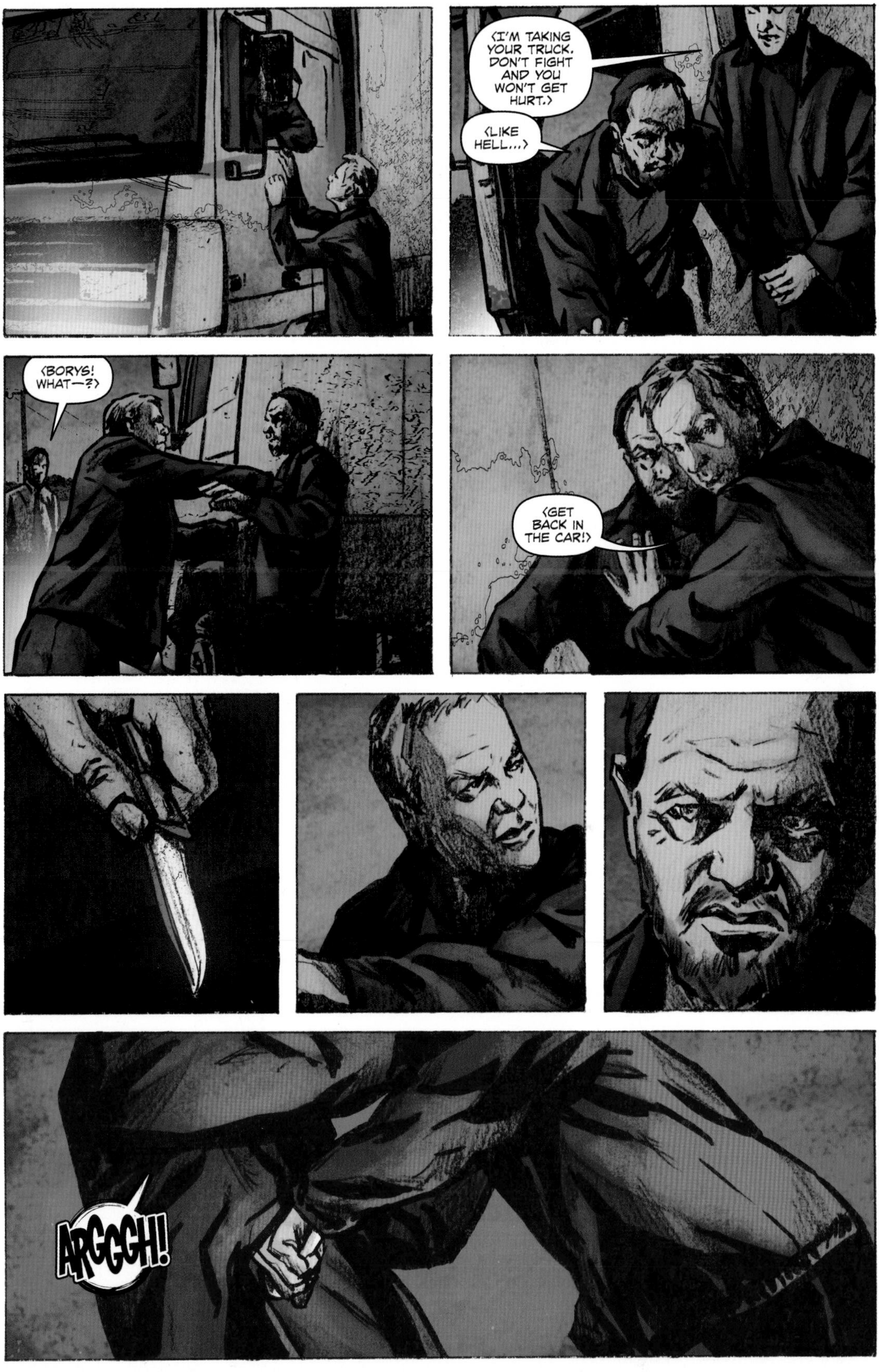
‹I'M TAKING YOUR TRUCK. DON'T FIGHT AND YOU WON'T GET HURT.›
‹LIKE HELL...›
‹BORYS! WHAT—?›
‹GET BACK IN THE CAR!›
ARGGGH!

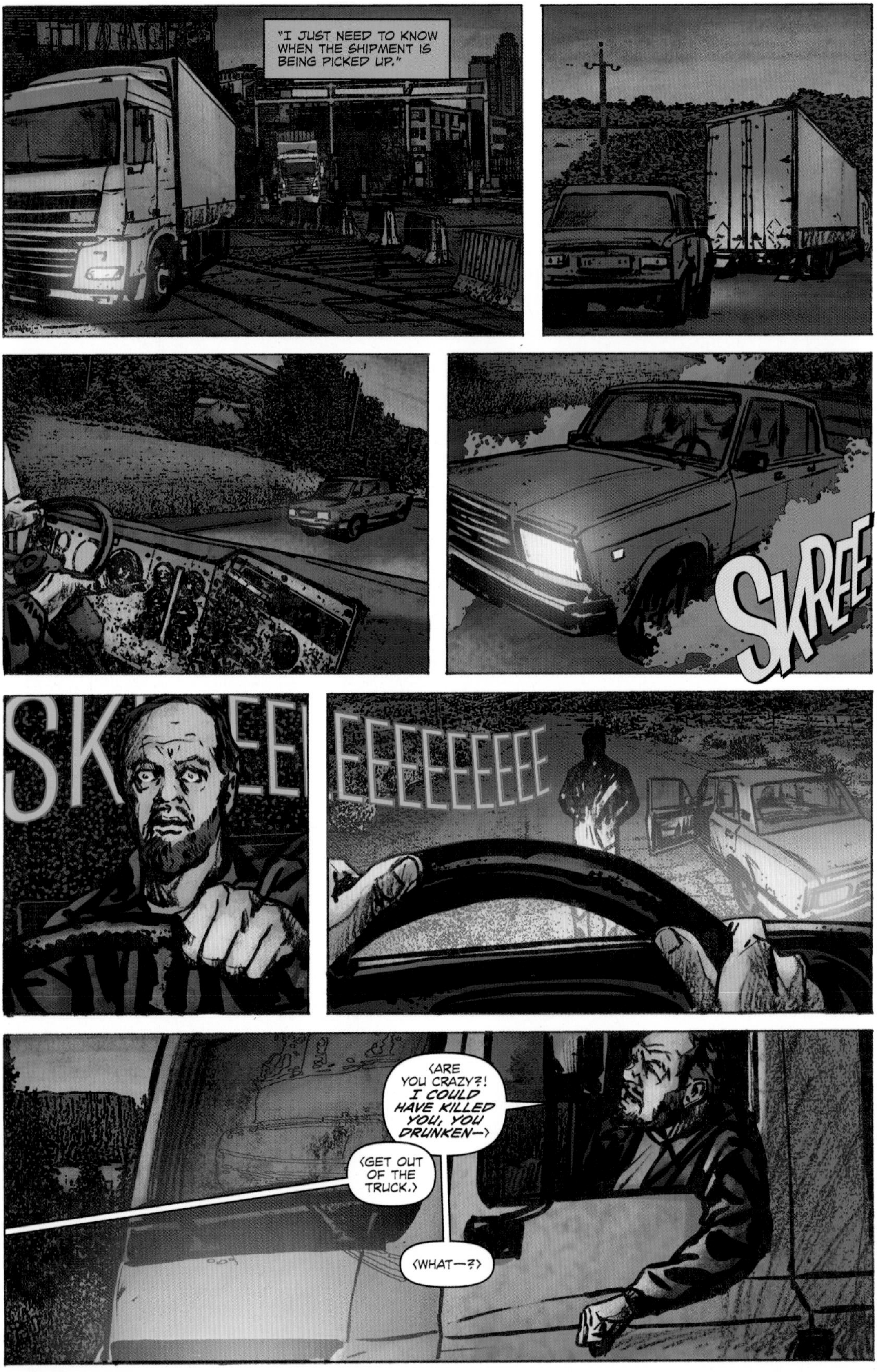
"I JUST NEED TO KNOW WHEN THE SHIPMENT IS BEING PICKED UP."
SKREE
SKREEEEEEEEEEEEEE
‹ARE YOU CRAZY?! I COULD HAVE KILLED YOU, YOU DRUNKEN—›
‹GET OUT OF THE TRUCK.›
‹WHAT—?›

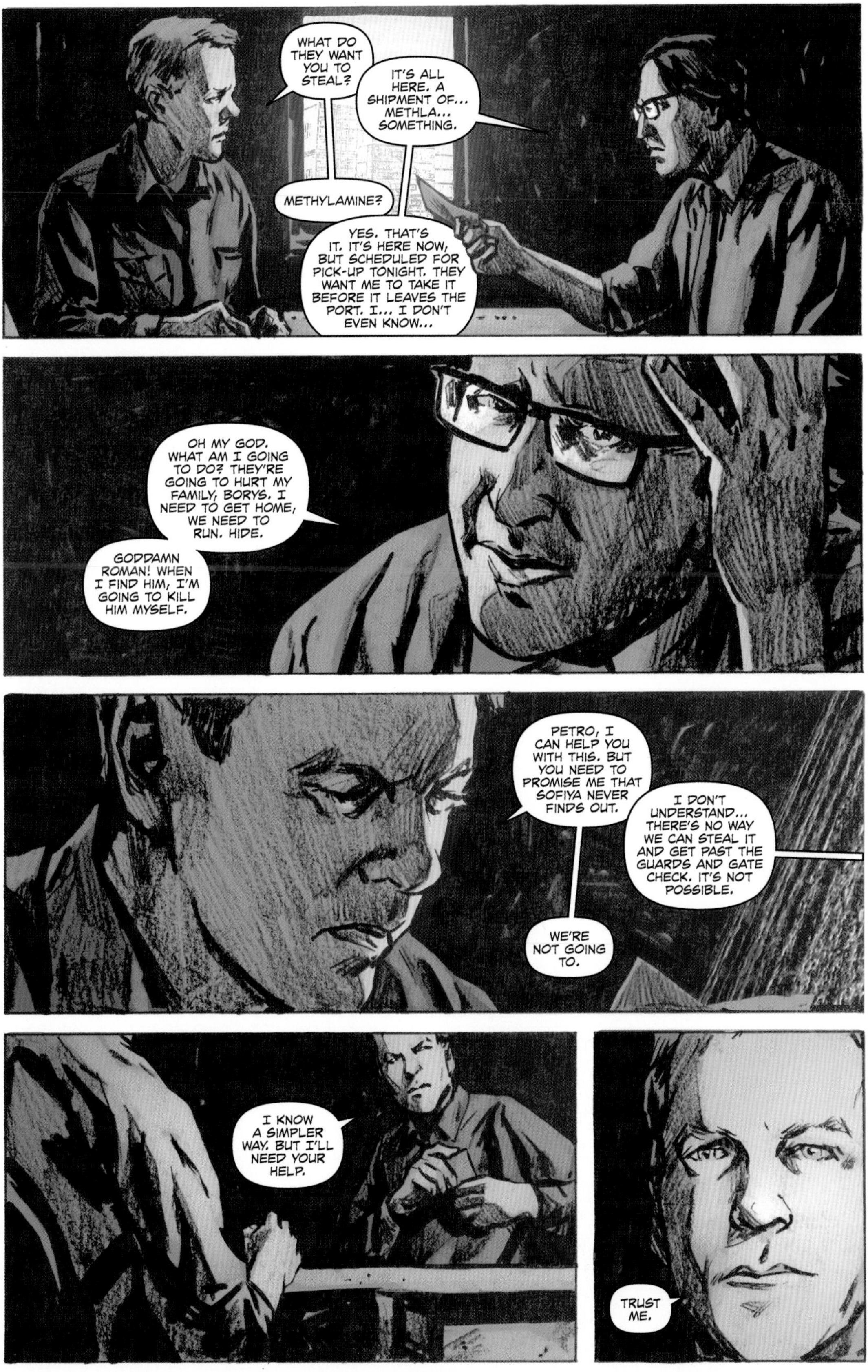
WHAT DO THEY WANT YOU TO STEAL?
IT'S ALL HERE. A SHIPMENT OF... METHLA... SOMETHING.
METHYLAMINE?
YES. THAT'S IT. IT'S HERE NOW, BUT SCHEDULED FOR PICK-UP TONIGHT. THEY WANT ME TO TAKE IT BEFORE IT LEAVES THE PORT. I... I DON'T EVEN KNOW...
OH MY GOD. WHAT AM I GOING TO DO? THEY'RE GOING TO HURT MY FAMILY, BORYS. I NEED TO GET HOME, WE NEED TO RUN. HIDE.
GODDAMN ROMAN! WHEN I FIND HIM, I'M GOING TO KILL HIM MYSELF.
PETRO, I CAN HELP YOU WITH THIS. BUT YOU NEED TO PROMISE ME THAT SOFIYA NEVER FINDS OUT.
I DON'T UNDERSTAND... THERE'S NO WAY WE CAN STEAL IT AND GET PAST THE GUARDS AND GATE CHECK. IT'S NOT POSSIBLE.
WE'RE NOT GOING TO.
I KNOW A SIMPLER WAY. BUT I'LL NEED YOUR HELP.
TRUST ME.

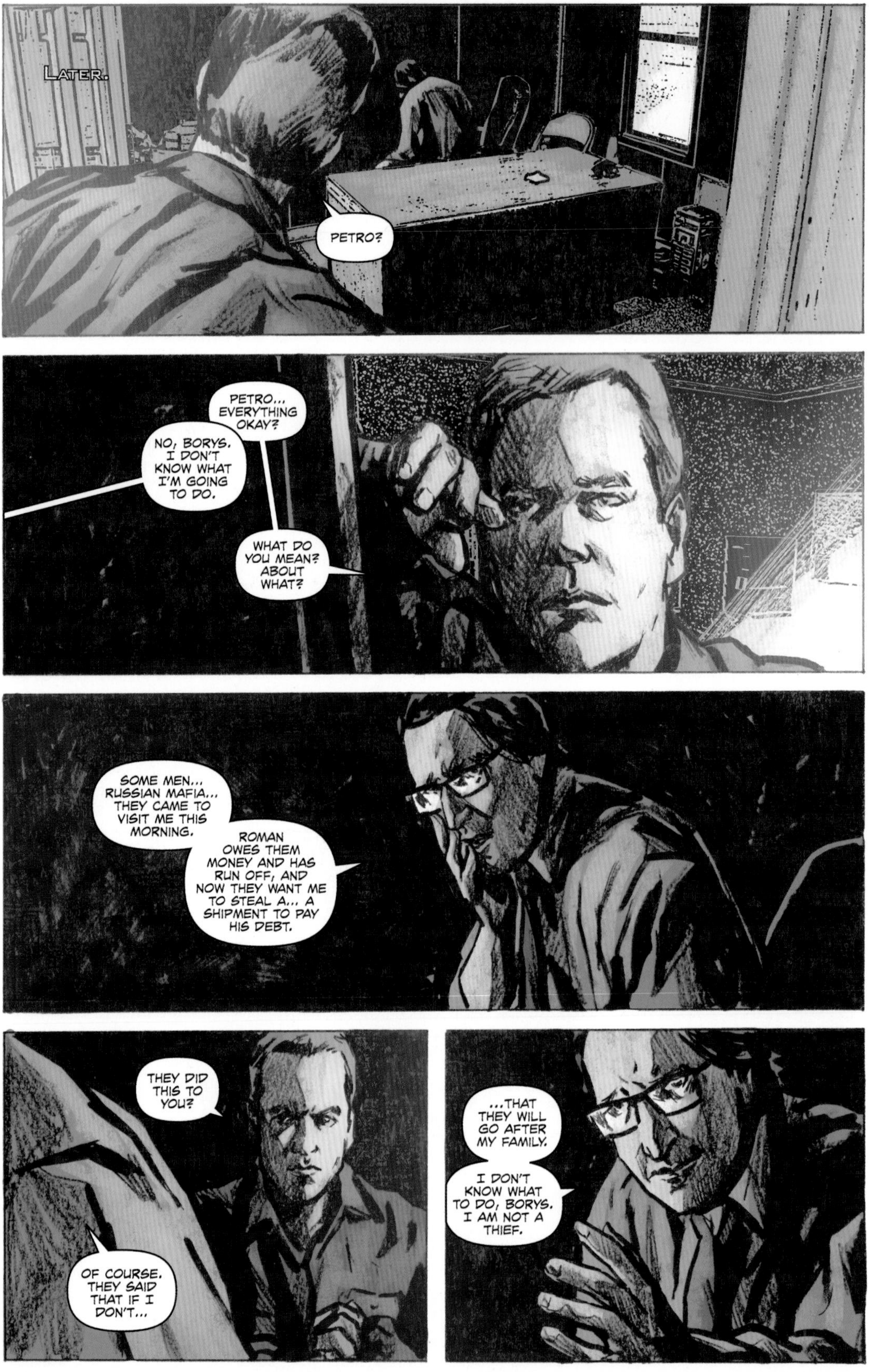
LATER.
PETRO?
PETRO... EVERYTHING OKAY?
NO, BORYS. I DON'T KNOW WHAT I'M GOING TO DO.
WHAT DO YOU MEAN? ABOUT WHAT?
SOME MEN... RUSSIAN MAFIA... THEY CAME TO VISIT ME THIS MORNING.
ROMAN OWES THEM MONEY AND HAS RUN OFF, AND NOW THEY WANT ME TO STEAL A... A SHIPMENT TO PAY HIS DEBT.
THEY DID THIS TO YOU?
OF COURSE. THEY SAID THAT IF I DON'T...
...THAT THEY WILL GO AFTER MY FAMILY.
I DON'T KNOW WHAT TO DO, BORYS. I AM NOT A THIEF.

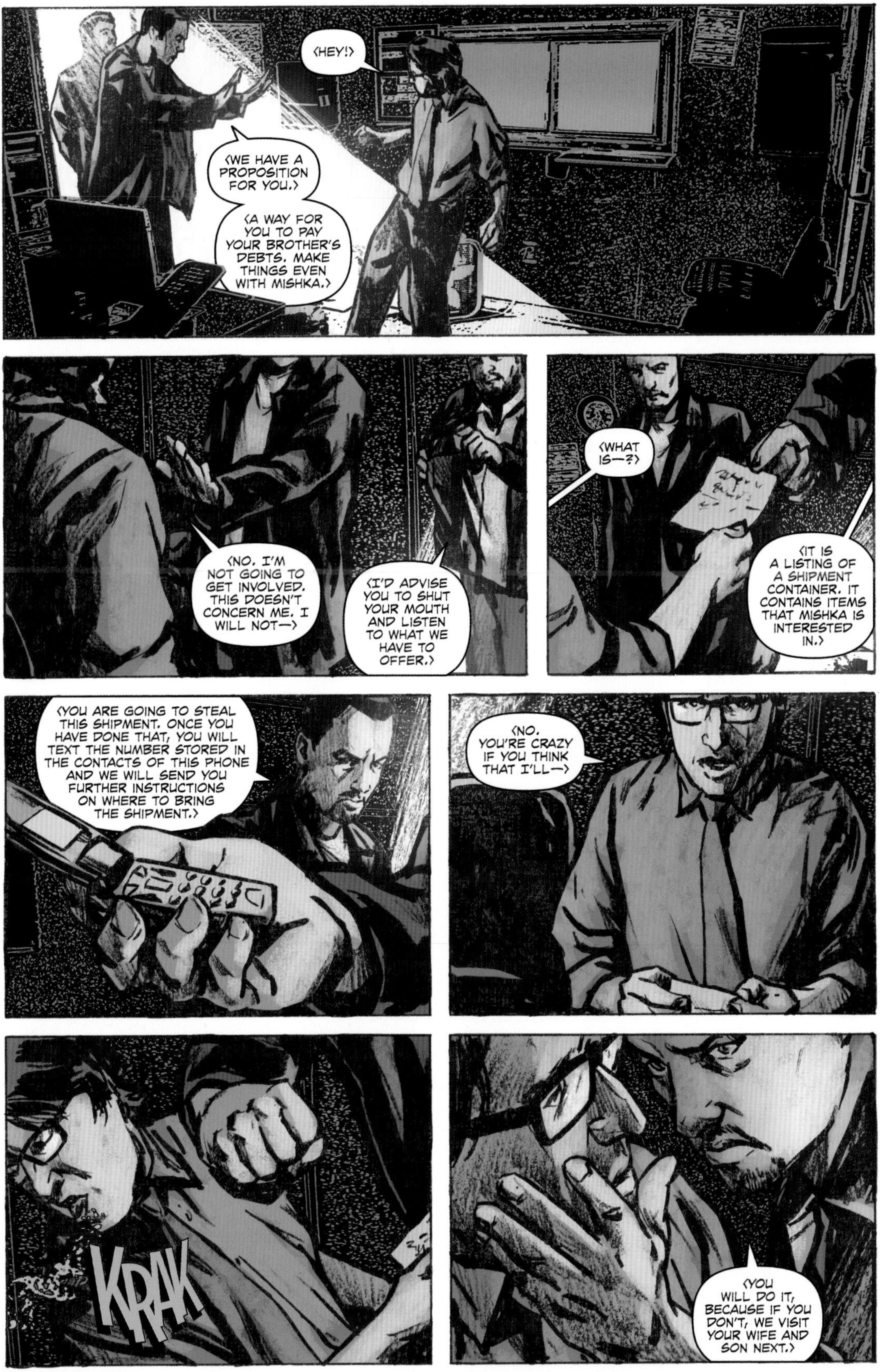

‹HEY!›
‹WE HAVE A PROPOSITION FOR YOU.›
‹A WAY FOR YOU TO PAY YOUR BROTHER'S DEBTS. MAKE THINGS EVEN WITH MISHKA.›
‹NO. I'M NOT GOING TO GET INVOLVED. THIS DOESN'T CONCERN ME. I WILL NOT—›
‹I'D ADVISE YOU TO SHUT YOUR MOUTH AND LISTEN TO WHAT WE HAVE TO OFFER.›
‹WHAT IS—?›
‹IT IS A LISTING OF A SHIPMENT CONTAINER. IT CONTAINS ITEMS THAT MISHKA IS INTERESTED IN.›
‹YOU ARE GOING TO STEAL THIS SHIPMENT. ONCE YOU HAVE DONE THAT, YOU WILL TEXT THE NUMBER STORED IN THE CONTACTS OF THIS PHONE AND WE WILL SEND YOU FURTHER INSTRUCTIONS ON WHERE TO BRING THE SHIPMENT.›
‹NO. YOU'RE CRAZY IF YOU THINK THAT I'LL—›
KRAK
‹YOU WILL DO IT, BECAUSE IF YOU DON'T, WE VISIT YOUR WIFE AND SON NEXT.›

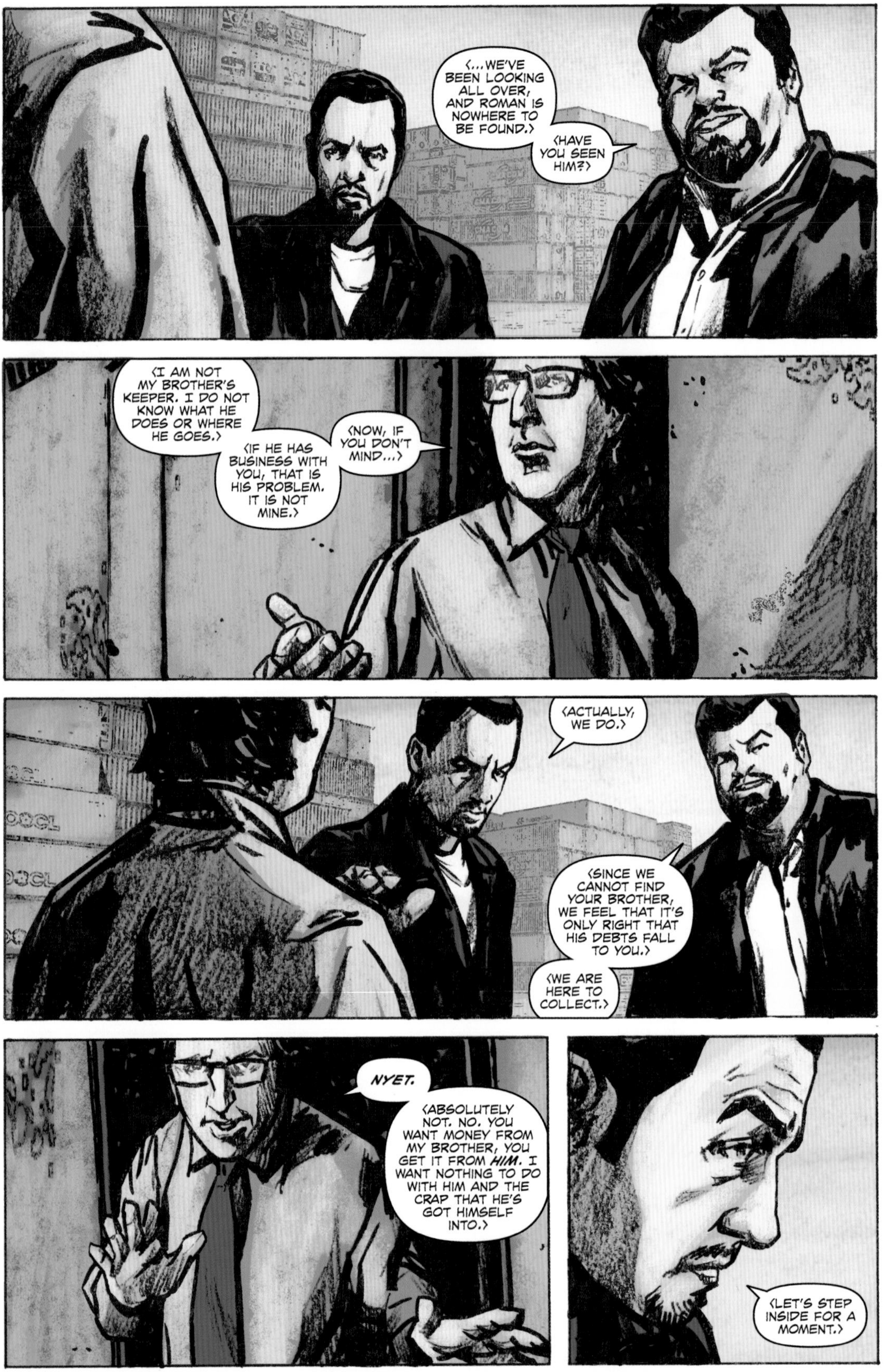
‹...WE'VE BEEN LOOKING ALL OVER, AND ROMAN IS NOWHERE TO BE FOUND.›
‹HAVE YOU SEEN HIM?›
‹I AM NOT MY BROTHER'S KEEPER. I DO NOT KNOW WHAT HE DOES OR WHERE HE GOES.›
‹IF HE HAS BUSINESS WITH YOU, THAT IS HIS PROBLEM. IT IS NOT MINE.›
‹NOW, IF YOU DON'T MIND...›
‹ACTUALLY, WE DO.›
‹SINCE WE CANNOT FIND YOUR BROTHER, WE FEEL THAT IT'S ONLY RIGHT THAT HIS DEBTS FALL TO YOU.›
‹WE ARE HERE TO COLLECT.›
NYET.
‹ABSOLUTELY NOT. NO. YOU WANT MONEY FROM MY BROTHER, YOU GET IT FROM HIM. I WANT NOTHING TO DO WITH HIM AND THE CRAP THAT HE'S GOT HIMSELF INTO.›
‹LET'S STEP INSIDE FOR A MOMENT.›

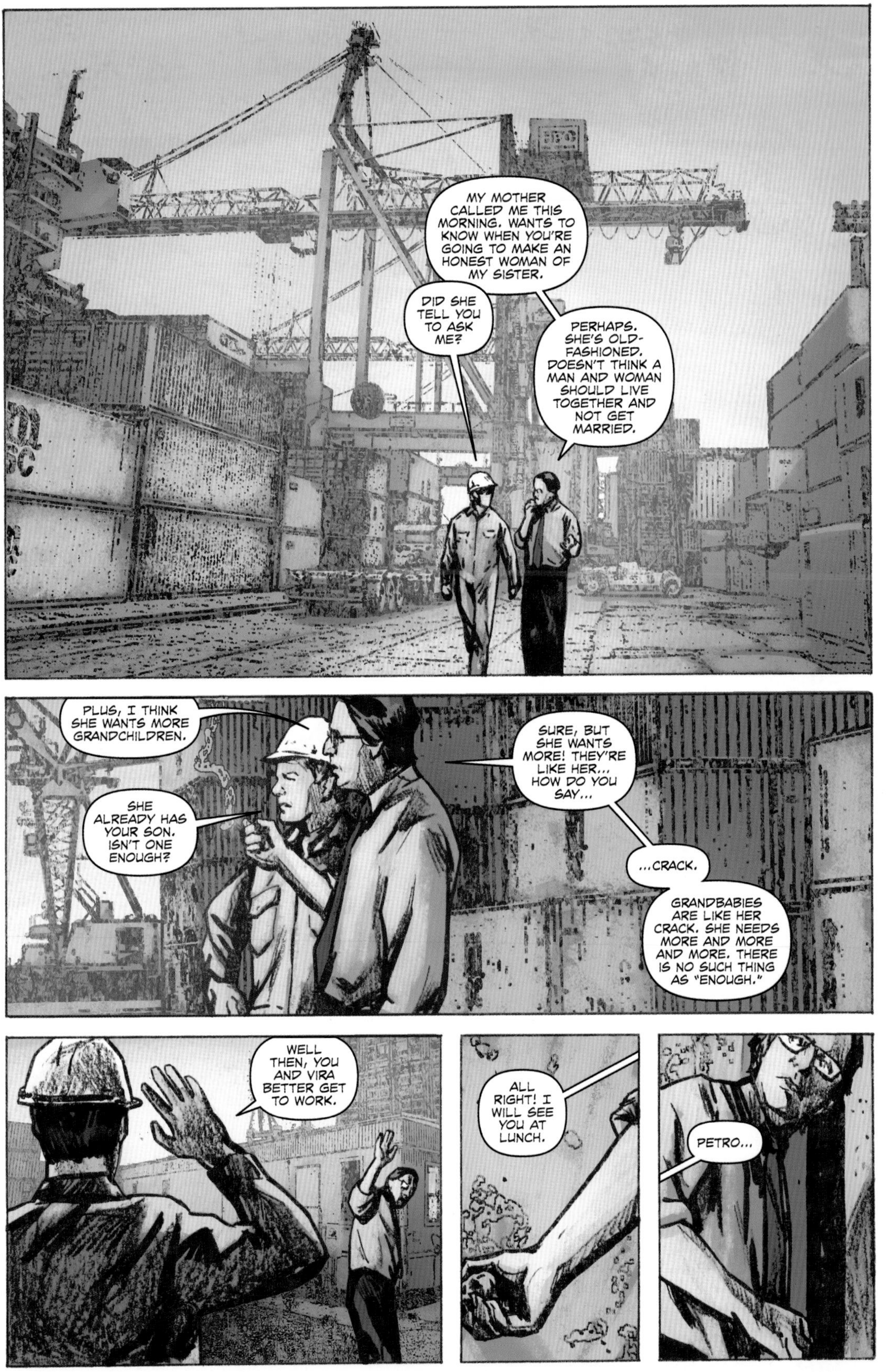
MY MOTHER CALLED ME THIS MORNING. WANTS TO KNOW WHEN YOU'RE GOING TO MAKE AN HONEST WOMAN OF MY SISTER.
DID SHE TELL YOU TO ASK ME?
PERHAPS. SHE'S OLD-FASHIONED. DOESN'T THINK A MAN AND WOMAN SHOULD LIVE TOGETHER AND NOT GET MARRIED.
PLUS, I THINK SHE WANTS MORE GRANDCHILDREN.
SHE ALREADY HAS YOUR SON. ISN'T ONE ENOUGH?
SURE, BUT SHE WANTS MORE! THEY'RE LIKE HER... HOW DO YOU SAY...
...CRACK.
GRANDBABIES ARE LIKE HER CRACK. SHE NEEDS MORE AND MORE AND MORE. THERE IS NO SUCH THING AS "ENOUGH."
WELL THEN, YOU AND VIRA BETTER GET TO WORK.
ALL RIGHT! I WILL SEE YOU AT LUNCH.
PETRO...

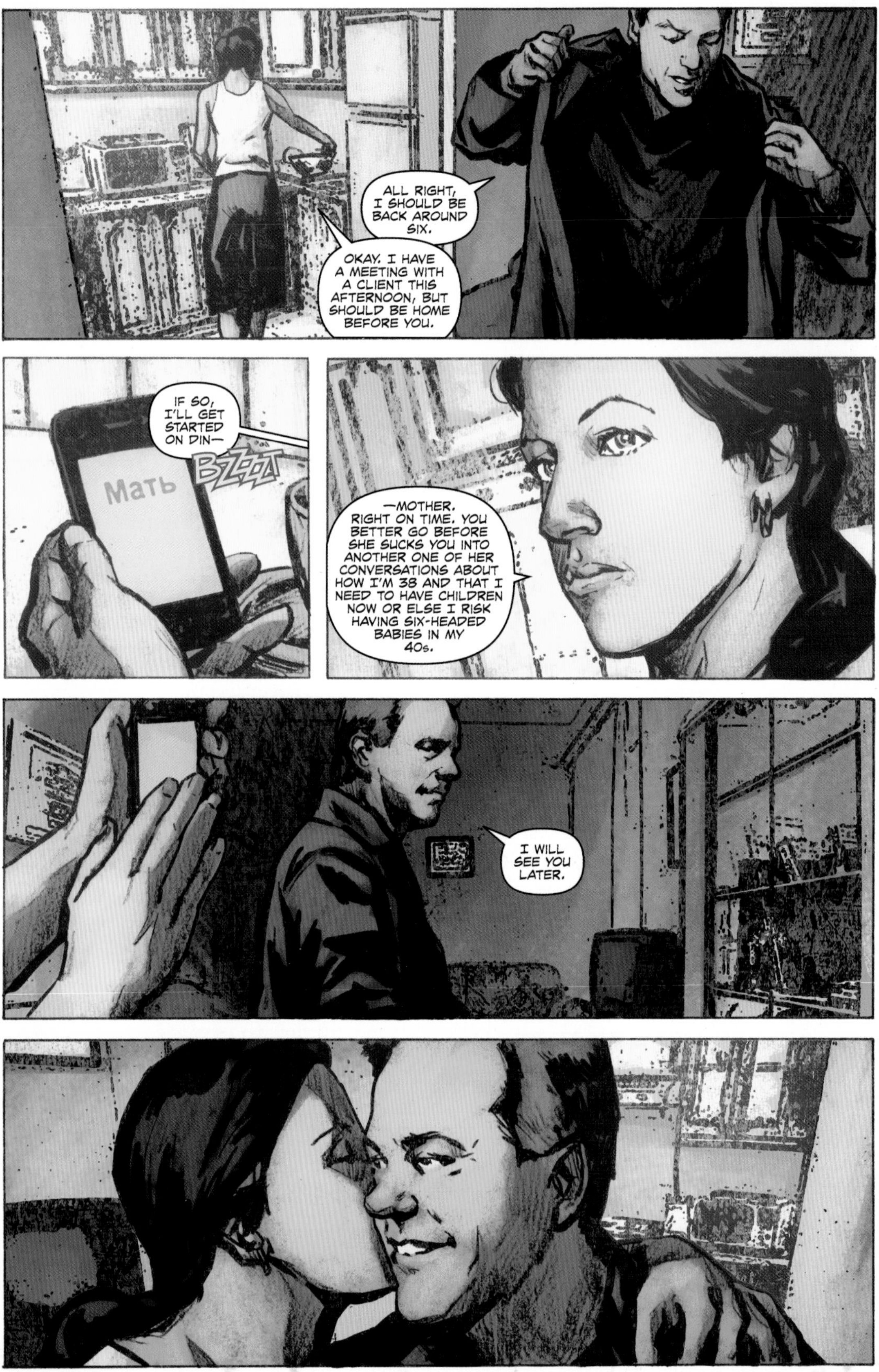
ALL RIGHT, I SHOULD BE BACK AROUND SIX.
OKAY. I HAVE A MEETING WITH A CLIENT THIS AFTERNOON, BUT SHOULD BE HOME BEFORE YOU.
IF SO, I'LL GET STARTED ON DIN—
BZZOOT
Мать
—MOTHER. RIGHT ON TIME. YOU BETTER GO BEFORE SHE SUCKS YOU INTO ANOTHER ONE OF HER CONVERSATIONS ABOUT HOW I'M 38 AND THAT I NEED TO HAVE CHILDREN NOW OR ELSE I RISK HAVING SIX-HEADED BABIES IN MY 40s.
I WILL SEE YOU LATER.

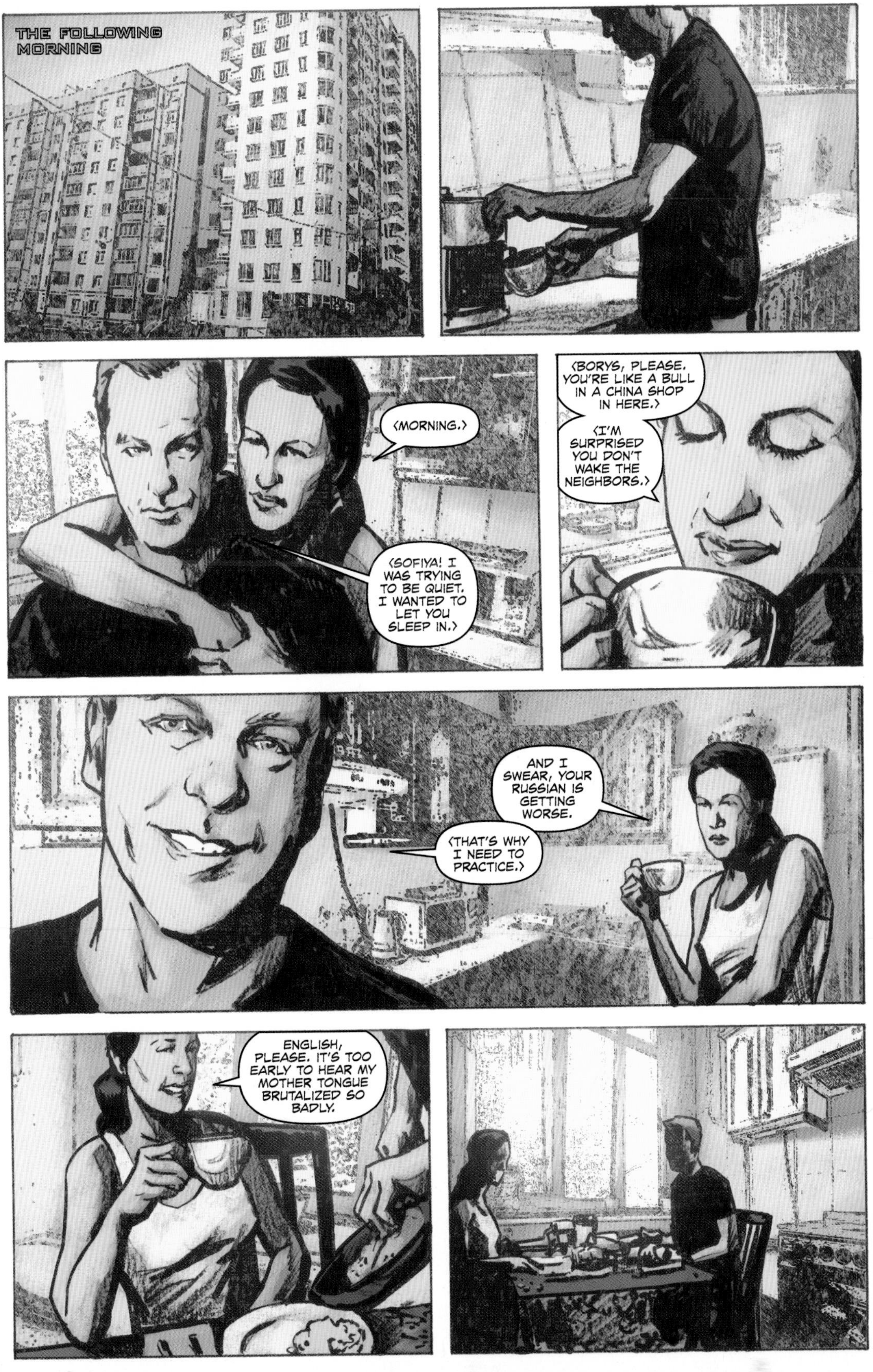
THE FOLLOWING MORNING
<MORNING.>
<SOFIYA! I WAS TRYING TO BE QUIET. I WANTED TO LET YOU SLEEP IN.>
<BORYS, PLEASE. YOU'RE LIKE A BULL IN A CHINA SHOP IN HERE.>
<I'M SURPRISED YOU DON'T WAKE THE NEIGHBORS.>
AND I SWEAR, YOUR RUSSIAN IS GETTING WORSE.
<THAT'S WHY I NEED TO PRACTICE.>
ENGLISH, PLEASE. IT'S TOO EARLY TO HEAR MY MOTHER TONGUE BRUTALIZED SO BADLY.

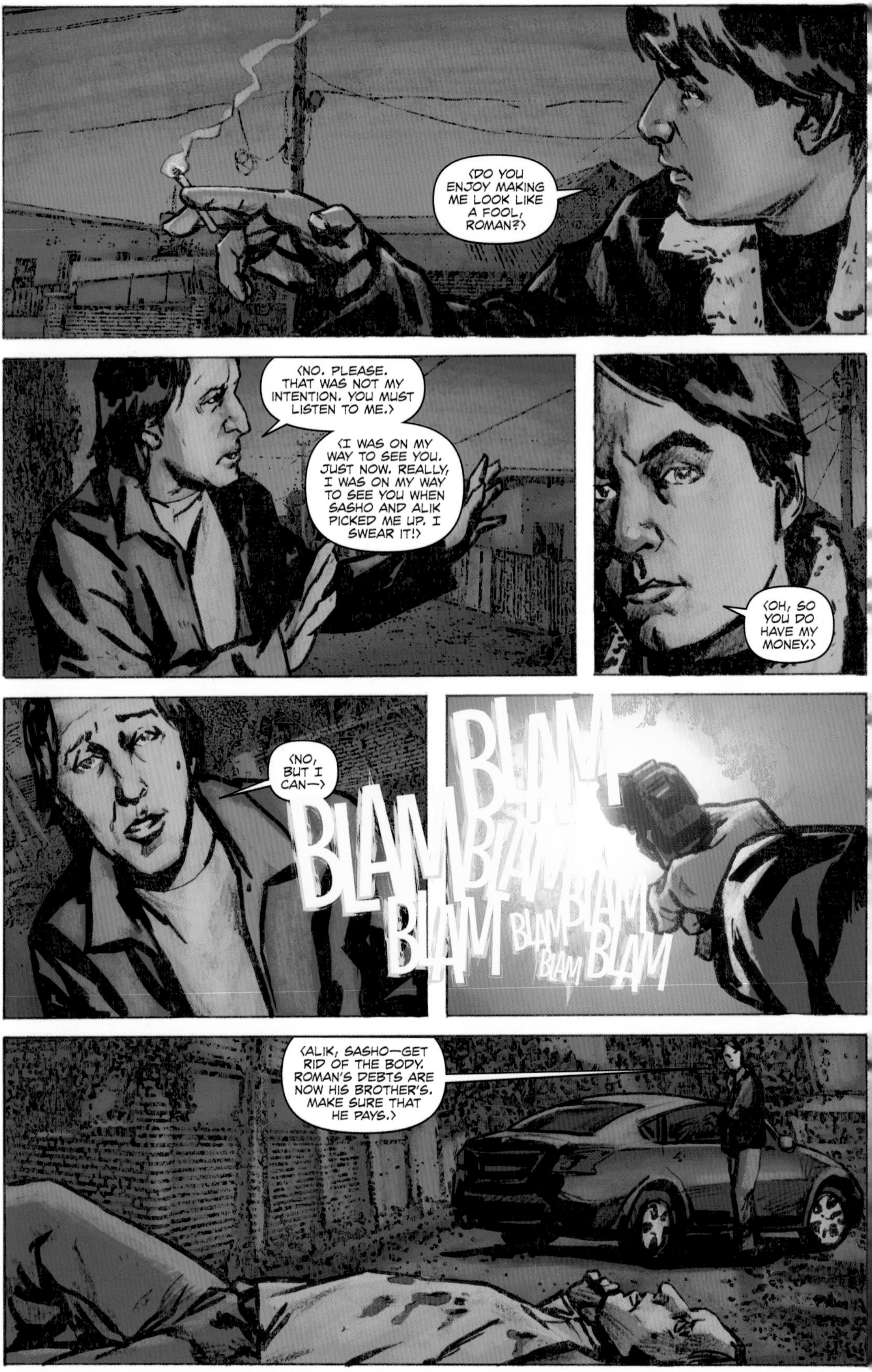

‹DO YOU ENJOY MAKING ME LOOK LIKE A FOOL, ROMAN?›
‹NO. PLEASE. THAT WAS NOT MY INTENTION. YOU MUST LISTEN TO ME.›
‹I WAS ON MY WAY TO SEE YOU. JUST NOW. REALLY, I WAS ON MY WAY TO SEE YOU WHEN SASHO AND ALIK PICKED ME UP. I SWEAR IT!›
‹OH, SO YOU DO HAVE MY MONEY.›
‹NO, BUT I CAN—›
BLAM BLAM BLAM BLAM BLAM BLAM BLAM BLAM BLAM BLAM
‹ALIK, SASHO—GET RID OF THE BODY. ROMAN'S DEBTS ARE NOW HIS BROTHER'S. MAKE SURE THAT HE PAYS.›

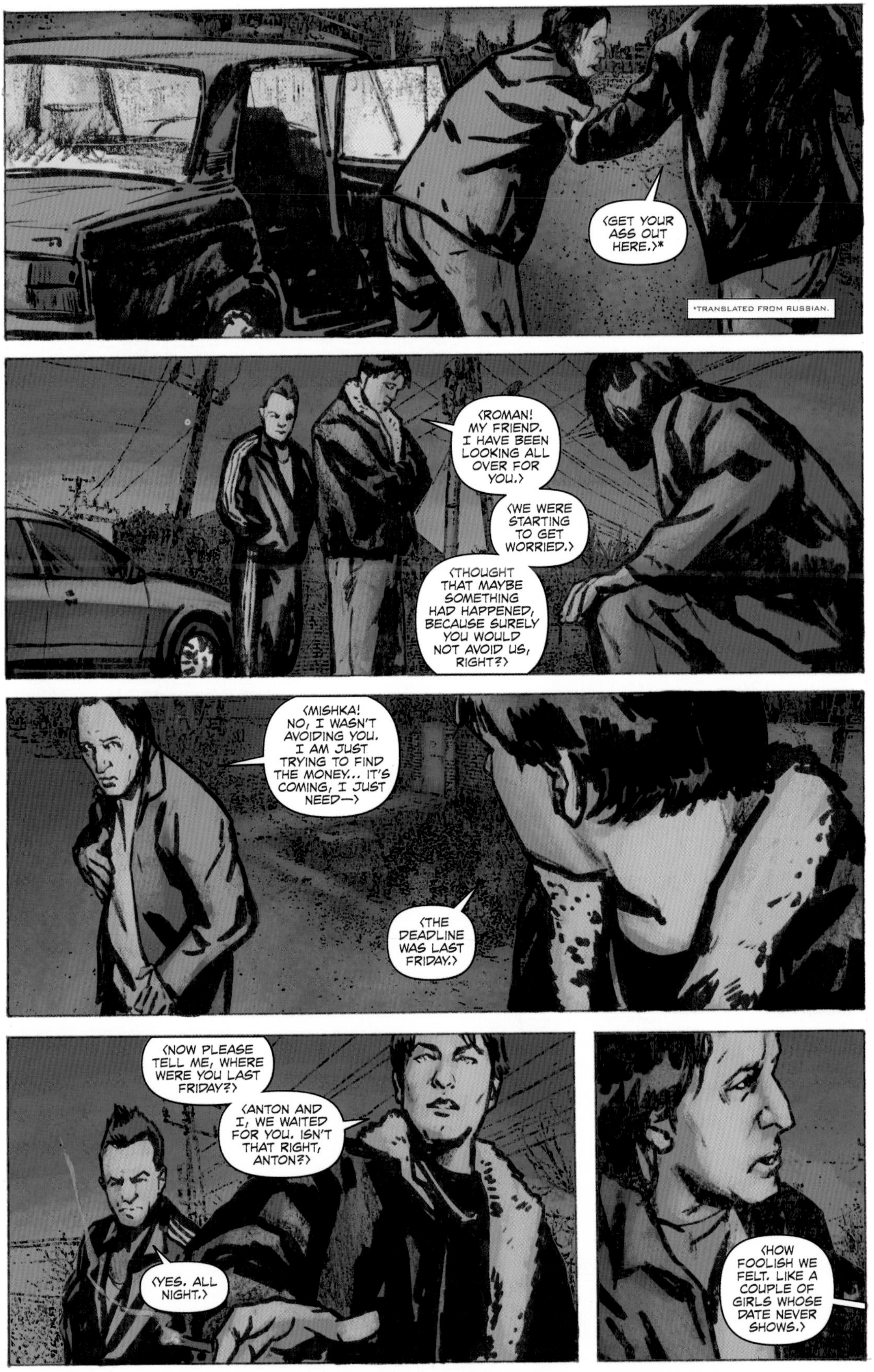

‹GET YOUR ASS OUT HERE.›*
*TRANSLATED FROM RUSSIAN.
‹ROMAN! MY FRIEND. I HAVE BEEN LOOKING ALL OVER FOR YOU.›
‹WE WERE STARTING TO GET WORRIED.›
‹THOUGHT THAT MAYBE SOMETHING HAD HAPPENED, BECAUSE SURELY YOU WOULD NOT AVOID US, RIGHT?›
‹MISHKA! NO, I WASN'T AVOIDING YOU. I AM JUST TRYING TO FIND THE MONEY... IT'S COMING, I JUST NEED—›
‹THE DEADLINE WAS LAST FRIDAY.›
‹NOW PLEASE TELL ME, WHERE WERE YOU LAST FRIDAY?›
‹ANTON AND I, WE WAITED FOR YOU. ISN'T THAT RIGHT, ANTON?›
‹YES. ALL NIGHT.›
‹HOW FOOLISH WE FELT. LIKE A COUPLE OF GIRLS WHOSE DATE NEVER SHOWS.›

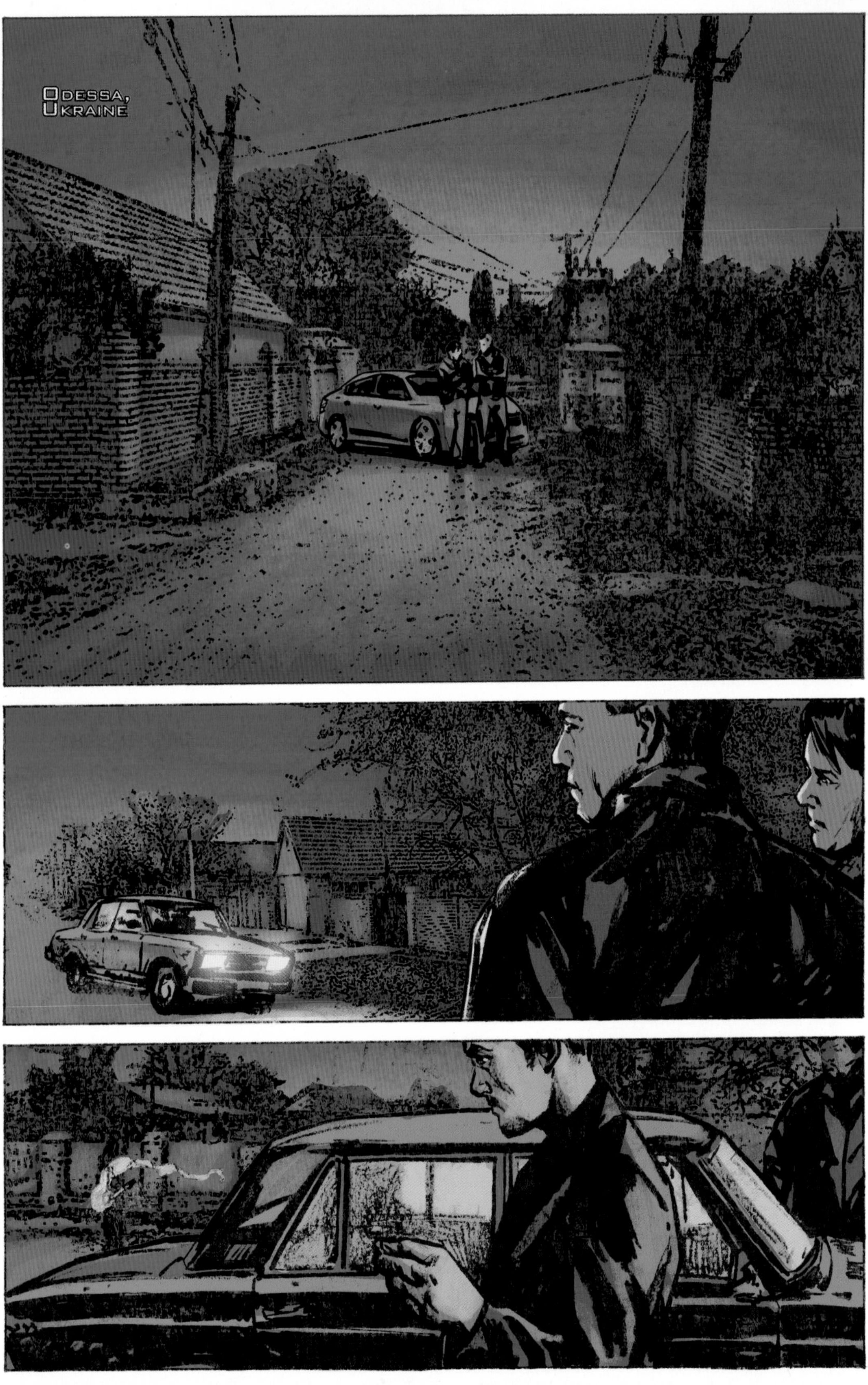
ODESSA,
UKRAINE

1 Art by Paul Shipper

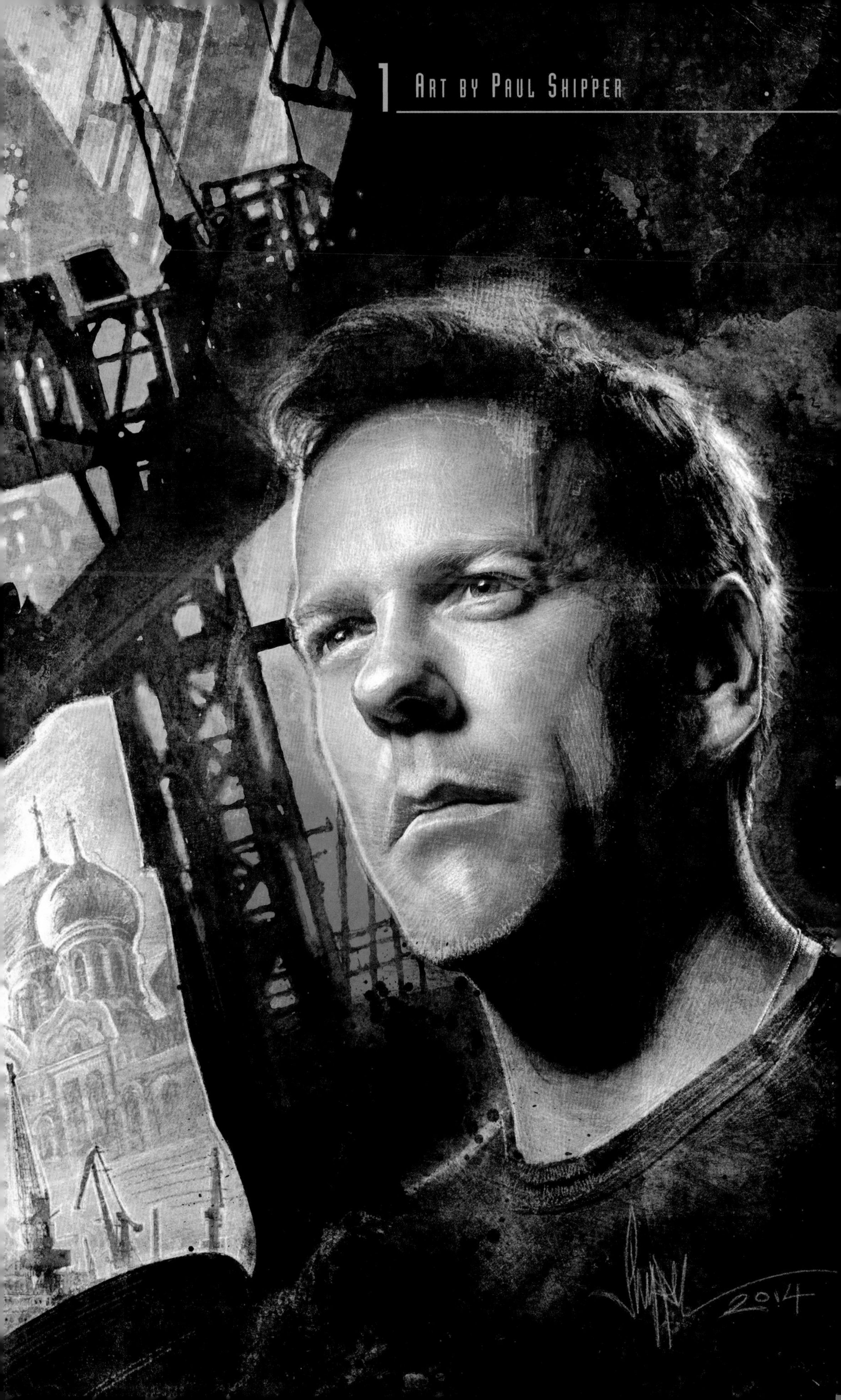

PREVIOUSLY ON *24*...

Four years ago, CTU agent Jack Bauer became a fugitive from justice. Soon, he will risk his life and freedom to avert yet another global disaster and LIVE ANOTHER DAY.

Jack spent the intervening years in exile, and now we reveal what happened during his time in the European UNDERGROUND...

WRITTEN BY ED BRISSON
ART BY MICHAEL GAYDOS
COLORS BY JOSH BURCHAM
LETTERS BY SHAWN LEE, ROBBIE ROBBINS,
AND NEIL UYETAKE
SERIES EDITS BY DENTON J. TIPTON

COVER BY DAVIDE FURNÓ
COLLECTION EDITS BY JUSTIN EISINGER AND ALONZO SIMON
COLLECTION DESIGN BY CLYDE GRAPA

19.99
3/13/15
NRN

Special thanks to Joshua Izzo and Lauren Winarski at Twentieth Century Fox.

IDW
www.IDWPUBLISHING.com
IDW founded by Ted Adams, Alex Garner, Kris Oprisko, and Robbie Robbins

Ted Adams, CEO & Publisher
Greg Goldstein, President & COO
Robbie Robbins, EVP/Sr. Graphic Artist
Chris Ryall, Chief Creative Officer/Editor-in-Chief
Matthew Ruzicka, CPA, Chief Financial Officer
Alan Payne, VP of Sales
Dirk Wood, VP of Marketing
Lorelei Bunjes, VP of Digital Services
Jeff Webber, VP of Digital Publishing & Business Development

Facebook: **facebook.com/idwpublishing**
Twitter: **@idwpublishing**
YouTube: **youtube.com/idwpublishing**
Instagram: **instagram.com/idwpublishing**
deviantART: **idwpublishing.deviantart.com**
Pinterest: **pinterest.com/idwpublishing/idw-staff-faves**

i140681.31

UNDERGROUND™